T0044165

PENGUIN BOOKS

MAGNA CARTA

Dan Jones is the *New York Times* bestselling author of *The Plantagenets*, *The Wars of the Roses*, *Magna Carta*, *Summer of Blood*, *The Templars*, and *Crusaders*. He wrote and presented the popular Netflix series *Secrets of Great British Castles* and appeared alongside George R.R. Martin in the official HBO film exploring the real history behind *Game of Thrones*. He is the historical consultant to *Knightfall*, an A&E drama on the legend of the Templars.

Magna Carta

The Birth of Liberty

DAN JONES

PENGUIN BOOKS

PENGUIN BOOKS

An imprint of Penguin Random House LLC

375 Hudson Street

New York, New York 10014

penguin.com

First published in the United States of America by Viking Penguin,
an imprint of Penguin Random House LLC, 2015
Published in Penguin Books 2016

ILLUSTRATION CREDITS

Insert page 1: (top) British Library Cotton Claudius D. II, f. 73; (bottom) SSPL / Getty Images

Insert page 2: (top) Manuel Cohen / Art Archive; (bottom) British Library Royal 14 C. VII, f. 9

Insert page 3: (top) DeA Picture Library / Art Archive; (bottom) Neil Holmes / Bridgeman Images

Insert page 4: (top) Bibliothèque Municipale Castres / Gianni Dagli Orti / Art Archive; (bottom) British Museum / Ealdgyth Wikimedia Commons

Insert page 5: British Library Additional MS 4838 / Art Archive

Insert page 6: (top) Granger Collection / Topfoto; (bottom) British Library Cotton MS Augustus ii. 106

Insert page 7: (top left) British Library / Art Archive; (top right) Jarrold Publishing / Art Archive; (bottom) Topfoto

Insert page 8: (top) Corporation of London / HIP / Topfoto; (bottom) Library of Congress

ISBN 9780525428299 (hc.)
ISBN 9780143108955 (pbk.)

Printed in the United States of America

Maps by Jeffrey L. Ward
Set in Adobe Jenson Pro

In memoriam
H. E.

But let no one, however rich, flatter himself that he can misbehave with impunity, for of such people it is written, "The powerful shall suffer powerful torments."

The Dialogue of the Exchequer
Richard FitzNigel, 1177–c. 1189

Contents

IV: Afterlife

England Under King John

SCOTLAND

Glasgow

Edinburgh

Berwick-upon-Tweed
TWEEDMOUTH
Tweed
NORHAM

ALNWICK

Newcastle

Carlisle

Durham

0 Miles 50 100
0 Kilometers 100

Pickering Scarborough

Lancaster
KNARESBOROUGH York

*North
Sea*

Irish Sea

Conwy *Conwy* Chester
Dee

Trent Lincoln

Nottingham Belvoir

The Wash

MONTSORREL King's Lynn Norwich
Leicester Great Yarmouth

Severn KENILWORTH
WALES *Wye* Kenilworth Bury St Edmunds *Orwell*
Worcester Northampton
Tewkesbury *Avon* NORTHAMPTON Bedford Cambridge
Hereford Brackley BENINGTON Colchester
Monmouth Evesham Dunstable HERTFORD Dunmow
St. Briavels Gloucester *Thames* Oxford St Albans
Pembroke Wallingford WINDSOR London ROCHESTER Sandwich
Cardiff MARLBOROUGH Windsor Runnymede Canterbury
Bristol Devizes Runnymede *Medway* Dover DOVER
Glastonbury Clarendon ODIHAM
Salisbury Winchester
Southampton Arundel
Exeter CORFE Portsmouth
Isle of Wight

English Channel

FRANCE

The Plantagenet Empire at Its Peak in 1189 and in 1215, After John's Losses

Rhine

Thames

London

North Sea

ENGLAND

Damme

BRABANT

Calais

Boulogne FLANDERS

Béthune Bouvines

English Channel

Crécy

HAINAULT

Barfleur

Rouen CHATEAU GAILLARD

VERMANDOIS

Seine

Reims

Caen LE VAUDREUIL

Falaise

Paris

NORMANDY

CHAMPAGNE

Milly

BRITTANY

MAINE

BLOIS

ROYAL FRENCH DEMESNE

VASSALS OF THE FRENCH KING

Rennes

Le Mans

ANJOU LOCHES

Loire

Nantes

Fontevraud

TOURAINE

BERRY

BURGUNDY

Chinon

Clairvaux

Atlantic Ocean

Mirebeau

POITOU

Poitiers

CHATEAU-ROUX

BOURBON

La Rochelle

CHALUS-CHABROL

LA MARCHE

AUVERGNE

Lyon

Saintes

SAINTONGE

ANGOULÊME

LIMOUSIN

AQUITAINE

PÉRIGORD

Bordeaux

Garonne

Lot

AGENAIS

CAHORSIN

Rhône

Avignon

GASCONY

Vassals of the French King in 1189

Territories held by the French Crown in 1189

Plantagenet territories in 1189

Plantagenet territories in 1215, after John's losses

ARMAGNAC

Toulouse

TOULOUSE

NAVARRE

ARAGON

0 Miles   50   100

0 Kilometers   100

CATALONIA

Mediterranean Sea

Barcelona

Magna Carta

Magna Carta

Introduction

EIGHT HUNDRED YEARS after it was first granted beneath the trees of Runnymede, by the fertile green banks of the river Thames, the Magna Carta is more famous than ever. This is strange. In its surviving forms—there are four known original charters dating from June 1215—the Magna Carta is something of a muddle, a collection of promises extracted in bad faith from a reluctant king, most of which concern matters of arcane thirteenth-century legal principle. A few of these promises concern themselves with high ideals, but they are few and far between, vague and idealistic statements slipped between longer and more perplexing sentences describing the "customary fee" that a baron ought to pay a king on the occasion of coming into an inheritance, or the protocols for dealing with debt to the Crown, or the regulation of fish traps along the rivers Thames and Medway.

For the most part the Magna Carta is dry, technical, difficult to decipher, and constitutionally obsolete. Those parts that are still frequently quoted—clauses about the right to justice before one's peers, the freedom from being unlawfully imprisoned, and the freedom of the Church—did not mean in 1215 what we often wish they would mean today. They are part of a document drawn up not to defend in perpetuity the interests of national citizens but rather to pin down a king who had been greatly vexing a small number of his wealthy and violent subjects. The Magna Carta ought to be dead, defunct, and of interest only to serious scholars of the thirteenth century.

Yet it is very much alive, one of the most hallowed documents in the world, revered from the Arctic Circle to the antipodes, written into the constitutions of numerous countries, and admired as a foundation stone in the Western traditions of liberty, democracy, and the rule of law. How did that happen?

The Magna Carta was a peace treaty born of a serious collapse in relations between John, the third Plantagenet king of England, and his barons. The reasons for that collapse will be discussed in this book, but the basic thrust of events was simple. A large party of John's barons, with the assistance of churchmen guided by the impressive archbishop of Canterbury, Stephen Langton, demanded that the king confirm in writing (and certify with his Great Seal) a long list of rights and royal obligations that they felt he and his predecessors had neglected, ignored, and abused for too long. These rights and obligations were conceived in part as a return to some semi-imaginary "ancient" law code that had governed a better, older England, which lay in the historical memory somewhere between the days of the last Saxon king, Edward the Confessor, and the more recent times of John's great-grandfather, Henry I.

The Magna Carta touched on matters of religion, tax, justice, military service, feudal payments, weights and measures, trading privileges, and urban government. Occasionally it reached for grand principle: Famously, John was forced to promise that "no free man is to be arrested, or imprisoned, or disseized, or outlawed, or exiled, or in any other way ruined, nor will we go or send against him, except by the legal judgment of his peers or by the law of the land" and that "to no one will we sell, to no one will we deny or delay, right or justice." But for the most part what was at issue in 1215 was a tight-knit, technical, and often quite dull shopping list of feudal demands that was mainly of interest to (and in the interests of) a tiny handful of England's richest and most powerful men. The Magna Carta's terms applied only to "free men," who were then at best 10 percent or 20 percent of England's adult population.

The main novelty of the Magna Carta, often overlooked, was the fact that it proposed a neat but flawed mechanism for ensuring that the king stuck to what he had promised to do. If John reneged on the charter, his barons would renounce their personal loyalty to the king, on which the whole feudal structure of society depended, and start a war. This grave threat was reflected in the words of the charter itself, in which John acknowledged that if he failed to keep the promises he had made, then his barons could "distrain and distress [him] in all ways possible, by taking castles, lands, possessions . . . saving our person and the persons of our queen and children."[1]

And that is precisely what happened. On Monday, June 15, 1215, John's barons compelled him to grant them a charter of rights and privileges, but the king began to wriggle out from beneath its terms almost as soon as the sealing wax was set. The original Magna Carta was legally valid for only a little more than two months, whereupon it was declared "shameful and demeaning . . . illegal and unjust" by the pope, who decreed that any man who observed the charter would "incur the anger of Almighty God and of St Peter and St Paul His apostles": a polite way of saying that they would burn in the fires of hell for all eternity.[2] This provoked full-blown civil war in which towns and castles were besieged, men were slaughtered, the royal treasure was (infamously) lost in boggy ground near the large river estuary in eastern England called the Wash, and the French king's heir was invited to England to replace John. The war was ended not by a chastened King John's agreeing to reaffirm the principles of the Magna Carta but rather by his death from dysentery during the night of October 18, 1216, after which his enemies rapidly began to lose their appetite for the fight. Little at the time would have led anyone to believe that the charter agreed at Runnymede in June of 1215 was anything more than a brave but flawed attempt to restrain an unpopular and overbearing king, which had failed in the most emphatic circumstances imaginable.

And yet. In the eight hundred years that have passed since that fateful day of June 15, 1215, when the Magna Carta was granted by King John *in prato quod vocatur Ronimed*—"in the meadow that is called Runnymede"—it has become the most iconic document in the Western liberal tradition, and the year 1215 has become in a sense "year zero" in the story of the struggle for freedom from tyranny.[3] The four surviving copies of the 1215 Magna Carta, held by the British Library, Lincoln Cathedral, and Salisbury Cathedral, are treated with the reverence normally accorded to ancient religious texts. Visitors to the U.S. National Archives in Washington, DC, will find that the Magna Carta is the first thing they see when they pass through the security zone: An edition of the charter dating from 1297, which was bought for more than $20 million at auction in 2007, sits, dimly lit, as the physical and metaphorical starting point for the history of American freedom. It is captioned with a quotation from President Franklin D. Roosevelt, who claimed that "the democratic aspiration is no mere recent phase in human history. . . . It is written in Magna Carta."

That democracy was the last thing on the minds of the men who conceived and agreed to the terms of the Magna Carta is in a sense beside the point. From surprisingly early in the thirteenth century the document's legend had begun to outgrow its terms, and that process has continued to the present day. The Magna Carta played an important role in the English Civil War and the Glorious Revolution of 1688. It provided a constitutional first principle for the rebellious colonists of New England who became the founding fathers of the United States and it informed the drafting of the Constitution. Its words are echoed in the clauses of the U.S. Bill of Rights and the United Nations' Universal Declaration of Human Rights, and it was cited by Nelson Mandela in his famous Rivonia speech in 1964. Three of the Magna Carta's sixty-three clauses remain law in England today, but as one scholar has recently noted, it has been quoted in constitutional debates more frequently than any other text except for the Bible.[4] As we consider the charter from eight hundred years' distance, the myth and symbolism of the Magna Carta have become almost wholly divorced from its original history. That fact is in its way as interesting as the content of the charter itself.

This book tells the story of the Magna Carta—its background, its birth, its almost instantaneous failure, its slow resurrection, and its mutation into the thing it is today: a historical palimpsest onto which almost any dream can be written. It looks at the Magna Carta's place in the history of medieval England and describes how the charter was exported to America and the wider world and how it came to be admired as the starting point in the story of Western liberty, democracy, and freedom under the law. It also presents the text in modern English translation so that readers can see what it was that so many of England's political elite were determined to secure as fundamental rights from their king.

At the book's heart lies a narrative of defiance and dispute between John and a group of his barons, who went about for a time under the name "The Army of God and the Holy Church." Mutual distrust and a fair deal of loathing had lingered between this group and the king for more than three years, but in the spring of 1215 their differences spilled over into naked constitutional crisis. In the autumn this turned to war and by the winter it seemed that this war was set to rival the very worst in living memory: the twelfth-century "Anarchy" that had pitted William the Conqueror's granddaughter Matilda against her cousin Stephen. So in the central chapters of this book we follow a short, eventful, and critical period in a wider struggle for a political settlement between a king and his leading subjects, looking not only at events in Runnymede but also at the clash of personalities, ideologies, and swords that gave birth to the Magna Carta.

In the course of that narrative I try to place the charter in the context of a year of change and upheaval beyond the borders of England. In France a long tussle for dominance between Plantagenet kings and their Capetian rivals was moving decisively in favor of the latter. The people of England were coming to terms with the consequences of the loss of Normandy, an event that held just as much significance as the Norman Conquest of 1066.

We cannot consider English politics and English society in this period without examining religious life during this extraordinarily muscular era in the history of Christianity. Neither should we ignore the fact that 1215 was the year that Pope Innocent III's Fourth Lateran Council met in Rome. The Fourth Lateran made substantial alterations to the lives of millions of people, issuing new commands on everything from the sacrament of confession to the identifying clothing that was to be worn by Jews and Muslims to the number of times that parish churches were to be cleaned. Many educated people would have considered it a much more important congress than the provincial gathering that took place at Runnymede in June of the same year.

I have tried here to write a history of the year that made the Magna Carta in the fullest sense. As well as describing the high politics of the year, I build up a picture of what life was like for people at every level of society: king and barons, knights and merchants, priests and peasants. This account of the Magna Carta is at least in part a history "from the bottom up" as well as "from the top down." And by the end I hope that readers will have a sense of 1215 not only as a year of world-changing importance but also as what it was for most people: just another year in the life of medieval England.

All this being said, it is essential to note that the Magna Carta had deeper roots than John's reign. While John's own often-appalling behavior was much to blame for the chaos that rained down upon him during his final years, he was not by any means the sole architect of his woes. This is a point recognized both by modern historians and by men who lived at the time. The chronicler Ralph of Coggeshall, writing in the middle of the thirteenth century, observed that the Magna Carta was not created simply to restrain John but also to end "the evil customs which the father and brother of the king had created to the detriment of the Church and kingdom, along with those abuses which the king had added."[5] Another chronicler, Gerald of Wales, who was always inclined to anti-Plantagenet hysteria in his writing, agreed, calling John a "tyrannous whelp," but admitting that he had "issued from the most bloody tyrants."[6] This was typical Geraldic exaggeration; nevertheless it nods us in the direction of an important historical truth: We cannot simply view the Magna Carta as a bill of protest and remedy aimed at the scandalous and unlucky John but must recognize it as a howl of historical complaint that was directed, at least on some level, against two generations of perceived abuse.

To begin this story, therefore, we must reach back sixty years before 1215 to the time of John's father, Henry II.

Dan Jones

Battersea, London

2015

I

Origins

I

The Devil's Brood

King John's father, Henry II, was a man who made an impression. Physically he was not much to look at—a little more than middling height, solidly built, with bowed legs and gray eyes that were said to flash when he grew angry—but the force of his character made him unforgettable. Henry possessed near-boundless energy. "Perpetually wakeful and at work," wrote the courtier and chronicler Walter Map, though this scarcely did justice to his sheer will and determination.[1] By the time Henry Plantagenet was crowned King of England on December 19, 1154, at twenty-one, he had also seized the titles of Duke of Normandy, Duke of Aquitaine—by virtue of marriage in 1152 to Eleanor of Aquitaine—and Count of Anjou, Maine, and Touraine.* Over the course of his long reign he would take effective command of Brittany and assert his right to the lordship of Ireland. His power therefore stretched from the borders of Scotland to the Pyrenees and encompassed virtually the entire western seaboard of France. Indeed, Henry's political tentacles stretched even further afield, for he had interests and alliances from Saxony to Sicily and from Castile to the Holy Land. Few European monarchs since Charlemagne had exercised control over such vast territories, and few medieval kings would rule with such political agility, ruthlessness, and skill.

*It is due to his possession of the County of Anjou that the continental holdings of Henry II and his sons Richard I and John are sometimes referred to as the Angevin Empire.

Henry's physical stamina allowed him to spend almost his whole life moving about his lands, "tolerant of the discomforts of dust and mud . . . travelling in unbearably long stages," and enjoying, according to Walter Map, the fact that his physical exertions prevented him from getting fat.[2] He astonished his rival rulers with the ability to pop up where they least expected him, and he both charmed and scared those who worked for him by dint of his tendency to slip in an instant from bluff good humor to foaming rage. During one infamous tantrum, Henry thrashed about on the floor of his chamber, gnawing at the straw from his mattress. But it was his innate talent for politics and government that most struck those who met him. Writing after the king's death, the Yorkshire chronicler William of Newburgh wrote that he "seemed to possess notable wisdom, stability, and a passion for justice" and that even from "his earliest days" he "conveyed the impression of a great ruler."[3]

Henry inherited the English crown in a political deal to end a civil war that had raged for nineteen years. Contemporaries called the war the Shipwreck; historians now refer to it as the Anarchy. It was a struggle waged between two grandchildren of William the Conqueror—Henry's mother, Matilda, and her cousin Stephen, both of whom claimed to be the legitimate heir of Henry I.* Neither could summon enough military might or political support to enforce their claim, and as a result England was torn for a generation between two hostile factions. Royal authority across the realm collapsed, and the horrors of civil war descended: arson, torture, bloodshed, murder, robbery, starvation, economic turmoil, and a widespread failure of justice. "Every man began to rob his neighbor," wrote the author of *The Anglo-Saxon*

*Matilda was Henry I's only legitimate daughter, and she used the title "Empress" following her marriage to Henry V, King of Germany and Holy Roman Emperor (d. 1125). Stephen's mother was Henry I's sister Adela of Blois. Stephen and Matilda were therefore first cousins.

Chronicle. "It was said openly that Christ and his saints were asleep."[4] In 1153 the Treaty of Winchester finally brought an end to the conflict by naming Matilda's son as Stephen's heir. When Stephen died the following year and Henry took power, his first duty was to restore firm royal rule to a land that had not known effective governance for a generation.

There were three determining conditions to Henry II's rule in England. The first was his urgent need to impose order after the Anarchy. The second was his need to create a political system that would allow him to rule his kingdom efficiently while he traveled across the rest of his territories fighting his enemies, chief among them Louis VII, King of France. The third was a constant need to raise money. Henry approached these problems with a natural instinct for strong, centralized government and a knack for financially squeezing his subjects—particularly those in England, the richest part of his empire. In doing so he put his personal stamp on the style and substance of all royal government in a way that would come to define the sixty years before the Magna Carta.

Henry loved control. Although in England, as in the rest of his lands, he was happy to delegate the business of government to trusted advisers, he made it very clear from the beginning that power stemmed ultimately—and only—from the king. At his coronation he imitated his Norman predecessors by issuing a charter that promised to protect "all the concessions and grants and liberties and free customs" that had been given to the Church and the great men of the kingdom by Henry I and likewise to abolish all the "evil customs" that had sprung up in the realm. But this was the last such concession that he would make. Although Henry II made a great effort to rally to his side as many of the great men of England as he could, he was prepared to break the power of the handful of English barons who dared to defy him while leaving the rest in no doubt as to whom they owed their positions of wealth and prestige. He razed castles that had been built during the civil war and expelled foreign mercenaries. He issued a new coinage and imposed heavy penalties on those who forged or clipped his coins.* He canceled all grants of land and office that had been made under Stephen, and those he saw fit to regrant were given back explicitly under his own authority. He refused to relinquish command of any territory or property where it might result in his own power being diminished, and he took great pains to punish anyone who opposed him. And, most important for the long-term history of England, Henry oversaw a legal and administrative revolution that allowed his authority to be felt in the realm even when he was absent—as he would be for around two thirds of his thirty-five-year reign. For England was only a part of Henry's huge patchwork of territories, and much of his life was spent defending his Continental lands from enemy attacks, largely carried out or sponsored by the king of France. This was extremely time-consuming. Even more important, it cost Henry a great deal of money.

"Wealth is obviously necessary not only in wartime but also in peacetime," wrote Richard FitzNigel, royal treasurer and bishop of London, in a practical guidebook to royal finance known as *The Dialogue of the Exchequer.*[5] FitzNigel completed his book in the late 1180s, around the time Henry died, and his words reflect a lifetime of service to a king whose need for money was always pressing. Under Henry's rule the Exchequer became the most important insti-

---

*Regulating and stabilizing the money supply was both a mark of kingly authority and a means of combating financial fraud. Coin clipping was seen as an especially pernicious activity: By shaving off the edges of coins, clippers could harvest the silver and mint their own fake coins.

tution of royal government, for it was there that royal revenues were accounted, on a large table, ten feet by five feet, which was covered with a cloth resembling a chessboard, and it was through the Exchequer that the king could levy heavy financial penalties on those subjects who displeased him. The Exchequer received fines imposed by the king's judges and it handled bribes paid by landholders who sought royal favor in disputes with their neighbors. Feudal dues— customary payments made by aristocrats for the king's permission to marry or inherit—came across the checkered cloth–covered table, and so did taxes such as "scutage," also known as shield money, a payment made by a baron to avoid sending his loyal knights to fight in the royal army (the money, in theory, might then be used to buy mercenaries).*

During the civil war the Exchequer had lost its teeth: Sheriffs— key royal officials in the shires of England—had stopped rendering their accounts before it, and the barons of England had avoided paying their feudal dues. But this decline was dramatically reversed under Henry. FitzNigel's handbook shows us just what a wide array of business came before Henry's Exchequer. Its officials counted and sorted silver coins, audited sheriffs' accounts for revenues raised in the shires, received scutage and fines paid by communities for murders committed where there was no culprit discovered (the law stated that in this circumstance the whole community stood to be punished), as well as taking in fines paid for abuses committed in royal forest land, which fell under a different set of laws from the rest of the realm. They took receipt of falcons and hawks given as gifts to the king and they handled the "queen's gold"—a tax

*"Feudalism" is a much-debated term, but in this period it refers to a hierarchical ordering of society whereby certain obligations (notably military, but also financial) existed in return for the possession of land, property, and other rights. At the top of the hierarchy was the Crown, from which leading men held land as "tenants-in-chief."

of one mark of gold for every hundred marks of silver owed to the king.*

The Exchequer was a huge and complex government department. Yet it is clear that Henry regarded it not only as a financial tool but also as a political institution. The marshal of the Exchequer had the power to arrest those who came before it insolvent. Powerful subjects could be ruined simply by the calling in of large debts they owed to the Crown. Equally, the king could reward men who were in his favor by reducing, rescheduling, or canceling their debts. Very few barons paid everything they owed to the Exchequer. Indeed, some of the king's close associates—such as Robert, Earl of Leicester, and Reginald, Earl of Cornwall—paid nothing at all on their debts.[6] Despite these selective exemptions, however, Henry's general insistence on tight financial governance bore fruit. Early in his reign about £13,000 a year crossed the Exchequer table. By the 1180s the flow of money stood at £22,000—testament not only to rising revenue, necessary to help the king defend his vast lands, but also to a king exerting a much tighter royal grip, even in absentia, on the great men of his realm.[7]

Having reformed royal finance, Henry set about changing the way that royal justice worked. Starting in 1163–66, sweeping reforms affected the way that the king's subjects interacted with royal law.† The Assize of Clarendon—a legal act of 1166—commanded that

---

*A mark—which was a unit of calculation rather than physical coinage—was held to be worth thirteen shillings and four pence, or two thirds of a pound.

†The chief point to remember regarding lawmaking at this time is that it was the era before Parliament and before statutes; laws were made by kings and their councillors; other laws and customs existed at local levels, while the Church stiffly and emphatically maintained its aloofness from secular laws, seeing its own ecclesiastical law as answerable to the pope—a cause of tensions that exploded in Henry II's conflict with Thomas Becket.

certain crimes in England be investigated by the Crown, regardless of any local jurisdictions held by the great lords of the realm. The investigating was to be done not by potentially corruptible sheriffs and local officials but by a high-powered commission of royal judges who traveled on a circuit known as the General Eyre and who tried cases with juries of twelve local men rather than committing defendants to judgment by ordeal of fire or water, as had been the case in the past. The assize meant that all murder, robbery, and theft now came under royal jurisdiction; ten years later the Assize of Northampton added arson, forgery, and counterfeiting to this list.

It was not only the scope of criminal law that expanded under Henry. There was also a revolution in the way that civil law in England operated. Land disputes were the source of a huge volume of litigation during the Middle Ages, and Henry made the process by which the Crown could intervene in cases smoother, easier, and more profitable. Since before the Norman Conquest it had been possible to apply for royal justice by seeking a "writ" from the government department known as Chancery. A writ was a short chit that could initiate legal action in royal courts or command a royal sheriff to carry out some form of action to remedy a wrong. These were generally ad hoc, nonstandard official devices. Henry made a series of standardized writs available, most importantly the writ of *novel disseizin*, the writ of *mort d'ancestor*, and the writ of right: Respectively these protected landholders from having their land illegally seized by lords or third parties, asserted the right to inherit land, and instructed a sheriff to "do right" by the holder of the writ. They were simple, formulaic, and straightforward to obtain, whether or not the king was in the country. The reach of the Crown thus began to extend deep down into English society as the royal law became more available, desirable, and widely used than ever before. Moreover, writs cost money, and their increasing popularity brought the Crown a handsome profit from litigants' fees and fines. Best of all, none of this required Henry's personal presence. A moneymaking bureaucratic machine was born.

Not everyone, however, was happy, and just as we can trace to Henry II's reign the origins of the royal system against which the Magna Carta was aimed, so we can trace the first rumblings of dissatisfaction and protest to which it responded. This dissatisfaction was most pronounced among two groups of Henry's subjects: members of the clerical establishment and England's most powerful barons, both of whom resented the curtailing of their authority and jurisdiction.

In 1163 Henry attempted to browbeat his erstwhile friend, servant, and boon companion Thomas Becket, whom he had appointed archbishop of Canterbury, into allowing the Crown to place on trial and punish "criminous clerks"—churchmen who had committed crimes. This was an age that still possessed a separate system of church law, and these proposals would have been a huge invasion of secular law into ecclesiastical jurisdiction. Becket's refusal to allow it prompted the famous breach between the two men, which ended with the archbishop's heinous murder before the altar of Canterbury Cathedral in 1170. His quarrel with Henry stemmed from a fundamental, unbridgeable divergence: The archbishop viewed the king as a tyrant who was riding roughshod over the law, while Henry saw only that he was exercising his royal prerogatives. When Becket went into exile from England between 1164 and 1170, he wrote a series of angry and insulting letters to and about the king, including one to Henry's mother, Matilda, in which he complained that Henry "is afflicting the churches of his realm beyond endurance and demanding from them unheard-of and unaccustomed things."[8] Cruel blows and bitter insults were thus being traded between English kings and the Church long before King John's reign. This tension would come to underpin the desire, fifty years later, to force the king to accede to a set of common rights and restrictions of royal power.

Henry II set the tone for early Plantagenet kingship—or so it would appear from the comfortable distance of his youngest son's reign. He set out a platform of aggressive, disciplined, rigorous central government that was highly adept at milking cash from England and channeling it to the Continent. He pushed the financial and judicial power of the Crown deep into the shires. He oversaw a dramatic reduction of the military power of the major barons, for as well as razing baronial castles following the Anarchy, Henry seized huge numbers of them following the rebellion known as the Great War (1173–74), when Henry's elder sons rebelled against him in alliance with the king of France and (most embarrassingly) their mother, Henry's wife, Eleanor. In 1154 the Crown held some 35 percent of England's 350 castles; by the 1180s that figure had risen substantially, and by John's reign nearly half of England's castles were in royal hands.[9]

Henry occasionally lived up to his ancestors' reputations for diabolical cruelty. Old family legend had it that the Plantagenets were descended from the devil, and there were Englishmen who saw something demonic in the character of the king. Writers hostile to Henry, such as Ralph Niger, accused him not only of demeaning the nobility of his greatest subjects but also of being an irreligious tyrant and a slavering womanizer. Even William of Newburgh, whose account was generally positive, recorded that in his day "he was hateful to nearly everyone."[10] This may have been an exaggeration, but Henry was certainly capable of a ferocity that tested the limits even of a violent age. His worst malice was shown in his treatment of Becket's followers, hundreds of whom were stripped of their possessions, sent into exile, or imprisoned in chains during Henry's quarrel with the archbishop. Clerics who attempted to proclaim the religious penalties imposed by Becket on the king could have their eyes put out or feet or genitals hacked off in punishment. Even messengers were not safe: A young boy who passed the king vexing letters from the pope was tortured by having his eyes gouged and being forced to drink boiling water.[11] And of course the archbishop himself was cut down, if not on Henry's orders then at least at his unwitting instigation. These deeds would not be forgotten by the generation that followed: Indeed, the murderous cruelty of the old king seemed to be the prelude to the even worse behavior of his sons.

The sons, indeed, were a dangerous bunch—relentlessly ambitious, rebellious, and untrustworthy—and Henry recognized as much. Toward the end of his life he had a mural painted in his chamber at Winchester Castle representing his family as he saw them. This is now lost, but according to Gerald of Wales it featured "an eagle painted, and four young ones of the eagle perched upon it, one on each wing and a third upon its back tearing at the parent with talons and beaks, and the fourth, no smaller than the others, sitting upon its neck and awaiting the moment to peck out its parent's eyes." Henry was fond of telling his friends that the eaglets were his sons, and the fourth and most vicious was John, "the youngest, whom I now embrace with such tender affection, [who] will someday afflict me more grievously and perilously than all of the others."[12] And so it would transpire.

Henry II died at the Plantagenet fortress of Chinon, in the Loire, during the hot summer of 1189. His later years had been made miserable by struggles with a new French king, Philip II, known as Philip Augustus, and wars with his impatient and rebellious children over their inheritances. On his deathbed he learned to his dismay that his beloved son John had joined a rebellion against his rule. It was said that the news finally broke his spirit. His eldest adult son with Eleanor, Henry, "the Young King," predeceased him (as did their third son, Geoffrey), and so it was Richard "the Lionheart" who was crowned King of England at Westminster Abbey on Sunday, September 3, 1189.

Richard would become one of the most celebrated kings in British history; he remains the only monarch to be commemorated with a statue outside the Houses of Parliament. This is ironic, for of all the kings who reigned after the Norman Conquest, Richard probably spent the least time—and took the least personal interest—in his English kingdom. His reign would see his father's reforms and policies pushed to greater extremes. It would also see the arrival on the political stage of Richard's controversial and deeply untrustworthy youngest brother, John "Lackland," the man who would come to suffer the consequences of all his family's misdeeds.

Lionheart and Softsword

RICHARD I'S HEART, leonine as it might have been, never truly lay in England. Today it can be found in Normandy, at Rouen Cathedral, where the mummified remains of the organ (removed from his body at death) have collapsed into a pile of grayish brown powder, mingled together with grains of frankincense, daisy, mint, and myrtle, the substances that were used to preserve it. But in the prime of Richard's life, this heart throbbed with a lust for warfare and adventure, which was fulfilled on battlefields from western France to the plains of the Holy Land.

Although Richard was born in Oxford, his mother, Eleanor of Aquitaine, raised him as a prince of the wild French south. He subsequently spent most of his adult life outside England and tended to return only when he was truly desperate for money. Nevertheless, the absent Lionheart's grand military ambition would have a profound effect on the realm that gave him his crown, and this most un-English of kings would have his own part to play in the history of that most enduring of English of documents, the Magna Carta.

Like many of the boldest young men of the age, Richard I was a crusader. He was crowned less than a week before his thirty-second birthday, by which time he had already taken the cross and promised solemnly to make an armed pilgrimage to "Outremer," as the Christian lands in the Middle East were then known. The Third Crusade had been called as a response to the fall of Acre and Jerusalem to forces under the great Muslim sultan Saladin. It galvanized princes across Europe, including the French king, Philip Augustus, and the Holy Roman Emperor, Frederick Barbarossa. The King of England had no intention of being left behind.

"The son, becoming greater and greater, enlarged the good works of his father, while the bad ones he cut short." Such was Roger of Howden's initial assessment of Richard's succession to the English crown.[1] But it is largely a piece of flattery from a writer who had close connections at court and who traveled extensively with his king about the Holy Land. It is true that Richard, like Henry II, promised at his coronation to protect the liberties of the English Church and to provide justice to his subjects. However, as Howden reports in a more truthful phrase, once the king was crowned and had taken oaths of allegiance from all his nobles, he "put up for sale everything he had."[2] Crusading was a dazzlingly expensive business, and Richard drained his new realm for all it was worth. As hired ships were loaded with thousands of salted pig carcasses, horseshoes, arrows, and other provisions necessary to fight a long war far from home, the king's leading subjects were exploited by every means available. Castles, offices, lands, and lordships were effectively auctioned off in a frenzy of selling before the king set sail. Henry II had designed a slick system of government that could raise money efficiently and operate in the king's absence. Richard drove the machine with single-minded vigor.

The pipe rolls of Richard's reign point to 1190 as a year of impressive financial exaction.* A special tax known as the Saladin tithe had been levied across the Plantagenet empire to help pay for the costs of crusading. This was supplemented with a year of intense royal fund-

*Pipe rolls were the annual records of royal finances kept by the Exchequer and were so called because the long documents (of parchment made from sheepskin) were rolled up to form pipe shapes. An almost complete run of these records exists from the midtwelfth century to the early nineteenth century and is held in the National Archives in Kew, England.

raising through the regular channels of government. While the regular royal income shown on the pipe rolls of Henry II's later years came to £22,000, in 1190 Richard managed to extract £31,089 from his realm—a jump of close to 50 percent.[3] The bulk of this rise came from two sources—the profits of justice and the exploitation of Richard's feudal rights as king. The former included fees charged for access to royal courts via writs, the sale of official positions (including most of England's shrievalties—the offices of sheriffs), and the confirmation of charters that had been previously granted by Henry II. On top of this the king imposed heavy feudal levies on his barons, significantly increasing the payments they had to make for permission to marry, to inherit, or to exercise wardship over underage heirs. The crusade inflation of these payments was sharp, and it must have been with some relief, as well as excitement, that England bade farewell to its energetic and zealous new ruler when he left Dover in December 1189, two months after his coronation, on his heroic quest to destroy the infidel armies and to chase them from Jerusalem. He would be gone for more than four years.

Richard's reputation in his day (and ever since) was founded on his peerless brilliance as a military leader. He had a good crusade, fighting his way through Sicily, conquering Cyprus, and arriving in splendor in Outremer just in time to participate in the last stages of the successful siege of Acre. Once the city fell, Richard reinforced Jaffa and Ascalon (Ashkelon today, in Israel), and secured a three-year truce with Saladin, during which time unarmed Christian pilgrims were granted safe access to Jerusalem. By the time he left the Holy Land in October 1192, Richard was famous across the known world and had made himself the object of Saladin's admiration. Unfortunately, he had also made some powerful enemies among his Christian allies, and on his way back to Europe Richard was shipwrecked off the northeast Italian coast, captured by Duke Leopold of Austria, and sold to the Holy Roman Emperor, Henry VI, who jailed him at Trifels Castle, high in the mountains of what is now southwestern Germany. The price of his freedom was a vast ransom of 150,000 marks (£100,000)—roughly the cost of another crusade—which had to be raised in a matter of months. For the second time in less than five years, England was bled to pay for the adventures of its charismatic ruler.

That England paid Richard's ransom at all was down to the efforts of the levelheaded and loyal men whom the king had placed in charge of the government during his absence. They included William Long-champ (bishop of Ely), Walter of Coutances (bishop of Rouen), and Hubert Walter (archbishop of Canterbury) and were directed by the king's "much-beloved" mother, Eleanor, now in her late sixties but still a regal force of nature.[4] Together they worked Europe's diplomatic channels, found hostages and ships when these were demanded by the king's captors, levied a 25 percent tax on income and movable posses-sions (i.e., property excluding buildings and land), requisitioned a whole year's supply of wool from England's Cistercian abbeys, and pressed Richard's personal request for English churches to send "the whole of the gold and silver" that they kept, which he promised to re-turn on his release.[5] Astonishingly, 100,000 marks—two thirds of the ransom—was raised within a year, and on February 4, 1194, Richard was released, quite literally, into the arms of his mother. He returned to England on March 13, wore his crown in a ceremony at Westmin-ster Abbey a month later, and went on a rapid tour of his kingdom. Then, on May 12, 1194, he put to sea at Portsmouth, leaving to defend Normandy and the rest of his Continental possessions from attack by King Philip Augustus. Another round of expensive military cam-paigning loomed. As it turned out, Richard would have five years more of fighting ahead of him. He would never see his kingdom again.

Between 1194 and 1199 Richard performed some mighty military deeds. During his crusade and captivity, his Continental lands had been sorely depleted, mainly thanks to the efforts of his feckless brother John. Although John had been bribed to stay out of England during the king's absence—he had been given a massive income from the revenues of six English counties and the Royal Duchy of Lancaster, as well as the Continental title of "Count of Mortain"—he had ignored orders, entering the country, provoking armed confrontations with Richard's officials, and trying to seize control of government for himself. Then, when his English machinations had faltered, John had gone over to the Continent, where he allied himself with the French king and agreed to grant away Richard's most strategically important lands and mighty castles in return for Philip Augustus's recognizing him as rightful ruler of Plantagenet holdings in France. When it was apparent that Richard was going to be released from his Austrian captivity, John joined with Philip Augustus in offering to pay the Holy Roman Emperor to keep Richard locked up for longer than the agreed term. Magnanimously, if not wisely, Richard forgave John almost immediately on his release in 1194—and then set about his war with France. The result was a long and bloody series of campaigns merely to restore his lands to their condition and extent at the time of his inheritance from Henry II.

Richard's sphere of operations stretched from the Vexin, a hotly disputed portion of land on the border between Normandy and the lands directly controlled by Philip Augustus, to Brittany, Berry, Poitou, and the Limousin. Costly alliances were made with men like Richard's former captor, Emperor Henry VI, as well as Baldwin, Count of Flanders, and a large number of other noblemen whose borders touched France. An extraordinary military supply chain was set up, connecting Portsmouth with the Norman castle towns along the Seine, culminating in a magnificent fortified palace at Les

Andelys known as Château Gaillard, which was built at massive expense (at least twelve thousand pounds, or half a year's English royal income) in just two years, between 1196 and 1198. The war was fought on land and from the sea, and it provided men like William Marshal, one of the most famous knights of the age, with a wealth of anecdotes and tall tales to tell his grandchildren.[6] It was supremely successful. By January 1199 Richard's enemies had been beaten into submission on every front and he was planning seriously to go east once again for the Fourth Crusade, proposed by a new pope, Innocent III.

A close look at Richard's accounts shows us that England paid dearly for this long process of restoration and reconquest. Analysis of the pipe rolls has shown that during the period 1194–98 the average revenue taken from England was nearly £25,000, peaking in 1196, when £28,323 went through the books.[7] Once again the proceeds of justice, the king's feudal rights, and taxation (such as scutage, levied notionally only in emergency, when the king needed to raise an army to defend the realm) were exploited to scoop money out of England for use across the Channel. And there were innovations too. In 1198 the king levied a "carucage"—a new land tax, initially assessed according to the size of estates as recorded in the great census of England carried out after the Norman Conquest that was known as the Domesday Book.* This raised £1,000 and appears to have been unpopular, as Richard's officials were obliged to investigate and punish with fines numerous instances of avoidance. In the short term such measures brought Richard the means with which to cow Europe with his untouchable military brilliance.

---

*A "carucate" was the amount of land that could be plowed by an eight-ox team in a year: somewhere between 100 and 120 acres.

In the long term, however, problems were starting to build that would spill over into his brother's reign.

Richard's death came suddenly, and shockingly, in the spring of 1199. While commanding a siege at the castle of Châlus-Chabrol in the Limousin on March 26, he was hit in the shoulder by a crossbow bolt fired speculatively from a battlement by a man using a frying pan for a shield. The wound was attended to by a field surgeon but went gangrenous, and by April 11 the Lionheart was dead.

Despite a marriage to Berengaria of Navarre, Richard had never had any children. He left his empire intact, the Crown somewhat impoverished, and his brother John as his heir. It was a combination that would have disastrous consequences.

✝

People loathed John. For all the attempts that have been made by historians to rehabilitate his reputation, any study of England's third Plantagenet ruler must account for the fact that he was a cruel and unpleasant man, a second-rate soldier, and a slippery, faithless, interfering, uninspiring king. It is true that at times John was no *less* ruthless than his brother Richard, nor any less manipulative than his father, Henry. Kings in this age were not supposed or expected to be nice. (Those who were too holy, such as Louis VII "the Pious" of France, were mocked behind their backs.) But if John's relatives shared some of his worst traits, he shared almost none of their best.

John stood slightly below average height at five feet six and a half inches. Middle age would gray his hair, although his teeth remained in good condition until the end of his life.[8] He wore expensive cloaks lined with miniver fur, and he loved jewels. (When he lost a necklace in 1202, John rewarded a man called Berchal, who happened to find it, with a generous annual income of twenty shillings.[9]) He was known for the changeability of his moods: In good humor he could be generous and openhanded, but it was hard to know at any moment what to expect from him. He was regularly seen sniggering with his closest companions, with whom he shared a sense of humor that delighted in others' misfortunes. When angered, John would dissolve into paroxysms of fury that reminded many of his father. The chronicler Richard of Devizes provided a sketch of his losing his temper: "Wrath cut furrows across his forehead; his burning eyes shot sparks; rage darkened the ruddy colour of his face."[10]

Our most famous image of John shows him hunting, colorfully dressed in a red tunic covered by a bright blue cloak, which billows around him as he charges on a great white horse tacked with gold stirrups and a gold bit.[11] This ink drawing was produced many years after the king's death and is certainly idealized; John is wearing his crown while chasing a stag, after all. But it still hints at the awesome spectacle of the monarch and his entourage. Certainly the king's servants' outfits were bright and regularly replaced: His greyhound keepers wore blue, his messengers green. John paid attention to the appearance of even his lowliest servants. His wife's washerwoman wore rabbit fur, paid for from the royal Exchequer.[12]

John was certainly an excellent administrator who knew his way around the departments of his own government, took an expert personal interest in the workings of royal justice, and kept a lavish, openhanded court. But these were not the primary measures by which men of his time assessed him, and even if we allow for the fact that some of the best surviving descriptions were written with hindsight by men who judged his whole life by the ignominy of its end, it is still clear that this was not a man who was considered fit for kingship.

Ralph of Coggeshall lived through John's reign and despaired of the king, pointing out his cruelty, his small-minded viciousness, his threatening manner, and his childish habit of ridiculing his subjects.

Ralph wrote from the distance of the 1220s, once John was dead and the Magna Carta had been reissued several times, but other, more strictly contemporary authors agreed with him. The writer known as the Anonymous of Béthune thought John was wicked, petty, and lecherous and made frequent references to John's lack of chivalry.[13] The southern French poet Bertrand de Born the Younger wrote that "no man may ever trust him / For his heart is soft and cowardly."[14] William of Newburgh, disgusted by John's treachery during Richard's imprisonment, called him "nature's enemy": a man who heaped "infinite curses on his own perfidious head."[15] Suspicious, paranoid, and absurdly secretive, John would establish elaborate codes and passwords to differentiate his real orders from fake ones, only to forget his own passwords.[16] His treatment of prisoners was also notoriously cruel: Those who fell afoul of him could expect to be fettered or chained in dungeons, where they would be starved or worse. John's reputation went before him, and it was a major factor in the political history of his reign.

By the time John came to the throne, in April 1199, he had already worked up quite a record for duplicity and troublemaking. Sent to Ireland in 1185 as a nineteen-year-old prince, he had offended the local lords as soon as he had landed. Gerald of Wales, who accompanied him on the expedition, recalled that he treated the natives "with contempt and derision, [and] even rudely pulled them by their beards, which the Irishmen wore full and long, according to the custom of their country."[17] Later John abandoned his dying father during the last war of Henry II's reign, in 1189. He then betrayed Richard by stirring up armed disputes in England during the Third Crusade and attempting to sell the family's lands to the King of France. Five years of muted loyalty to Richard, between 1194 and 1199, did very little to turn popular opinion John's way, and when the news of Richard's death spread across the Plantagenet lands, there were large numbers of people who objected very strongly to the announcement that his brother had been named as successor.

It was, in fact, only with some difficulty that John secured his succession at all. His former dealings with Philip Augustus had been craven enough to convince the French king that John was a man who could be dominated by aggression. (As Richard had put it, John was not a man who could conquer a realm by force if there was force to oppose him.[18]) Philip's judgment was correct. As soon as Richard's death was known, the French invaded the Duchy of Normandy and Philip Augustus encouraged his allies up and down the rest of the Plantagenet dominions to rise up in rebellion. As a result, John began his reign fighting a defensive war on several fronts, and in 1200 he was forced to accede to the terms of the Treaty of Le Goulet, which compelled him to pay homage to the French king and acknowledge the loss of a considerable chunk of his lands in Normandy and claims to overlordship elsewhere. The chronicler Gervase of Canterbury, commenting on John's willingness to accept the unfavorable terms of Le Goulet, wrote that he "would rather achieve peace by negotiation than fight for his own terms, and because of this his enemies and detractors call him John Softsword."[19]

From the beginning John was troubled by the existence of a rival candidate for his lands and titles: Arthur, Duke of Brittany, the son of John's late elder brother Geoffrey. Born in 1187, Arthur had just turned twelve when Richard died, but his claim to the Plantagenet crown was considered by some, including the King of France, to be superior to John's. Indeed, in 1190 Richard had actually named Arthur—then less than three years old—as his successor should he die on crusade. Arthur and John were therefore direct rivals, a fact gleefully exploited by Philip Augustus. For the next three years—and indeed for quite some time beyond—Arthur of Brittany would be a thorn in John's side.

John had been crowned king at Westminster Abbey on May 27, 1199, but, much like his brother, he made it a very brief visit to England. Even after the Treaty of Le Goulet his main preoccupation was with defending his lands from further incursions by Philip and Arthur. This required his near-constant presence on the Continent. It looked as though England were going to experience a third successive absentee king with a chronic need for financial support. In that sense at least it was business as usual. And despite being married for ten years to Isabel of Gloucester, John, like his brother Richard, had no heir.

Soon, however, everything would change. In August 1200 John, having secured an annulment of his marriage to Isabel of Gloucester, took as his wife a young girl from Aquitaine called Isabella of Angoulême. That she was twelve years old was no great outrage by the standards of the day. That she was already betrothed to someone else was more problematic. Isabella's intended was Hugh de Lusignan, and the marriage was due to draw together the two most prominent, troublesome, and mutually hostile families of the Gascon south. By effectively kidnapping Hugh's bride, John achieved the impressive feat of pushing these enemy clans into each other's arms and giving Philip Augustus an excuse to launch, in 1202, a fresh round of punitive invasions of Plantagenet territories.

During the subsequent war John managed to capture Arthur, during an impressive military operation at Mirebeau, in Anjou. But this was a rare success. John consistently antagonized and alienated his own allies, many of whom abandoned or turned on him. Within a year Anjou, Maine, Touraine, and parts of Poitou had all fallen to Philip, ripping the heart out of the Plantagenet empire. John retreated to Normandy, taking Arthur with him. Just before Easter

1203 Arthur disappeared, almost certainly murdered at Rouen, possibly by a drunk and angry John himself—he was said to have crushed the sixteen-year-old's head with a heavy stone and thrown his body into the river Seine.[20]

In the summer of 1203 Philip invaded western Normandy and laid siege to Château Gaillard, the greatest symbol of Richard the Lionheart's muscular kingship. This castle was built to be invincible: It had cost twice as much as the greatest defensive castle in England, the one at Dover, and Richard was said to have claimed its position, high above the Seine, was so good that he could hold it even if the walls were made of butter. John holding it was another matter. With Normandy falling around him, John was said to have gone into a paranoid decline, fearful to ride the open highways in case of attack and convinced that traitors lay all around him. Gossips had it that he spent all day lying in bed with his young bride, Isabella.[21] Whether or not this was true, in December 1203 John abandoned Normandy, sailing for England and leaving his duchy to its fate.

The following summer the supposedly impregnable Château Gaillard fell and Caen, Rouen, and—farther south—Poitiers all surrendered. On March 31, 1204, John's spirited but ancient mother, Eleanor of Aquitaine, died at eighty-two. Her formidable presence had kept some order in the empire's south, but her death prompted the King of Castile to invade Gascony. Together all this amounted to a sudden and catastrophic collapse. Within five years of John's accession to the throne, he had lost virtually the whole Continental empire that had been so painstakingly assembled and defended by his father and brother. All that remained loyal was a coastal strip of Aquitaine around Bordeaux. This fact of geography had very pronounced long-term implications for John and the future shape of government in the English-speaking world. For the first time in more than half a century, a Plantagenet King of England would be obliged to live among the English people.

✠

The loss of Normandy is often described as one of the great turning points in England's medieval history. It was obviously a terrible military defeat for John, an illustration of his low stock as a leader, and a blow to his reputation. There were also financial implications. The wealth—and thus the military power—of the King of France, Philip Augustus, had been growing steadily since the 1190s, boosted by territorial acquisitions including the rich Flemish county of Artois and the Vermandois. Sucking Normandy, Anjou, Maine, and Touraine back into the orbit of the French Crown made Philip's position even stronger. Under Henry II and during Richard's early years the Plantagenet Crown had been much richer than the French Capetian royal house. Now those roles were decisively reversed.

Ejection from Normandy therefore redrew the political and conceptual map of western Europe. English kings had been dukes of Normandy since William the Conqueror had stood victorious at the Battle of Hastings in 1066, and during those 138 years the two territories had become tightly bound together. Many barons loyal to the English king held lands on both sides of the Channel. There was a common Anglo-Norman aristocratic language and culture, and trade, commerce, warfare, and society operated on the assumption that the realms were linked by a common ruler. Wrenching apart the kingdom and the duchy would have profound consequences for the men and women for whom this duality was the normal order of life.

As Philip Augustus rode imperiously about Normandy, landholders there were forced to come to a decision. Feudal practice did not permit a man to pay homage to two vying lords, because one of the conditions of submitting to a king was to promise to serve him

in war. In 1204, therefore, men with lands in England and Normandy had to make a choice: They could either lay their allegiance
at the feet of the English king or submit to France. Those who sided
with John kept their English estates but were liable to lose the land
they held across the Channel. Those who decided to safeguard their
Norman property were almost instantly cut off in England.

Whenever John learned that one of his lords had decided to throw
in his lot with Philip Augustus, he immediately ordered that lord's
English lands to be seized by the Crown and his name to be entered
onto a register known as the *Rotulus de valore terrarum Normannorum*
("Roll of the Values of the Lands of the Normans").[22] Some barons—
including men like William Marshal—attempted to work around
feudal protocol and hold onto some or all of their lands across the new
divide, with limited success. Only a tiny minority could make such
arrangements work. It may be an exaggeration to say that the loss of
Normandy drove a permanent cultural wedge between two peoples
divided by the Channel, for it was not until the fourteenth century
and the Hundred Years' War that the English and French began to
regard each other as enemies and opposites. Nevertheless, the year
1204 demanded a clear choice from the Anglo-Norman nobility. Were
they English subjects or not? And if so, what did that imply? The idea
that England was a "community" with collective rights would underpin much of the philosophy of the Magna Carta in 1215; it was a feeling
that was accentuated by the loss of Normandy in 1204.

In King John's own eyes the loss of Normandy demanded revenge.
He was tormented by the sense that he had to win back the homeland
and heartlands of his ancestors. For the next ten years John did everything within his power to amass enough treasure, troops, and foreign
allies to return to the Continent and reconquer what he had lost. But
this was now a doubly difficult business. Without Normandy John
lacked both a beachhead in northern France from which to advance his

armies and a supply chain of fortresses along the Seine. He had also lost the duchy's revenues. Normandy had paid for some portion of its own defense during the reigns of Henry and Richard, but now any expedition would have to be financed in full from England. So the task was enormous. Yet John was not daunted. This single-minded obsession would lead him into a fateful trial of strength with his own barons.

In the years that followed 1204 England got to know its new king. Whereas John's father and brother had spent very little time in their kingdom, now there was nowhere else for the monarch to go. For the first five years of John's reign he would have been known to many of his royal subjects only from his coins, from which a wrathful cartoon face glared out, eyes popping from the thin features, with flowing locks of hair and a short beard. Now John made his presence strongly felt.

Like his father, John was an irrepressibly energetic traveler. He spent his whole life on the road, his court snaking out behind him in a caravan train that was driven along at an unholy pace of up to thirty miles a day. The court never stayed in one place for more than a month and only rarely lodged anywhere for longer than a night or two. Even before the loss of Normandy John had shown himself inclined to visit the forgotten corners of his realm, including towns of the north like York and Newcastle, where people had previously set eyes on a Plantagenet king only once in a generation.[23] But this was no mere tourism. John's determination to tramp even the chilliest highways of his kingdom sprang from a deep desire to see that his government was as efficient, wide-reaching, and profitable as possible.

Despite the many demands that had been placed on England during the earlier Plantagenet years, John's realm was rich—and getting richer. Several years of acute inflation around the turn of the century wobbled but did not seriously damage a rapidly diversifying economy, which one recent historian has described as experiencing "an exceptional period of overall expansion . . . fuelled to a great extent by a tremendous surge in commercial activity."[24] New towns, markets, and fairs were being founded at a record rate. Goods were being transported faster and farther as England's farmers switched to horses (rather than oxen) to pull carts whose wheels were often clad in iron around the rims to prevent them from shattering on long journeys along potholed roads. An international trade in wool and cloth was beginning to boom, bringing great quantities of produce and coin in and out of the ports of the southeast.[25] This was a realm from which a king fixated on fighting an expensive war of reconquest could quite reasonably decide to take his cut.

John took to his task with gusto. In his methods he stayed true to his Plantagenet predecessors: He exploited the profits of justice through the royal courts and via his rights over royal forests, maximized his income from feudal payments, squeezed sheriffs for ever-higher returns from their administration of the shires, and imposed one-off taxes such as scutage with increasing and unprecedented frequency. A handsome trade was done too in selling exemptions from royal justice: The king could, and did, sell immunity from lawsuits at the shire courts, and he charged aristocratic widows vast sums for the right to remarry the man of their choice rather than being subjected to forced marriage, as the king technically had the right to do. Areas defined as royal forest were subject to special royal jurisdiction, and fines against those who breached the forest law produced lucrative profits—making this another area that received John's merciless attention. During John's reign and the reigns of Henry II and Richard I before him new swaths of the countryside had been designated as forest—which could mean moorland and agricultural land as well as thick patches of trees. On forest land hunting deer and boar was forbidden, as was collecting firewood, felling trees to clear the land, or erecting buildings. Harsh fines and corporal punishments could be levied on those who transgressed. The forest was the king's personal property and lay outside the normal scope of the law. When more and more of the English countryside was being classified as forest, this became a burden on an increasing number of people, or as Richard FitzNigel, author of the *Dialogue of the Exchequer* had put it: "Those who have their homes in the forest may not take wood from their own woodlands for use in their own homes."[26]

None of these measures were wholesale innovations: All had their roots in the practices of his father and brother. What made John different was the sheer scale and relentlessness with which he bled his realm. Over the course of his reign his average annual income was at least £37,483—far higher than either his father or his brother had ever achieved.[27] But his need was greater still.

John attempted to invade France in the early summer of 1205 and then again in 1206. Neither mission was successful. In the first instance the English barons refused to turn out in support of the king's invasion fleet, and in the second John was kept firmly at bay by the armies of Philip Augustus and had to settle for a two-year truce. Yet the Plantagenet king never gave up believing that he was obliged—perhaps even destined—to one day return to the lands he had lost and reclaim them. The consequences of this urge for revenge and restoration would be severe, both for John and for his kingdom, in which he was now so firmly stuck.

3

Interdict and Intimidation

T HE TEN YEARS that followed the loss of Normandy saw John achieve a form of mastery over England and the British Isles that, although brief, was scarcely bettered by any medieval king after him. Hobbled in France, John made it his business to stamp his authority over Wales and Scotland, to plunder and command the English Church, and to impose his will on the barons under his authority. If he did not exactly make himself popular or well loved, he nevertheless grew into his role as a fearsome lord. By the end of the first decade of the thirteenth century, the writer known as the Crowland Chronicler could write that "in Ireland, Scotland and Wales there was no man who did not obey the nod of the King of England— a thing, which it is well known, had never happened to any of his forefathers."[1] For a time, at least, John was supreme. But beneath the mastery he was amassing serious problems.

The area of policy that earned John the most infamy among the monastic chroniclers of his day was that of his relations with the pope. Across western Christendom, kings were engaged in a grand struggle with the papacy to mark out the extent of their control over the Church—an argument that frequently focused on the issue of ecclesiastical appointments. Kings claimed the right to appoint bishops in their own kingdoms, but popes were seldom happy to allow this and reserved their right to confirm appointments—or veto those that displeased them. Just such a debate blew up in 1206 between John and Pope Innocent III.

In the summer of 1205 Hubert Walter, a highly capable but essentially pliant archbishop of Canterbury, suffered a high fever brought on by an infected carbuncle and breathed his last. This was a loss to the Crown, but it was also an important opportunity for John to appoint a new man who would, like Hubert (and unlike Becket, his father's nemesis), serve the needs of the king with at least the same diligence with which he served those of his flock. John's choice was his former Chancery clerk and close ally John de Gray, bishop of Norwich. Because the monks of the cathedral chapter in Canterbury claimed the privilege of electing the new archbishop, John leaned on them to choose his man. The monks had other ideas. Instead of electing de Gray they picked a man called Reginald, subprior of their chapter, and packed him off to Rome to seek papal confirmation for his new post.

John was livid and lobbied the pope to respect his choice. Innocent hesitated for a few months and finally, after much petitioning and deliberation, he made up his mind. His decision was altogether unexpected: He rejected both claimants and imposed his own candidate, Cardinal Stephen Langton. An Englishman by birth and a brilliant Continental scholar by training, Langton was supposed to be a compromise appointment. He would turn out to be anything but.

Langton's appointment was enraging to John, and not simply because his royal authority had been overridden from Rome. The man whom Innocent wished to impose on him as archbishop had been born in Lincolnshire to a family of minor nobles and had spent twenty years as a star theologian at the University of Paris—the capital city of John's most hated rival. In hundreds of lectures given in Paris, Langton had developed ideas that clashed directly with John's view of kingship. Langton condemned "the avarice . . . of modern kings," criticizing those who "collect treasure not in order that they may sustain necessity, but to satiate their cupidity." He recommended that kings apply themselves diligently to studying (and, by implication, observing) the law and that they refrain from pursuing their subjects without proper judicial process.[2] He toyed with the idea that, as he put it, "when a king errs, the people should resist him as far as they can," considering even that "if they do not, they sin."[3] In short, Langton was a scholar in the tradition of Becket and of the distinguished and prolific theologian John of Salisbury—both of whom had been severely critical of Plantagenet kings and had gone to great lengths to defend the principle that ecclesiastical authority outranked the power of princes. For all his intellectual concern with the corruption and correction of kings, Langton would, through his actions, demonstrate a remarkably pragmatic attitude to earthly politics. Nevertheless, in 1206 he was hardly a promising candidate for a peaceful coexistence between Church and state. When Innocent secured his election at Canterbury and consecrated him personally at Viterbo, north of Rome, in June 1207, an almighty standoff began.

John's rage at being thwarted was always spectacular. He was not cowed by the fact that his opponent in this instance was God's anointed vicar-in-chief. In response to Langton's consecration John seized all the lands belonging to Canterbury and threw the monks who had dared to defy him out of England. But in Innocent he had a more than worthy opponent. The pope was a reformer, a crusader, and a strict clerical authoritarian. He was an unbending believer in Roman supremacy who disliked any show of willfulness by mere princes. So in response to John's heavy-handed behavior, in March 1208 Innocent laid an interdict on England.

An interdict was a severe sentence. It forbade all church services, effectively placing the souls of everyone affected by it into limbo. Marriages could not be consecrated, most baptisms could not take place, and the dead could not be buried with the usual Christian rites. The bells of England's churches fell silent. The Mass went uncelebrated. This was a punishment felt far beyond the household of the king who had invited it. But if there was one man in England who was entirely unbothered by the interdict, it was John.

John saw his falling-out with Rome in simple terms: It was an unmissable financial opportunity. As soon as the interdict was pronounced, he began confiscating ecclesiastical treasure, land, and property. Some of it was ransomed back to its owners; the rest was simply used to provide income for the king. Churchmen's mistresses were arrested and sold back to their unhappy lovers. The ample revenues of the Church were diverted straight into the royal coffers, and John's castles and strongholds, where he stockpiled his own money, began to fill with silver at a rate his ancestors could only have dreamed of. This was, in short, clerical extortion on a dizzying scale. And it tossed religious life in England into disarray for more than five years.

+

The English Church had been established in the late seventh century and by John's time, nearly five hundred years later, it was rich, institutionally self-confident, and knitted into politics, law, government, culture, the economy, education, art, and architecture at every level of society. The Church baptized and buried virtually every single person born in England. Most people who married did so in accordance with the rites and laws of the Church. Thousands of parish churches, scattered the length and breadth of the realm and overseen by seventeen English (and four Welsh) bishops, were hubs for both villagers and townsmen. The bells that rang in their square stone towers kept the hours of the day and their services (whether or not attended) were a reassurance to the general population that God was being honored and his favor sought. This was more than a matter of theology. People believed that there was a real life after death and that one's destination in the afterlife—be it heaven, purgatory, or hell—could be affected by deeds done on earth. The Church therefore bore an enormous responsibility for the spiritual well-being of every man, woman, and child in the realm.

A large section of English society was bound to the Church by employment, training, or consecration. Indeed, by John's time as many as one sixth of all Englishmen were clerks of some description: entitled among other things to tax relief and the right to be punished for crimes by the more lenient Church courts rather than the king's courts, which sentenced many miscreants to mutilation or death. The institutional hierarchy of the Church consisted of bishops, priests, deacons, and subdeacons, known collectively as the "major orders"; but there were many other sorts of clerics who had received some form of church training and wore the tonsure to mark them out from the rest of the population. The minor orders included porters, who looked after church doors; lectors, who read from the New Testament at Mass; exorcists, who maintained a supply of holy water and were therefore involved in baptisms and blessings; and acolytes, who assisted the priest during the Eucharist. Beyond these were "secular" clerics working outside the hierarchy of the Church. They ranged from priests employed in the private chapels of lords and kings to educated administrators who had been schooled by the Church in reading and writing and could therefore work as secretaries, scribes, or teachers. All were expected to wear the tonsure, to avoid trouble and taverns, to dress plainly, and to refrain from bearing arms. Many did so, although not all. Violent clerics were a bugbear of Henry II—and the issue of disciplining them had been the source of his dispute with Becket in the 1160s. At the great reforming Fourth Lateran Council late in 1215

the pope would issue decrees against churchmen who were ignorant, decadent, or sexually deviant.*

The Church also included monks, canons, and nuns living
under various rules, from crusading orders like the Templars to
ordinary brethren who lived together in monastic communities
promising obedience to an austere rule that celebrated chastity and
poverty and rejected individual indulgence of any sort.† Benedic-
tine monks followed the rule of St. Benedict and were known as
"black monks" thanks to their dark attire (symbolizing their commitment to penance), but there were plenty of other "white monks"
such as the Cistercians (named for their origin in Cîteaux, in Burgundy), who deliberately tried to pursue an even more austere and
physically grinding lifestyle than the Benedictines, mostly living in
monasteries located in remote areas. (In 1203 John himself had
founded and richly endowed a Cistercian abbey in Hampshire: It
was known as Bellus Locus Regis, or "the beautiful place of the
king," shortened and Francified to "Beaulieu." This was the place
where he intended to be buried.) The few Carthusians in England
were more self-denying still—living in tiny communities and
spending most of their time alone in contemplation and suffering.
Then there were canons, who also obeyed a rule (usually that of St.

---

*The stereotype of the randy or roguish priest was a staple throughout the Middle
Ages, with some justification. In popular culture it was summed up nowhere better
than in the genre of bawdy poems known as fabliaux, which were popular from the
twelfth through the fourteenth centuries. Surviving fabliaux include the tale of a sly
priest who tricks a guileless peasant into giving him a cow but then loses two cows to
the peasant as his punishment and another of a pompous bishop who finds a sparkling, jeweled ring on the path and takes it for himself, only to find to his horror that
it is a magic ring that bestows uncontrollable virility on the wearer, giving the bishop
a mighty erection that bursts through his breeches and drags along the ground.

†Despite the austerity of their rule, monks employed large numbers of servants to
farm, cook, and clean. Some monastic orders included lay brothers: unordained, usually poor and illiterate men who lived separately and performed the more onerous
menial tasks in the monastery.

Augustine) and lived in communities but were generally associated
with cathedrals or other public places of worship and performed
more priestly functions. Nunneries were less common than monasteries: There were around 500 male religious houses in England in
1215 and only around 150 female ones.[4] (There were basic practical
difficulties in establishing female religious houses when women
were not able to become priests as this meant that they could not
celebrate the Mass alone; nunneries were thus generally attached
to—and very often built near—monasteries.)

This was, in short, a society in which the Church loomed large
and stood as the ultimate guarantor of the spiritual health of the
realm. The imposition in 1208 of an interdict by Pope Innocent was
a severe sentence on all of John's subjects. England's collective soul
was placed in peril.

In 1209 Innocent attempted to sharpen his threat against the
English king by personally excommunicating him—at which point
every bishop in England except for two of John's closest allies left
the realm. Again John brushed it off—and with good reason. The
author of the thirteenth-century financial manual known as the
Red Book of the Exchequer reckoned that the interdict enriched John
by perhaps £100,000 above and beyond his normal income—the
equivalent of about four years' royal revenue. More recently it has
been estimated that around half of this sum would have come in
the form of ready cash paid not into the Exchequer but directly into
John's hands via the Royal Chamber.[5] Rather gallingly for the English Church, much of that wealth was spent in diabolical ways:
Large parts of the revenues of Christ Church, Canterbury, were
spent on lavish clothes and jewels for the royal household, hunts-
men and hounds, new costumes for the king's lion and its keeper,
and two thousand crossbow bolts and military uniforms.[6] John's
coronation oath obliged him to protect and defend the interests of

the English Church. He had done nothing of the sort, but for the three or four years that followed the interdict it scarcely seemed to matter. John was, momentarily at least, the richest English king in history.

✝

If John's plunder had been limited to the Church, all might still have been well. But the cost of reconquering his French lands exceeded even what he could squeeze from clergy. From 1207 he began increasing his extortions more generally. That year a tax of a thirteenth—the heaviest of his reign—brought in nearly £60,000.* John claimed that this tax was levied with the agreement of "the archbishop, bishops, abbots, priors and magnates of our kingdom"; in fact he had taken no such advice. The levy had been conceived and agreed at a meeting with a small number of his intimates and favorites.[7]

Several other punitive taxes were levied on England's Jews, including a collective imposition of 66,000 marks in 1210. The law regarded the Jews as the king's personal property—ultimately answerable to him for their lives, livelihoods, and freedom to work. Affection toward his charges was nowhere to be seen in John: According to the chronicler Roger of Wendover, those who would not or could not meet the king's demands were beaten until their teeth fell out.† Meanwhile, the standard practices of Plantagenet king-

---

*A "thirteenth" meant a thirteenth of the value of all portable property ("movables").

†Wendover was writing after John's reign, and he is generally to be treated with caution when discussing the king's excesses; all the same, his description of John's harshness toward England's Jews is in keeping with common attitudes at the time. The thirteenth century in England was a time of vigorous anti-Semitism. Jews were heavily involved in finance across Europe, since unlike Christians their religious beliefs did not prohibit them from charging interest on loans. For protection they were heavily reliant on royal favor, which was not always extended. Widespread riots against the Jews took place at

ship were maintained: The profits of justice kept on rising. Most significant of all, so did feudal levies and the ruthless pursuit of indebted barons.

There were just over two hundred barons in England in 1215, of whom the twenty most senior were earls.* Great lords' lands were measured at the time by a unit known as the "knight's fee": It was an inexact unit, as it varied depending on the richness and disposition of the land, but one knight's fee corresponded to the amount of land necessary to provide enough income to sustain a single knight for one year.† At the time only around 130 men held more than ten knight's fees—a level of landholding that would mark them out as barons.[8]

Entry to the baronial class was not an exact science: Some men were born into it, some came to it by marriage or canny acquisition of lands, and some found themselves propelled into noble life by the favor of the king. In a very broad sense the English barons recognized themselves as a class with close family relations, similar interests,

---

the time of Richard the Lionheart's coronation. Subsequently John had targeted Jewish wealth in his drive to raise a war chest: Jews were stripped of their wealth and possessions and often violently mistreated. There was precious little sympathy for their plight. Reporting the "holocaust" (*holocaustum*) that accompanied the Lionheart's coronation, the chronicler Richard of Devizes wrote that Jews were "bloodsuckers" and "worms" and had been "immolated to their father, the Devil." J. T. Appleby, ed. and trans., *The Chronicle of Richard of Devizes* (London: Thomas Nelson and Sons, 1963), 3–4.

*The title of "earl" arrived in England with the Norman Conquest. At the time of the Domesday Book in the 1080s there were seven earls—the ranks had swelled with the most recent creation in 1208 when John made Saer de Quincy Earl of Winchester.

†From the term "fee" we derive the word "feudal" and the notion of the "feudal system," which describes the theoretical relations between all of the free and landed men in England in this period of the Middle Ages. The king was, in theory, the sole "owner" of all land in the country. His barons held the land in return for feudal services. They then subleased it for either cash or further feudal service to other men. There was thus a pyramid of landholding with the king at the top. For every knight's fee's worth of land he held, the baron was obliged to render the service of a knight or pay a fee of the same value when the king demanded it.

agreed standards of behavior, and a collective role to play in the political life of the realm. And yet the barons knew that they owed their position in society to the sponsorship of the king. Every one of them would have knelt before the king, hands clasped inside his, and promised that he would be a faithful servant to his lord. This ceremony of homage was the ritual glue that bonded England's political society. Once made, a promise of fealty could be unmade only in the direst circumstances, for to renege on the oath of loyalty was to become an enemy of the realm.

Once he had paid homage to the king, a baron could comport himself like a miniature king. He held court in a castle, kept a large household of dozens (sometimes hundreds) of male and female servants, took counsel from knights and lesser barons, made judgments in his private courts, sponsored religious houses, commissioned fine chapels in which he and his family would eventually be buried, authenticated documents with his special seal, and identified himself in tournaments and on the move with a heraldic shield and flag emblazoned with his personal coat of arms. Because the upper classes were inevitably involved in warfare, a baron would be dubbed a knight, usually at a young age, and would be aware of (even if he did not always observe) the emerging code of chivalry, designed to give spiritual, social, and ethical guidance to men of great means. Ramon Llull, the thirteenth-century author of *The Book of the Order of Chivalry*, wrote that the duties of a chivalrous man included upholding justice, guarding the highways, defending peasants, "persecuting traitors, thieves and robbers," as well as "going about armed, taking part in tournaments, holding Round Tables, fencing, hunting deer, bears, wild boars, lions and other things similar." He was to reject stealing, gambling, boasting, and sleeping with other lords' wives. [9] These values were also transmitted by some of the most popular stories of the day: the tales of King Arthur, which had been popularized by the gripping, if essentially fanciful, pseudohistory of Geoffrey of Monmouth.*

Barons lived a life of conspicuous wealth and luxury. To do otherwise was seen as shameful. They wore fine, fur-trimmed clothes of imported silk and embroidered cloth. Both the barons and their sons wore expensive armor and could wield a variety of weapons: swords, maces, lances, and daggers. They had sufficient leisure time to enjoy the entertainment of minstrels and acrobats and to play dice, bowls, or chess. (The famous Lewis Chessmen, made from walrus ivory and probably imported from Scandinavia, suggest the opulence of noblemen's luxury trinkets at this time.)[10]

Many of the English barons tasted the king's disfavor during the first decade of the thirteenth century. In 1207 John confiscated the lands of the Earl of Leicester, accusing him of having failed to pay his debts. The East Anglian baron Roger Bigod found himself under such tremendous financial pressure as a result of the Crown's feudal demands that he was forced to strike a deal by which in 1211 he paid the Exchequer £1,333 (twice the fine he had been charged simply to claim his inheritance)—just to have respite from the demands for

---

*Geoffrey of Monmouth was a brilliantly imaginative cleric who lived in the first half of the twelfth century. His *Historia Regum Britanniae* (*History of the Kings of Britain*), completed in 1136, purported to be a translation of a more ancient text relating British history from ancient times. In fact it was a work of Geoffrey's own invention. It was very influential and wildly popular in the Middle Ages, read across Europe and in some cases treated uncritically as a work of scholarship rather than fantastical storytelling. Geoffrey's narrative of King Arthur related the story of a great king who attempted to fulfill the prophecies of Merlin, conquered the Saxons, Picts, and Romans, married Queen Guinevere, and was eventually killed in A.D. 542 following a great battle with the treacherous Mordred. The legend and cult of Arthur bloomed in the centuries following the completion of Geoffrey's *Historia* and continue to fascinate readers today. The evidence for a "real" Arthur, however, is extremely ambiguous and slight. Of the many, many books on the subject, readers might wish to begin with G. Halsall, *Worlds of Arthur: Facts and Fictions of the Dark Ages* (Oxford: Oxford University Press, 2013). For Geoffrey's work in modern translation see L. Thorpe, *Geoffrey of Monmouth: The History of the Kings of Britain* (London: Penguin Books, 1966).

payment. In early 1214 John forced another East Anglian baron, Geoffrey de Mandeville, to agree to a monstrous fine of twenty thousand marks in return for marrying Isabel of Gloucester—John's own now-forty-year-old former wife. Even by the standards of his family these were savage financial impositions. John deliberately pushed numerous barons to the brink of bankruptcy, a state in which they became highly dependent on royal favor. And no one suffered so much as the de Briouze family, whom John hounded mercilessly, combining his mastery of the royal law with his appetite for extreme and unflinching personal brutality.

William de Briouze had been a close associate of both Richard I and John. He had served as a royal sheriff and as a justice of the eyre. He had defended royal interests in Wales and had risked his life numerous times fighting against the insurgent Welsh. He had been at the siege of Châlus-Chabrol on the day that King Richard had died and had helped smooth the path for John to succeed to the Plantagenet crown instead of Arthur of Brittany. He had been with John at Rouen on the day Arthur disappeared and almost certainly knew what had happened to the boy. He was, in short, an impeccably reliable baron, and as reward for his loyal service he had accrued many lands and titles in England, Wales, and Ireland. Yet the obvious side effect of acquiring lands was the financial obligation to pay the king fees for the privilege; de Briouze was therefore entirely typical of a certain high-ranking, loyal sort of English lord in that he had been both rewarded and placed in enormous financial jeopardy as a result of having loyally served the Crown.

Then, in 1208, de Briouze fell out with the king. The reasons are somewhat obscure but may well have resulted from an indiscreet comment made by de Briouze's wife, Matilda, concerning the suspicious circumstances of Arthur of Brittany's death. John heard—or learned of—the comments and, typically, flew into a fury. Suddenly the vast debts incurred on de Briouze's climb through Plantagenet favor became John's chief weapon with which to abuse his friend. Citing nonpayment of debt, John sent his men to seize the de Briouze estates. Fearing for his life, de Briouze fled to Ireland, where he was sheltered for a time by William Marshal. John continued to pursue him, leading an army across the Irish Sea, crushing those who opposed him, and seizing lands as he went. He threatened military action against those who harbored de Briouze and released an open letter in which he used tightly legalistic arguments to justify his dreadful behavior toward a loyal man and insisted that he had acted "according to the laws and custom of England."[11] This may have been so, but because John's position as king allowed him to make and manipulate the law and to enforce it vigorously through his Exchequer, this was of little comfort to those who heard the king's claim explained. When de Briouze's wife, Matilda, approached the king to attempt to negotiate, John prevaricated before taking Matilda and her eldest son as hostages and throwing them into one of his dungeons at Corfe Castle.

William de Briouze escaped to France, where he died an outlaw and an exile in 1211. (His funeral was attended by another exile, Archbishop Stephen Langton.) But William's fate was gentle compared with that of his family. In 1210 Matilda and her son had been starved to death on the king's orders: It was said that when the door to their cell was finally opened they were found huddled against each other in a grotesque knot of death. The mother had died insane with hunger. Her last earthly efforts were to try to eat her child's face.

John's pursuit of the de Briouze family had taken him into Ireland and Wales, which coincided with a broader policy of muscular imposition of English royal power over the Celtic lands in Britain. From 1208 he set about attacking the native princes of North Wales, first humiliating Gwenwynwyn ap Owain, Prince of Powys, and subsequently, in 1211, launching a massive military raid into Gwynedd, smashing the power of Llywelyn ap Iorwerth, known as Llywelyn the Great, and commanding him to forfeit everything east of Conwy to the English Crown. This period of dominance was matched across the Irish Sea. In 1210 John's expedition in pursuit of the de Briouze family had coincided with a brutal campaign of subjection in which Anglo-Norman and native Irish lords alike were brought to heel and English administrative procedures and offices were forced upon Irish territories.

In Scotland similar ultra-aggressive methods were pursued. In 1174 Henry II had forced William I "the Lion," King of Scots, to accept the Treaty of Falaise, under which William had explicitly recognized English overlordship of his kingdom and submitted to the English king "as liege lord."[12] Richard had granted independence back to the Scots in his fire sale of rights before the Third Crusade. But in 1209 John determined to make William, aged and ill, recognize the feudal situation as it had stood thirty-five years earlier. He learned that the Scots had destroyed an English castle at Tweedmouth and that the king was planning to offer one of his daughters in marriage to a Frenchman, thereby securing an alliance with the King of France, Philip Augustus. In response John marched an army north and forced the Lion to agree to the Treaty of Norham, a town in Northumberland. Under the terms of the treaty John was paid fifteen thousand marks and given around thirteen extremely valuable Scottish hostages, including William's daughters Margaret and Isabella, whose marriages John claimed for his own sons, two-year-old Henry and a baby called Richard born in January 1209. "We and the king of Scotland and our sons will help each other for as long as we live," wrote John, describing the terms of the treaty to his subjects in England. "And all ills moved between us will cease in perpetuity."[13] This faux-reasonable tone was absolutely characteristic of John and used most often when he was describing a situation in which he had menaced an enemy into total submission.

By 1212 John had done much to justify the chroniclers' opinions that he had achieved a cruel mastery over his kingdom. He was vastly, almost unimaginably, wealthy, his castles heaving with silver. He oversaw a pitilessly efficient legal and financial administration with which he could crush any baron who was even merely suspected of having slighted him. He had terrorized his neighboring princes into submission. And he appeared impervious to—even slightly amused by—the wrath of Innocent III, one of the most formidable popes ever to wear the tiara. His judicial and financial policies continued apace, with plans for a new judicial commission, known as an eyre, to punish offenses on the king's forest; a scheme by which debts to the Jews would be funneled directly into the king's coffers; and an inquiry into feudal rights, which was intended to squeeze yet more value out of the king's royal prerogatives.[14] This was Plantagenet kingship at its most ruthless and uncompromising. All that now remained for John was to return to France to destroy the armies of King Philip Augustus and recover the lands and castles beyond the Channel that had been lost in 1204.

It was to be his undoing.

4

Crisis and Catastrophe

MIGHTY AS JOHN must have felt in the spring of 1212, his problems with France remained firmly unresolved. The better part of a decade had passed since he had retreated to England from the shores of Normandy, yet still the duchy and the rest of his family's Continental lands lay under the command of Philip Augustus. This was an intolerable situation for any Plantagenet king, and John now had enough silver stockpiled in his English castles to invade Jerusalem if he so wished. The journey to Caen, Rouen, Le Mans, and the rest was hardly prohibitively far, and the mood around Europe was ripe. It was time for John to make his move.

Across western Europe other rulers were beginning to chafe against Philip's bullish lordship—they included the Count of Boulogne, the Duke of Brabant, and others neighboring France, including, most prominently, Otto of Brunswick, the son of John's sister Matilda and her husband Henry, the onetime Duke of Saxony and Bavaria. Otto had been raised at the court of Richard I before embarking on a spectacular political and military career in Germany and Italy, which had seen him rise to become Holy Roman Emperor (as Otto IV) in 1209. These were all serious allies, and all were interested in goading the English king into open hostility with France. Thus, in 1212 John resurrected the policy, once favored by his brother Richard, of creating an anti-French alliance to the north and east of Philip's frontiers, all paid for handsomely with pensions and gifts to these Continental friends. Then, in June, he sent out a feudal summons for an army of his own to meet at Portsmouth. Everything seemed set for an invasion. Instead it was the moment when everything began to fall apart.

John's problems began in Wales. His aggressive treatment of the native princes in 1211 returned to haunt him during the summer of 1212 in the form of a massive revolt under Llywelyn ap Iorwerth. John angrily ordered that a couple of dozen Welsh hostages be hanged, but he was still forced to divert his feudal muster from the south coast of England to Chester, in the northwest. Worse followed. During the summer a hermit known as Peter of Wakefield became briefly notorious for prophesying the king's death; in August the prophecy gained ominous substance when John was told of a plot led by two of his barons—Eustace de Vesci and Robert FitzWalter—to kill him outright or else betray him to the Welsh. John had always tended to be suspicious of his subjects, even those who considered themselves his friends. After this time he would slip into near-constant paranoia.

Undoubtedly de Vesci and FitzWalter had their reasons for plotting against the king. Gossip of the time suggested that John had attempted to seduce both de Vesci's wife and FitzWalter's daughter. Perhaps there was some truth in this. More pertinently, though, it seems that the opposition of these two lords represented two early strains of a more general disaffection with John's reign and the whole system of Plantagenet government. De Vesci was a man of the north, a region of England that had been exposed for the first time, under John, to the full attention of a Plantagenet king and an area that would provide many more rebel barons in the months to follow. As a group England's northern barons felt most aggrieved at the level of royal incursion into previously lightly governed countryside. They had the least historical interest in Normandy—which was, after all, not much nearer than Norway to many of them—and most resented the provision of troops or the paying of scutage for royal expeditions across the Channel. They had the greatest sense of themselves as an independent political group whose interests overlapped and could be threatened by outside interference.

FitzWalter was not, though, a man of the north. He was one of the wealthiest barons in East Anglia and the southeast—indeed, in the whole of England—and had been close to John for many years. He had significant interests in London and the international wine trade. He was also a quarrelsome, violent hardhead. A series of relatively petty clashes with the king appear to have pushed FitzWalter to the fore of baronial opposition, where he would remain for the next three years. He was hardly an ideologue, but he was nevertheless a product of an environment, largely of John's creation, in which the English barons had become so disillusioned, exasperated, and threatened by their king that they were prepared to countenance his murder.

De Vesci and FitzWalter both fled with their families and households, running to Scotland and France respectively, when John discovered their plot. They were outlawed in the county courts. But they were not the only plotters, and their departure neither rid the realm of trouble nor soothed the increasingly agitated mind of the king.

By 1213 John's position was a great deal more precarious than it had been a year earlier. In aborting his invasion of France the previous summer, he had handed the military initiative to Philip Augustus, who commissioned his son and heir, Louis, known (like the king of Scots) as "the Lion," to invade England and seize the Crown and then began raising a massive fleet of his own at Damme and in the mouth of the river Zwin. The French king was emboldened by John's continued estrangement from Rome, for as an excommunicate heretic John was not protected by the pope's blessing. More than that, indeed, at the beginning of 1213 Innocent III had threatened to have

John deposed and sanctioned the King of France to lead a mission against him as an enemy of Christ. While John had been courting Philip's enemies, a counterattack with all the righteous fury of a crusade now seemed to be imminent.

In this circumstance John showed a flash of diplomatic genius. On May 13, 1213, he met the papal legate Pandulf Verraccio, who was serving as envoy to the English court, and agreed to return to the obedience of Rome, to accept Stephen Langton as archbishop of Canterbury, and—most astonishing of all—to hand over England and Ireland as fiefs of the papacy. On May 15 he humbly submitted in public to papal overlordship, paying a mere thousand pounds by way of a tribute. This was nothing given what he had appropriated from the English Church, although it must have caused him some personal vexation to swallow his pride and accept an end to his extortion of the English Church. Nevertheless, the reward was that John could now claim special protection from all his enemies as a personal vassal of the pope.

In July Archbishop Langton arrived in England, traveled to Winchester to meet John, and absolved the king in person of his excommunication. According to Roger of Wendover, the king stood with Langton and several other bishops in the doorway of Winchester Cathedral and swore on the Gospels he would "love the holy church and its ordained members, and would, to the utmost of his power, defend and maintain them against all their enemies; and that he would renew all the good laws of his ancestors, especially those of king Edward, would annul bad ones, would judge his subjects according to the just decrees of his courts, and would restore his rights to each and all."[1] The next month, in London, Langton preached to the citizens gathered at St. Paul's cathedral, taking as his text lines from Psalm 27: "My heart has hoped in God and I am helped."[2] It was the most astonishing volte-face, and it required John to trust that Innocent would put more stock in the principle of Christian forgiveness than he did in the human instinct for bearing a grudge. As time would tell, John gambled correctly: His abrupt reversal of his long-standing policy toward the Church would turn out to be a political masterstroke.

For the English barons who opposed John, and for the French king who had been preparing to topple him from his throne, everything was now turned upside down. The French invasion was finally seen off on May 30, when a number of English ships sneaked into the mouth of the Zwin and burned the French fleet as it bobbed at anchor there. Somehow, against all odds, John had survived a genuine crisis. But his relief would soon turn once again to despair.

For all the trouble that his plans for Continental warfare had caused him, John had no intention of leaving France alone. During the rest of 1213 he continued to fund—at vast cost—a proxy war between Philip and the barons of Flanders. At the same time he made preparations for his next personal invasion. Once again, however, he found that a hard core of the English barons was entirely unmoved by his appeals for support. Others acquiesced, sending knights and paying scutage, but they did so uneasily. On November 1, 2013, following a short military tour of the northern counties that was designed to overawe his subjects, John held a meeting with the northern barons at Wallingford, in Oxfordshire. There he attempted both to mollify them by promising a program of reform and to scare them by surrounding them with his heavily armed knights. Once this heavy-handed business was finished with, John went back to assembling a fleet and an army to take Normandy from the south. It was an awesomely grand undertaking, and John threw all he had into it.

For some time now the fines that John had been levying on his subjects had been ratcheted up to outrageous levels. When Baldwin of Béthune, Count of Aumale, had died in 1212, John had forced his widow, Hawise, to pay him five thousand marks to be excused from a forced remarriage to one of the king's favorites. In the months before his invasion of France the sums became even more dizzying. John extorted ten thousand marks from William FitzAlan in return for the latter's right to inherit his family's title. John de Lacy was charged seven thousand marks for a similar privilege. Geoffrey de Say was persuaded to offer the king fifteen thousand marks for lands he claimed had been wrongfully taken from him by another baron. And then, of course, there was the egregious twenty-thousand-mark fee levied on Geoffrey de Mandeville for marrying the king's former wife. Each of these grossly inflated charges was underwritten by a promise on the payee's part to forfeit all of his or her lands and tenements* to the king if they could not keep up with payments. Meanwhile, barons whom John suspected of disloyalty were forced to pledge lands, castles, and their children as hostages as security for their good behavior.[3] Even by John's standards this was a time of severity, mistrust, extortion, and tyranny, which hardly inspired any greater love for him among his subjects. When he sailed for Poitou in February 1214, John left his castles in the north of England well garrisoned as a precaution against any immediate disquiet. He knew that his realm might spring into rebellion at any moment. What he did not know was that he was walking into the defining crisis of his reign.

✝

Many flags flew over the two large armies that met on that warm summer Sunday afternoon at Bouvines, a tiny village next to a bridge across the river Marcq, in what is today the Nord-Pas-de-Calais. The banners that most impressed men on the battlefield belonged to John's

---

*A tenement was land (perhaps including property) held by the tenant of a manor.

nephew Otto of Saxony, Holy Roman Emperor, and Philip Augustus, King of France. William the Breton, an eyewitness, described Otto's banner, pushed around on a cart: It consisted of a long pole around which twined a dragon, "its tail and wings bloated by the winds, showing its terrifying teeth and opening its enormous mouth. Above the dragon hovers Jupiter's bird with golden wings while the whole of the surface of the chariot, resplendent with gold, rivals the sun and even boasts of shining with a brighter light." Philip's banner was simpler. It was the Oriflamme, the sacred banner of France, "a simple silken cloth of bright red," which "has the right to be carried in all battles, ahead of every other banner."[4] John's flag, bearing the Plantagenet lions—or lions passant guardant, or leopards, to use their alternative heraldic name—was nowhere to be seen. This was because John was not present at the Battle of Bouvines. Instead, on July 27, 1214, he was waiting four hundred miles away near La Rochelle, ignorant of the action taking place farther north, despite the fact that he had paid for a significant part of Otto's army himself.

John's military strategy during the preceding months had been straightforward. The plan had been for him to make a summer landing at Poitou, gather up his southern allies, and raid north through French territory. Meanwhile, his coalition of well-paid allies, led by his half-brother William Longuespée and his nephew Otto of Saxony, would punch down from the north, pincering Philip between them and—ideally—laying siege to Paris. But all of this had started to unravel from an early stage. John did land in Poitou as planned and enjoyed some early success, but he was unable to fully distract Philip. The French king went north, leaving his son Prince Louis to face down John. This was enough to cause John's local allies to lose their nerve. They abandoned him and John was forced into a red-faced retreat. Placed under the slightest pressure, one half of the pincer had simply snapped. In the north, meanwhile, Philip's and Otto's armies shadowed each other for some time until battle could no longer be avoided. They lay poised for a confrontation as the sun rose on Sunday, July 27.

It was thought very low to contemplate fighting on Sunday, the holiest day of the week, but this did not seem to trouble Otto, who, like John, had been excommunicated from the Church as a result of a long-running dispute with Innocent III. Though some companies of Otto's men decorated their armor with small crosses made from strips of fabric, it was the view of at least one chronicler that these were the cynical badges of a bad bunch, worn "much less for the glory and honor of Christ's cross than for the growth of their wickedness."[5]

The forty-nine-year-old French king, Philip, was sitting under an ash tree enjoying some respite from the midsummer's blaze when his messengers informed him of his enemies' approach. This presented Philip with a dilemma: to disgrace the conventions of holy warfare or to stain his own honor by retreating and being thought a coward. The decision did not take long. Although no French king had fought a pitched battle for more than a century, Philip buckled on his armor, made a quick trip to a church to pray, and prepared to fight.

The battle site that had been chosen was close to a marshland that spread out from the banks of the Marcq. It was large enough for the two armies to array in long lines facing each other. Heavily armored horses shuffled on both sides, ridden by similarly well-protected men: "Each knight covered his members with several layers of iron and enclosed his chest with armor, pieces of leather and other types of breastplate," wrote William the Breton. Emperors, kings, dukes, earls, and counts commanded the various divisions of cavalry and foot soldiers. It was highly unusual for these men to be preparing to do battle in an open field, for the preferred mode of warfare in this period was the siege: a slower but far more predictable and less sudden means of conflict. Nevertheless, this was a golden age for tournaments, and the best men in both armies would have experienced fighting in the melee: a codified form of sparring between armed knights that mimicked most of the aspects of real fighting and that was designed, in theory at least, to prepare a man for a day like Bouvines. Despite the inherent novelty of a battle, men on both sides stood ready and willing to fight. Trumpets blared. The fighting began.

The sun beat down on pure carnage. While knights and commanders were considered too valuable to kill—the ransoms that could be earned from capturing noblemen were enormous—a savage range of weapons were brought to the battlefield. "Lances are shattering, swords and daggers hit each other, combatants split each other's heads with their two-sided axes, and their lowered swords plunge in the bowels of the horses," wrote William the Breton.[6] A number of bishops rode into battle wielding maces and clubs instead of swords. This was a strictly literal view of the Church's ruling that men of God ought not to spill blood: It was reasoned that although churchmen could not wield bladed weapons, a bishop could crack a skull with a blunt instrument and remain within the favor of the Lord.

Some of the worst violence at Bouvines was committed against horses, because attacking a man's beast was a sure way of sending him tumbling, vulnerable, to the ground. (At one point Philip Augustus himself was knocked from his mount, but he rose quickly to continue fighting.) William the Breton saw terrible things that day: "You could see horses here and there lying in the meadow and letting out their last breath; others, wounded in the stomach, were vomiting their entrails while others were lying down with their hocks severed; still others wandered here and there without their masters and freely offered themselves to whomever wanted to be transported by them: there was scarcely a spot where one did not find corpses or dying horses stretched out." Amid all this some men stood bewildered, shocked by the brute chaos of war. "Here a caval-ryman, there a foot soldier voluntarily surrender, fearing more to be killed than to live vanquished."[7]

After hours of this melee, the orderly lines in which the armies had begun had splintered. John's brother William Longuespée was taken prisoner, the emperor Otto fled the battlefield, and the counts of Flanders and Boulogne were captured. A final stand of coalition cavalry, whose knights made sorties out against the French from within a circle of pikemen, was eventually overwhelmed. The day thus ended with a resounding victory for Philip Augustus. It was, recorded William Marshal's biographer, "a large-scale rout."[8]

It took a number of days for the news to make its way south to Poitou. When it did, John realized the game was up. In short order he made expensive arrangements for the release of his half brother, agreed an eighteen-month truce with Philip Augustus, and returned home to face the music. For Philip this was total vindication. "After this, no one dared wage war against him," wrote the chronicler known as the Anonymous of Béthune. For John, Bouvines was a catastro-phe. He had gambled his reputation and most of his fortune on the outcome of a single battle in which the Almighty would speak to the rectitude of his cause. The God-given answer was that John was now a busted flush. He left French soil on October 13 and never came back. "And thereafter began the war, the strife and criminal conflict between the King and the barons," wrote Marshal's biographer, with evident disdain.[9]

After the debacle of Bouvines, John, his foreign policy and mili-tary reputation now severely tarnished, returned to England to find the chorus of baronial anger at his high-handed brand of kingship louder than ever. His kingdom was teetering dangerously on the brink of civil war. It was a war he could neither avoid nor afford to pursue. John had either forsaken or exhausted his most lucrative sources of income during the preparations for the war that preceded Bouvines. Having lost that war, John had been forced—according to the chronicler Ralph of Coggeshall—to pay sixty thousand marks for a five-year truce with Philip Augustus. There could not have been a worse time to fund a war at home. Yet it was clear that his enemies, led by the barons of the north, now expected a fight.

II

Opposition

5

Trouble at the Temple

ON CHRISTMAS DAY 1214, King John listened as the clergy-men of his private chapel sang "Christus Vincit." He had promised them a handsome fee to do so.* The Latin words swirled sweetly, alternating between the voices of the two accomplished soloists and the collective chorus of the congregation, gathering toward a triumphant refrain: *Christus vincit! Christus regnat! Christus imperat!* "Christ conquers! Christ reigns! Christ commands!"

The theme of this particular chant lay close to John's heart, for when sung before a monarch, "Christus Vincit" (a song of the type known as *laudes regiae*) was nothing short of a hymn to lordly—and thus kingly—magnificence. It had been chanted at royal coronations across Europe since the time of Charlemagne, who had been crowned Holy Roman Emperor by the pope on another Christmas Day in the year 800, and its popularity had not waned since.† The practice had come to England with the Norman invasion and John had heard "Christus Vincit" at his own coronation in May 1199 and at that of his wife in October of the following year. Throughout his reign he had paid for it to be sung at Christmas and Easter and now he listened again as the singers called for the blessing of a long

---

*When the time came to settle his bills the following month, the two men who had led the plainsong chant, Robert of Saintonge and James the Templar, received twenty-five shillings each—about a week's wages.

†"Christus Vincit" remains popular today: It was sung at the inauguration mass of Pope Benedict XVI in 2005.

list of holy men and women: from St. Peter and the Virgin Mary to St. Thomas Becket and St. Etheldreda, a seventh-century East Anglian nun who had successfully avoided being ravished by a lascivious king. The well-trained male voices prayed together that their king should enjoy prosperous times. They called for piety and joy. They asked for the peace of Christ to descend on the realm. "To the king of the English, crowned by God, salvation and victory," they sang.[1] That year there could have been no more fitting Christmas wish.

John was celebrating Christmas in Worcester, a favored stopping point for kings since the days of the Norman Conquest.[2] Worcester, like Gloucester below it and Hereford to the west, rose out of the fertile borderlands between England and Wales known as the Marches, where lush green countryside was watered by the rivers Wye and Severn as they ran down from the Cambrian Mountains. This was the westernmost point of civilization, for beyond the Marches roamed the Welsh, a strange, wild, quarrelsome people, by turns generous and musical, bold and barbarous, witty in their speech but fierce when they were met riding into battle, the men fighting barefoot with their mustaches grown long and their faces painted brightly.[3] The Welsh were half respected and half feared by their English neighbors. John's father, Henry II, who had fought a number of times both against and alongside Welshmen, once said that they were "so brave and untamed that, though unarmed themselves, they do not hesitate to do battle with fully armed opponents."[4] The walled city of Worcester had been fortified against these strange and ancient Britons since the time of William the Conqueror—John's great-great-grandfather—and it remained a royal stronghold after two generations of Plantagenet rule.

Besides being safe, one of Worcester's main attractions at Christ-

mastime was simply that it was large enough to handle the royal entourage. Buildings within the grounds of the town's castle, described
as the "king's houses" in official documents, could cater for the small
army of cooks, servants, clerks, scribes, and workmen who formed
the core of the royal retinue. The monks of the nearby priory could
be counted on to provide lavish living quarters for the most presti-
gious guests, including the king himself, his noble companions, and
the knights of his household. The monks would also be tasked with
hosting a party fit for the royal presence: On any given day, let alone
a feast day, the king was surrounded by dozens or even hundreds
of hangers-on whom convention and honor required him to treat
generously. Of course, the forty-seven-year-old King John was not
universally celebrated among his subjects for honor or generosity.
Indeed, there were many who thought him a greedy scoundrel whose
name was synonymous with perfidy. Even so, he was expected to rise
to the occasion for Christmas.

A Christmas court at this time required considerable planning.
The chief midwinter festival was usually celebrated for a full twelve
days, from the Nativity on December 25 to Epiphany on January 6.
Along the way it took in the traditionally raucous Feast of the Circumcision on January 1, which, according to a hymn by the twelfth-
century poet and theologian Walter of Châtillon, was both a festival
of "disorder" organized "to promote fun" and one in which "vice" should
be "cut off" (*amputetur vitium*), because "this is the mystery signified by
Christ's circumcision, when his foreskin was removed following Jewish
custom."[5]

Whatever the case, Christmas was expensive and conspicu-
ously indulgent. The daily costs of the court might rocket to seven
or eight times their normal levels. In 1206 John had stopped in
Winchester, near the south coast of England, and the royal kitchens

had taken delivery of fifteen hundred chickens, five thousand eggs, twenty oxen, one hundred pigs, and one hundred sheep.[6] In 1213 an even grander Christmas had been held at Windsor: The court had then gone through four hundred pigs' heads, a dizzying sixteen thousand hens, ten thousand salted eels, and fifteen thousand herrings.[7] Recipe books from later in the Middle Ages record traditional Christmas dishes, such as broiled venison basted in wine and ginger and served in a pepper sauce thick with bread crumbs and animal fat; and huge pies stuffed with six or seven different types of fowl.[8]

This year too the revelers would expect to be well fed. Seven weeks earlier the king had ordered his servants in Yorkshire to go into the forest at Pickering and start catching pigs to slaughter. One hundred were to be taken, the carcasses salted, and the heads preserved in wine or beer.[9] John's long-standing counselor, administrator, and gambling partner Hugh de Neville had bought fifty goats and forty pigs to Worcester from the royal hunting lodge of St. Briavels in the Forest of Dean, and twenty silver bowls had come up from the recently refurbished kitchens at Marlborough Castle.[10] Supplies would also have been ordered in from the rest of the realm, including huge quantities of wine imported from royal lands in southern France, stored in large barrels in the cellars of castles all over England, and moved around by horse and cart in accordance with the royal itinerary.[11] (A large and frequently visited royal castle like Corfe would have taken deliveries of thirty barrels of wine at a time—a consignment of several thousand liters.)

The presence of the royal household would have been both a curse and a boon for the people of Worcester. The dense flow of human traffic from the royal court would have ensured that the town's streets were left piled with the dung, bones, and rotting waste that were a feature of life in any busy medieval town.[12] True, the chance for local merchants to profit from the presence of the court would have been gladly received, and there were times when the king would give something back to the towns, as he did to Worcester in 1204 when he ordered the rebuilding of a gatehouse in stone rather than timber following a devastating fire,[13] but taxes on the town had risen by 500 percent in the last decade, and that painful fact would have outweighed any municipal delight at the new gate.

Although John had paid rather a lot of money to lay on feasting and to hear his favorite song, in truth he had no wish to linger over the celebrations, nor any intention of staying in the city a moment longer than was necessary. A couple of days devouring wine-pickled swine heads was more than enough distraction from the pressing business of saving what remained of his shattered inheritance. The twelve days of Christmas were to be spent on the move. On the Feast of St. Stephen, December 26, John ordered that his possessions be packed away onto the horse-drawn carts that formed the royal caravan train in which he traveled up and down his kingdom and set out in the direction of London.[14] He knew when he got there he would find a large number of his disgruntled barons waiting for him.

✝

The road that carried John and his entourage from Worcester down to London was one of England's great highways. It passed through the gently rolling landscape of the Thames valley, connecting London— by far the largest city in the realm—with the important town of Gloucester. Other major medieval roads ran from London to Dover and Colchester in the southeast and York and Chester in the north. In places these followed the course of the great Roman roads like the Fosse Way, Watling Street, and Ermine Street, which had been dug out and paved in stone during the Roman occupation. Mostly, though, medieval roads were wide, unengineered tracks laid by generations of footsteps. The biggest highways had originated during Saxon times as simple paths to join the ports and settlements with places of worship and trade. Smaller ones were slowly carved into the landscape by the wanderings of merchants and animal herders, soldiers and messengers, pilgrims and funeral processions.[15] Whatever the road, the sight of a Plantagenet king's court in motion—"with carts and sumpter horses, pack-saddles and panniers, hawks and hounds, and a concourse of men and women," in the words of Walter Map—was extremely impressive.[16]

Besides the large numbers of men, women, and hunting dogs who rode with the king, the royal baggage train would have included weapons, money, treasure, precious cups and plates, food, wine, tents, and even a pop-up chapel containing saints' relics.[17] On average the king moved his court thirteen times every month, seldom staying anywhere for more than a few days. Although his main business was done in a roughly diamond-shaped patch of central England with its corners at Dover, York, Worcester, and Exeter, John visited corners of his kingdom that had not seen a king for centuries: In 1201 he had been the first king since William Rufus in 1062 to visit the remote northwestern town of Carlisle. This restlessness was one of the traits he had either inherited or learned from his father. One writer vividly recalled seeing Henry II riding at the head of his band of knights and clerks, deep in conversation with a trusted counselor, the two of them trying to stifle their laughter when a monk tripped in the road before them, his habit blowing up to display his bare buttocks.[18] Exactly the same image could be conjured of his son, with one small but important difference: John would have laughed.

Following his abrupt departure from Worcester, John moved south to Tewkesbury, where he kept a house that had once belonged to his first wife, Isabel of Gloucester. Then the royal train swung west toward Temple Guiting in Gloucestershire.[19] The distance between each of these stages was about fifteen miles—for the fully laden court with its ten to twenty carts and wagons, this probably represented a full day's travel.

As John traveled he kept up a heavy stream of business. His orders were sent out on small chits of parchment, whose contents were copied out for reference by the king's clerks in his Chancery onto long membranes of vellum (stretched, bleached, and treated parchment made of calfskin), which were stitched together and rolled up for easy storage and transport. These survive today as close rolls and patent rolls: Close rolls contained private orders and were sent sealed shut, while patent rolls were delivered open.

John was a keen-eyed and capable administrator, and the breadth of government business that he could deal with, quickly and personally, was astonishing. It ranged from deciding the disposition of property that had come into royal hands and granting letters of safe conduct for merchants, soldiers, and envoys to gifting trinkets and animals to those who had found royal favor. At Tewkesbury on December 28 he had sent a blizzard of orders to men including the mayor of London, the barons of his Exchequer, and the sheriffs of Essex, Gloucester, Bedford, and York, ordering everything from the payment of bills and the transfer of servants to the regifting of two "hawks of good breeding" that had been sent to him by the King of Norway.[20] His scribes worked furiously, copying out a vast array of names and orders and sending them out to the most far-flung places in the kingdom. John's bureaucratic machine working at speed and on the hoof must have been an awe-inspiring thing to behold.

One of the orders he sent out that day permitted the Marcher lord and sometime outlaw Fulk FitzWarin to capture five deer from the royal forests in Leicestershire. It is usually but wrongly assumed that the mythical English outlaw Robin Hood was active in John's reign. In fact the earliest known ballads of Robin Hood are set in the reign of John's descendant Edward III and in the forms we have them come from the fourteenth and fifteenth centuries. Fulk FitzWarin, however, was very much an outlaw of the early thirteenth century, a real-life dispossessed nobleman—albeit from Shropshire and not Yorkshire or the Midlands—who fell into dispute with John in 1200 when he was denied his rightful inheritance. Fulk and a number of his relatives rebelled and he spent nearly three years as an outlaw before being received back into royal favor in November of 1203. His story was romanticized in the poem "Fouke le Fitzwarin," which was probably written in the second half of the thirteenth century and included fanciful episodes such as the young John and Fulk falling out over a game of chess.[21] Over the years, some of Fulk's supposed escapades have been rolled up into the myth of Robin Hood, which has endured with far more popularity.

✚

John arrived in London on January 7. He lodged, as he often did when visiting the capital, in the New Temple, the London headquarters of the Knights Templar, the vastly rich crusading order established in Jerusalem around 1119, whose power and interests reached across Europe to the Holy Land. Their distinctive Temple church, with its round nave of Caen stone, Purbeck marble pillars, and elegant Gothic arches, was at the heart of a much larger complex of riverside buildings in which John evidently felt at home. His friends—men like Alan Martel, a future master of the order—walked the grounds dressed in white robes decorated with a bright red cross to symbolize their willingness to shed blood and die in defense of a Christian Holy Land.

The Templars wore their hair cropped short, while their beards flowed down to their chests in obedience to the rule of their order, which forbade them from shaving. They slept four hours a night, attended up to seven Masses a day, and fasted three times a week. Templar Knights vowed to remain chaste, to refrain from anger and cursing, to refuse gifts, and never to indulge in luxury, a commitment that specifically included rejecting gaudy horse bridles and shoes with laces, which the original rule of the order considered to be "abominable things [that] belong to pagans."[22] It was muttered that their diligence had slackened over the course of the decades as their wealth had accrued, but it remained a basic fact that the duty of a Templar Knight was to concentrate on religious observance and hard military training. These men were not raucous company, but they did make for highly effective bodyguards.

The New Temple was a convenient spot for a king to stay, standing as it did outside London's thick Roman walls on Fleet Street, the road that connected the western entrance to the city, known as the Ludgate, with Westminster, the administrative village a mile or so up the Thames. It was also an attractive set of lodgings with an orchard and gardens and cloisters in which the knights lived and worked, abutting the waterfront of the Thames, which thronged with river traffic. An earth-and-stone wall ran around the main precinct and across Fleet Street was the Templars' jousting ground, known as Fittes Field.[23]

John was fond both of the Temple and the Templars, who loaned him money and provided the Crown with semiformal banking services, as they did for princes across Europe. In return the knight-monks thought unusually highly of the king. During his stay in January of 1215 John awarded the brothers land worth ten pounds a year at Radnage— a manor nestled at the edge of the low Chiltern Hills in south Buckinghamshire and made a personal gift to Brother Aymeric, grand master of the Templars in England, of all the houses and palaces in Northampton that had been seized from the wealthy Jewish financier Aaron of Lincoln. Years after John's death the Templars would maintain priests specifically to sing Masses in the Temple church for his soul as it passed through purgatory.[24]

John had come to London to attend to difficult business. A dozen bishops and at least as many barons of the highest rank had come to town to meet him at the Temple.[25] Some were friendly, or at least neutral—these included Stephen Langton, archbishop of Canterbury, and William Marshal, Earl of Pembroke. But there were far more barons in London whose fidelity John had cause to suspect. They too had spent Christmas trudging along England's highways, descending on London from all over the realm for a prearranged meeting set to begin on Thursday, January 8. And they had come armed.

The purpose of this meeting was to thrash out business that had been outstanding since the previous autumn, when John had returned from his French lands in disgrace. The issues at stake were many and varied and ranged from matters entirely of John's making to bones of contention they had been gnawing over for more than fifty years.

Prior to his failed invasion of France, John had encountered truculence and in some cases downright refusal when he had demanded that his barons fulfill their feudal obligation to send him troops or pay the tax known as scutage, which was assessed according to the number of knights each baron was liable to raise. But in early 1215 the resistance was beginning to take shape in a more organized fashion than ever before.

According to Roger of Wendover, a baronial meeting had been held at Bury St Edmunds, near Cambridge, around the time of John's return from Bouvines, under the cover of a pilgrimage to the gold-encrusted shrine to the ninth-century Saxon king Edmund.* At Bury, says Wendover, the barons "discoursed secretly . . . for some time."[26] The same account goes on to claim that Stephen Langton, the archbishop of Canterbury, had advised the assembled barons that the best way of restraining the king who was vexing them so sorely was to demand that he confirm the coronation charter of Henry I, whereupon "they all swore on the great altar that, if the king refused to grant these liberties and laws, they themselves would withdraw from their allegiance to him, and make war on him, till he should, by a charter under his own seal, confirm to them every thing they re-quired; and finally it was unanimously agreed that, after Christmas, they should all go together to the king and demand the confirmation of the aforesaid liberties to them."[27]

The coronation charter of Henry I had been issued at a time of political weakness: Henry had snatched the throne from beneath the nose of his elder brother, Robert Curthose, and was obliged to do as much as he could to endear himself to the English nobles whom he claimed, rather tenuously, to rule. He had therefore offered the aboli-tion of "evil customs by which the kingdom of England has been un-justly oppressed." These included a vow to avoid unjustly battering

---

*St. Edmund ruled the kingdom of East Anglia from around A.D. 855 to A.D. 869, when he was killed by a band of Vikings known as the Great Heathen Army. The story of his martyrdom held that he was shot to death with arrows and then be-headed, his head recovered only after a talking wolf summoned faithful Christians to the woodland spot where it had been discarded. His shrine was one of the greatest in England, richly decorated in precious stones and metals. John himself had promised the monks a large ruby set in gold for the shrine, to be handed over on his death. R. Yates, *History and Antiquities of the Abbey of St Edmund's Bury*, part 2 (London: Nich-ols, 1843), 40. The shrine was destroyed during the Reformation.

barons with demands for feudal payments, to guarantee the financial rights of widows, to write off old debts to the Crown, to avoid imposing a range of newfangled and unpopular taxes, and to keep the peace.[28]

Whether or not this meeting happened quite as it was described is a matter of some uncertainty. Certainly Archbishop Langton was not quite the out-and-out inciter of rebellion that Wendover portrayed. On the other hand, much of his political thinking developed in Paris rested on the notion that kings should govern in accordance with the law. What is clear, however, is that tense political discussions had taken place among the barons before Christmas, that the realm was in mutinous spirit, that a charter similar to that granted by Henry I on his coronation in 1100 was being demanded, and that if John did not accede to the reformers' demands he could expect serious and potentially violent consequences.[29] But if ever there was a king likely to wriggle when he was pinned, it was John. For the better part of a week at the Temple, John listened to the angry complaints of his subjects imploring him to reconfirm Henry I's charter. Deftly he sidestepped and stalled. He declared himself unprepared to concede to the barons' demands, which he condemned as a "novelty," and countered by saying that he would come to terms only on the condition that the barons swear a general oath of obedience "to stand with the king against all men" and promise never to make similar demands of him again.[30] Crucially, just as he had done in the autumn, John played for time. He proposed to give his barons a final answer at Easter, banking on the fact that they were restive but not yet so angry as to make war.

By Thursday, January 15, the meeting at the Temple broke up without a binding resolution or a full descent into violence. At this point John must have known that England was teetering on the brink of full mutiny, because on the previous day, a Wednesday, he had prepared orders asking major landowners between London and the far north to provide safe conduct for those "who came to London at Epiphany . . . to appeal to us over their grievances."[31] Still, he was not ready to concede. Bidding farewell to his hosts, the king ordered his mobile court packed onto its wagons and rolled out once more onto his country's ancient high roads. He was heading west, and he had a plan.

Taking the Cross

WALTER MAUCLERK ARRIVED in Rome in the middle of February 1215 feeling rather unwell. His journey from England had begun with an unpleasant winter crossing of the Channel and a long ride south through France. A thirteenth-century map made by the St. Albans chronicler Matthew Paris shows the several routes from London to Rome: One could sail from Dover to the ports of Calais or Boulogne, ride on via Paris or Reims to Lyon, and then cross the Alps through the Mont Cenis pass, a route trodden by generations of pilgrims. Travelers would then descend through northern Italy via Lucca and Siena and approach Rome from the north.[1] All this seldom took less than three or four weeks, but the trip had taken Walter longer than usual because, as he wrote in a letter home to King John, "I was detained by serious illness."[2]

In an age when travel was hard, slow, and physical, crossing the Continent in faltering health was no light undertaking. Yet this trusted royal confidant, who described himself to the king as a "faithful and devoted clerk always and everywhere," had done his duty and eventually arrived in the Holy City on Tuesday, February 17. He presented himself at the Lateran Palace armed with a package of letters from King John asking for papal support in the tussle against England's barons and was soon granted an audience with one of the most formidable men in the recent history of Christendom: Pope Innocent III.

Born Lotario de' Conti, Innocent had been elected pope in

January 1198 at the unprecedentedly young age of thirty-seven. A fresco painting at the monastery of St. Benedict in Subiaco, idealized but unquestionably striking, shows a youthful man with an almond-shaped face and thin features, his brown hair cropped above his ears, dressed in rich red ecclesiastical vestments offset by a butter yellow pallium embroidered with blue crosses. The magnificence of the image is fitting: During his seventeen years as pontiff, Innocent had done everything in his power to raise the prestige of the papacy and the authority of Rome.

Despite his youth, Innocent was well suited to high office. He came from a distinguished family (Pope Clement III had been his uncle) and was an exceptional scholar whose training at the universities of Bologna and Paris had left him equally gifted in the fields of canon law and theology. He had written several important theological works, including one called De contemptu mundi ("On the Contempt of the World"), which, despite its gloomy title, would be hugely popular for centuries and would come to be translated and adapted by Geoffrey Chaucer as "The Man of Law's Tale" in his Canterbury Tales.

Few previous popes had ruled with as much self-confidence, political acuity, and success as Innocent. He was by turns ruthless and sensitive, personally domineering yet able to unite and command great swaths of Christendom by reconciling princes who were more naturally inclined to tear one another's throats out. Innocent was as exacting and precise in his handling of the disputes of rival claimants to the title of Holy Roman Emperor as he was in his handling of petty cases concerning the humblest men and women. In 1204 he took on the memorable case of an Italian woman who had left her new husband on discovering that he was impotent to marry a lover better able to satisfy her needs. (Her bishop had forced her to return to the first husband, who, unable to stand the humiliation, had entered a monastery and promptly died of shame.) Innocent took pains to familiarize himself with the details of the case, and his ruling redefined the Church's entire position regarding impotence and marriage.[3]

Innocent had extended or reclaimed Rome's power over neighboring states, as well as over the Norman kingdom of Sicily and the principalities of Germany. The greatest kings in Christendom had felt the sting of his displeasure: The pope had intervened in the affairs of the King of France; the Holy Roman Emperor and his rival the Duke of Swabia; the kings of León, Portugal, and Aragon; and even the King of Norway. A brutal campaign to stamp out the Cathar heresy in southern France had triggered seven years of slaughter, mainly around Toulouse, and the sickly Walter Mauclerk may have been regaled with tales of heretics being run through with swords, used for target practice, and dragged behind horses as he passed near that terrorized region on his way to Innocent's court.*

In his sixteen years at the Vatican Innocent had also embarked on an ambitious program of artistic improvement in Rome. To reflect the rising might of the papacy, the Lateran Palace, the main residence of popes, had been dazzlingly restored under his supervision, such

---

*Cathars were members of a Christian sect that spread to southern France and northern Italy from the eastern Roman (Byzantine) empire around the middle of the twelfth century. Influenced by Manichaean thought, believers identified two gods—one good and one evil—and considered the material world the creation of the evil deity. Catharism was a direct assault on the Church's fundamental principle of monotheism. Innocent III initially attempted to reason with the Cathars, sending missionaries to convince them of the error of their ways. But in 1208 a papal legate was murdered after excommunicating the Count of Toulouse for his failure to deal sufficiently harshly with the Cathar heresy. Innocent declared the dead man a martyr and launched a full military assault, led by one Simon de Montfort (father of the later English earl and rebel) and known now as the Albigensian Crusade. For good general introductions to the subject see J. Sumption, *The Albigensian Crusade* (London: Faber and Faber, 1978) and more recently R. I. Moore, *The War on Heresy: Faith and Power in Medieval Europe* (London: Profile Books, 2012).

that the poet Dante Alighieri would write around a hundred years later that it "outsoared all mortal art."⁴ To be granted an audience with Innocent III in the halls of this awe-inspiring palace was to stand before a true colossus of his age—perhaps the greatest of all the medieval popes. Yet, as Mauclerk was aware, this was a man with whom his king had a rather tarnished history. More concerning still, baronial ambassadors were circling the papal court, attempting to put forward their own version of events. For the sake of peace in England—and perhaps even of his master's crown—it was vital that he make a good impression.

"I found the Lord Pope at the Lateran and that same day went to him, saluting him with due reverence on your behalf and presenting your letters to him," Mauclerk wrote to John, reporting on his progress in Rome. "Receiving these with beneficence he asked diligently about you and the peace of your realm. As soon as he understood, thanks to my answer, that all went well with you, he rejoiced, giving thanks to the Almighty."⁵ Mauclerk went on to tell the king that men sent by the barons were lobbying the pope to complain about the bad-tempered meeting that had taken place at the New Temple in January. They were claiming (fairly accurately) that "in breach of your proper oath, you showed contempt towards conceding their ancient and customary liberties." Mauclerk advised the king to send more men to Rome to ensure that the royal side of the argument was both up to date and strongly pressed. Otherwise, his letter fairly bubbled with confidence about John's prospects of securing papal approval for his position.

"Your lordship should know . . . I have acquired much grace for your reverence," he wrote, "both in the sight of the Pope and in the eyes of all the cardinals, so much so that it is said in the curia that there was never anyone from your land who found greater favour."⁶ Mauclerk was right to be positive. Innocent's pragmatism and his eagerness to assemble secular allies who might help to further his military ambitions in the east far outweighed any personal rancor he might have held toward the English king. Following John's apparently recondite return to obedience in 1213, Innocent stood squarely behind him and would remain a staunch supporter. The fact of John's submission alone would probably have guaranteed this, but on March 4, John went one step further still. Two short weeks after Walter Mauclerk's happy audience with the pope, following in a long Plantagenet tradition, he swore an oath promising to take up the cross and lead an army on crusade.

✝

By 1215 the crusading movement was more than one hundred years old, but enthusiasm in the west for traveling to the Holy Land burned as hot as ever. Gerald of Wales provided a neat summary of the mood of an entire century when he wrote that "the whole of Christendom . . . is excited to battle and to vengeance, so also are all the nations of the heathen and the people of the infidels excited to resistance and rebellion; from which causes there arose so great a disorder upon the Earth and so great a concussion in the world as had not been heard of for many ages before."[7] Under Innocent III the Church had asserted its power to remit the sins of men who went on crusade. This was a direct and very attractive spiritual pact. Pain and suffering on earth could be written off against the far greater tortures that awaited in purgatory.

Pope Urban II had preached the First Crusade in 1095. It had led to the capture of Jerusalem four years later and the establishment of a Christian kingdom in the Near East, which stretched at its peak for the whole length of the Levantine coast. Since then the peoples of western Christendom (known generally as "the Franks") had been engaged in a sporadic but basically ceaseless war to defend this kingdom from attack by Islamic forces around the eastern Mediterranean. In the summer of 1187 that struggle met with calamity. Christian forces were slaughtered at the Battle of Hattin, where they lost a precious wooden relic believed to be the remaining part of the True Cross. Months later Jerusalem had been recaptured by forces under the great sultan and founder of the Ayyubid dynasty, Salāh ad-Dīn Yūsuf ibn Ayyūb, better known in the West as Saladin. To the Muslims of the region this was "a magnificent triumph to Islam" and proof of "the grandeur of Muhammad's law . . . [whose] might exceeded that of the Christian religion."[8] To Christians both in Outremer and at home, it was a scarcely fathomable catastrophe.

The Third Crusade, in which John's brother Richard the Lionheart had been a prominent leader between 1191 and 1194, had failed to recapture Jerusalem, and no successful attempt had been made on the city since. In his first year as pope Innocent III had stated his intention to "arouse the nations of Christendom to fight the battles of Christ," but the Fourth Crusade, launched under his authority, had been a comprehensive failure, achieving only the embarrassing sack in 1204 of Constantinople, another Christian city. The pope was disappointed but not deterred. In 1213 he issued a papal bull known as *Quia maior*, in which he claimed personally to have foreseen the collapse of Islam, writing that Muhammad had "seduced many from the truth" and reassuring the Christian faithful that God had given him a sign that "the end of this beast approaches."[9] This marked the beginning of the Fifth Crusade, and although in 1215 no troops had yet departed for the East, Innocent still regarded the organization of another assault as a matter of urgent, near-apocalyptic importance. But it was one thing for a pope to predict the eradication of the heathen enemies of Christ and another entirely for the armies of the Christian west to travel three thousand miles to the eastern Mediterranean to see that this actually happened.

John had good reasons for taking his crusader's vow. For one thing, it ran in the family. John's paternal great-grandfather, Fulk V of Anjou, had been King of Jerusalem from 1131 to 1143, and many of the subsequent kings were John's cousins. But beyond that a crusader was allowed remittance from debts and a three-year period of grace to fulfill secular obligations. In other words, any concessions that might be wrung from him by his irate barons during the spring of 1215 could be deferred until at least 1218 on the grounds that his highest priority was to prepare for the crusade. It is fair to wonder if John took his crusader's vow seriously or whether, like his father, who had taken the oath and died before getting around to the journey, he was simply suggesting as much for his own short-term political ends. The English barons certainly had a view on the subject: According to the Crowland Chronicle, they thought the king was not behaving "out of piety or for the love of Christ" but rather that the whole thing was a fraud.[10]

The best crusade preachers could rouse huge crowds into a frenzy, combining foaming visions of the Apocalypse with promises of the remission of sins. In the text of one surviving anonymous crusading sermon, the preacher warned that "there is nothing in this world except bitterness. The sea reeks and this world is foul. . . . Before the Lord's countenance, the soul of the corrupt sinner stinks more than every corpse piled together at once would reek." He enjoined his listeners to "vomit up every sin" and join the crusade, for "he who takes the cross will cross over to the Lord through a shortcut and profitable way."[11] People would be encouraged to make a private oath to God, declaring that they intended to travel east to fight the infidel, but the main drama involved the "taking of the cross," as cloth strips were cut or torn in the shape of a cross and sewn onto the right shoulder of the would-be warrior's cloak or tunic, marking him out from the rest of society.

A sense of the fervor that could greet crusading drives is captured in an account of Bernard of Clairvaux's preaching the Second Crusade in the presence of King Louis VII of France: "The Abbot ... was there at the time and place appointed together with the very great multitude which had been summoned.... A wooden platform was built for the Abbot in a field outside of Vezelay, so that he could speak from a high place to the audience standing around him. Bernard mounted the platform together with the King, who wore the cross.... [After Bernard had preached,] the people on all sides began to clamor and to demand crosses. When he had ... passed out the parcel of crosses which had been prepared, he was forced to tear his clothing into crosses.... He labored at this task as long as he was in town."[12] The most zealous crusaders might forgo the cloth and cut the shape of the cross into their skin, keeping the wound fresh by applying herbs. One clergyman was even recorded as having branded the shape of a cross onto his forehead.[13]

Of course, there were those who found themselves possessed by the crusading spirit, only to regret it later on. The thirteenth-century poet known as Rutebeuf wrote sardonically: "When your head is swimming with wine by the fireplace, you take the cross without a summons. Then, you intend to go to inflict great blows on the Sultan and his people.... When you get up in the morning, you have changed your talk."[14] Changing one's talk, however, was a problem, as reneging on a crusading oath was severely frowned upon. Gerald of Wales heaped scorn on John's father, Henry II, for substituting his vow to journey to Jerusalem with the foundation of three monasteries. (Gerald quoted St. Augustine, saying, "You can lie to God, but you cannot deceive God."[15]) In 1196 a monk from Evesham called Edmund had a vision in which he saw the sufferings in purgatory of a young knight who had discarded his cross: He was forced by demons to endure every night all the pains he had avoided in life.[16]

John took the cross on Ash Wednesday, which fell that year on March 4, while he was staying in the Tower of London. It was a highly symbolic moment: the first day of Lent, a day of overt penitence, when Church liturgy fittingly allowed for the marking of a cross of ashes on believers' foreheads. We do not have a record of John's ceremony, but it most likely followed the form laid out in a contemporary text known as the Lambrecht Pontifical.[17] A knight taking the cross would first hear Mass and then lie on the floor of the church or chapel with his arms outspread in the shape of a cross. He would place his cloak near the altar and listen to psalms sung by the congregation, then the *Kyrie eleison* and the Lord's Prayer, followed by more prayers. The priest would ask God to free him from his enemies, to grant "bodily health and protection for [his soul]" and a smooth path toward heaven, and to preserve him from "every diabolical attack" and "enemy ambushes upon the way." Then the crusading crosses on his clothes would be sprinkled with holy water and perfumed with incense while the congregation sang an antiphon celebrating Christ's own wooden cross, the "wondrous sign through which the Devil is vanquished," which would enable crusaders to "frustrate the impious deeds of our adversaries . . . that we might be able to seize the port of salvation [i.e., Jerusalem]."

Blessings and prayers were offered for the crusading ship and for the staffs and purses, the ceremonial ornaments carried by all crusaders to indicate that they were pilgrims as well as soldiers. Finally the priest called on God to "help your servants . . . through all the ways in which they will be travelling . . . so that no adversary may harm them, no difficulty hinder them, but rather everything be salutary, everything prosperous for them, so that . . . whatever they might strive after with righteous desire, they might attain with speedy accomplishment." This, surely, would have been music to John's ears.

Innocent had been informed of the king's intention to take the cross, and on the day of the ceremony in London the pope was already preparing a letter in Rome commending John for his devotion and addressing him as "glorious king." What a remarkable reverse this was, and it speaks to both the political dexterity of John and the remarkable moral flexibility of Innocent, who blended seamlessly the Christian principle of forgiving one's enemies with a willingness to consort with almost anyone who he thought could help him achieve his heartfelt desire to smite the Muslims of the Middle East.

Insofar as we can infer anything of the king's mood around the time that he promised to wager his immortal soul on the war in the east, he was in more than simply a devotional frame of mind. He quickly resumed his domestic tasks and prepared to indulge in his favorite pastime: hunting. He arranged for horses and grooms to be moved around the country, paid expenses run up by the keepers of his greyhounds, bloodhounds, and beagles, settled the bills of his fishermen, who needed new nets, and made careful instructions for the keeping of his falcons and hawks, which were to be guarded by mastiffs and fed on "plump goats and sometimes hens" and once a week "the flesh of hares." He gifted his half brother William, Earl of Salisbury, one hundred pikes to stock one of his fishponds, redecorated the chapel altar at the manor of Kingshaugh in Nottinghamshire, and commanded a refitting of the royal traveling kitchens with a new linen tablecloth, new bread baskets, fresh leather and canvas coverings for the pantry carts, and new kitchen vessels, which were to be delivered to the scullion, Robert.[18]

Despite this industry it is clear that John believed war was coming. Throughout January and February he had been keeping up negotiations with his rebellious barons through William Marshal,

Earl of Pembroke, and Stephen Langton, archbishop of Canterbury, while simultaneously mustering Continental mercenaries and sending crossbowmen, horses, light weapons, and heavy artillery (in the form of giant wooden catapults known as ballistae) to his castles. These were mixed messages indeed. Marshal and Langton did their best to convince the rebels that the king was willing to review the evil customs that had developed over the past sixty years of Plantagenet rule. But at the same time, royal fortresses at Nottingham, Colchester, Hertford, Winchester, and elsewhere were heavily reinforced. A large team of professional diggers were hired to enlarge the moat at Corfe Castle in Dorset.[19] John's visit to the Tower to take his crusading oath prompted him to order structural—probably defensive—work on London's main royal bolt-hole. (Ten oaks were felled in the woods of Essex to provide timber for the job.[20])

John traveled around London, Surrey, and Kent during the first half of March before heading north around March 18 to spend three weeks in and around Nottinghamshire. In April he headed back down to the Thames valley, moving between Oxfordshire and Berkshire. By now Easter week was drawing close, and with it the deadline for coming to terms with his fractious barons. John was waiting—increasingly anxiously—for word to return from his men in Rome. He had done everything within his power to cloak his realm with the protection of the Church. Now all he could do was hope that the word of the pope, whenever it came, would be enough to dissuade his barons from taking up arms.

Confrontation

KING JOHN HAD PROMISED his barons that he would meet
them to settle their long list of grievances in Northampton at
Easter, which fell that year on April 19. He did no such thing. Instead he spent Easter in London, staying at his favored spot, the
New Temple, just outside the city walls.

Holy Week was the most solemn festival in the whole Church
calendar. It began on Palm Sunday, when processions marked the
passage of Christ into Jerusalem. The week that followed was a swell
of ritual and liturgical ceremony. Churches burst into color and song
after the austere solemnity of Lent as they prepared to mark the awesome occasion of the Passion and Resurrection. John was the first
English king to observe Maundy Thursday by washing the feet of a
few (carefully selected) paupers, who had in years past been presented
with robes and cash gifts as a mark of royal penitence. Elsewhere in
England men busied themselves by having their hair and beards
trimmed to prepare for the festival ahead.[1]

On a typical Good Friday England's parishioners came to church
to hear a reading of the whole Passion as recounted in the Gospel of
John, after which a crucifix was unveiled at the high altar so that the
clergy and congregation could crawl barefoot to kiss its base in the
ceremony known as "Creeping to the Cross."[2] On Easter Sunday
King John entertained himself just as he had done at Christmas:
with a performance of "Christus Vincit." This time the chorus was
led by Master Henry of Cerne and Robert of Xanton. (One had come

from Dorset and the other from near Poitiers in France, although both were described in the chit for payment that was issued a couple of days later simply as "clergymen in our chapel."[3])

John's choice of music was as traditional and triumphant as ever, and it matched his bullish mood. All across his realm military preparations continued apace: Towns were barricaded, castles staffed with extra soldiers, and catapults and crossbows ordered, and mercenaries continued to muster. Tens of thousands of square-headed crossbow bolts were supplied to royal strongholds.[4] The royal forests of Essex, Northamptonshire, Hertfordshire, and Yorkshire creaked with the sound of trees falling to provide timber for defensive building works.[5] A couple of weeks before Easter, John ordered from London five new tabards (short, sleeveless, decorated jackets) and five banners with the Plantagenet royal arms of three lions embroidered on them in gold. Yet for all the king's magnificent bluster, his grip on his kingdom was far from secure.

✛

In Rome on March 19, Innocent III had finally decided to give his response to the month of lobbying by English representatives of king and barons, sealing three different letters outlining his thoughts on the various points of contention between them. The letters were addressed to John, to Archbishop Stephen Langton and his bishops, and to the magnates collectively. Assuming that it would have taken four weeks for their transmission from Rome, Innocent's letters probably arrived in England at or immediately before Easter.[6]

The tenor of all three letters was almost painfully favorable to the king. To the barons Innocent wrote that the news of their rebellion was a source of "grievous trouble to us" and that their dissatisfaction with John's rule would "cause serious loss unless the matters are set-tled quickly by wise counsel and earnest attention."

He continued: "By apostolic authority we denounce as null and void all leagues and conspiracies set on foot since the outbreak of dissension between the kingdom and the priesthood, and under sentence of excommunication we forbid the hatching of such plots in future—prudently admonishing and strongly urging you to appease and reconcile the king by manifest proofs of your loyalty and submission. . . . If you should decide to make a demand of him, you are to implore it respectfully and not arrogantly, maintaining his royal honor."[7]

To Stephen Langton and England's churchmen the pope was even blunter. "We are forced to express surprise and annoyance," he thundered, "[that] you have until now ignored the differences between [the king] and certain barons, magnates and associates of theirs, willfully shutting your eyes and not troubling to mediate for a settlement. . . . Some indeed suspect and state that . . . you are giving help and favor to the king's opponents."[8] The enormous respect Innocent had held for Langton, which had, after all, led him to place England under interdict for more than five years in support of Langton's right to become archbishop, now seemed to be draining away. No doubt this was extremely galling to the archbishop, who had in fact spent much of the early part of 1215 doing his best to reconcile John with the barons: a truly thankless task.

To John, however, it must have seemed that all his careful wooing had paid off: He had secured a papal judgment entirely in his favor. But would it have the hoped-for effect? Although Innocent's letters were sympathetic, they were not in any way conciliatory and their impact was not remotely that which he had hoped. The ire of the English barons was not doused: It was stoked. The papal letters made it abundantly clear that there was no prospect of bringing the king willingly to terms. John's vision of peace was his boot on his barons' throats as they croaked out miserable apologies. From this point on, a number of them decided that they had no alternative but to make war on their king. If excommunication was to be the price, then so be it.

✝

Not all of the barons—perhaps not even a majority—went into open opposition to the king at Easter 1215. Nevertheless, what John experienced following the publication of the pope's letters was the worst rebellion against the Plantagenet Crown since the Great Revolt of 1173–74, which had very nearly cost his father his throne. The barons' leader, one of John's most prominent opponents, was Robert FitzWalter, Lord of Dunmow.

FitzWalter had been among the plotters of 1212 who had, with Eustace de Vesci and others, planned to have John murdered by Welshmen and replaced by the French nobleman Simon de Montfort. He was combative by nature and uncowed by the magnitude of his task. His silver seal die, which survives today in the British Museum, shows him mounted on the back of a large horse, draped in heraldic trappings, and heavily armed. He wears a solid, square-topped helmet, a shield is carried in front of him, and chain mail covers his entire body, from a padded collar around his neck down to his wrists and ankles. His outstretched left hand brandishes a sword as long as his arm, with a tapering, double-edged blade. As he kicks the horse forward, FitzWalter is preparing to swing his sword in the direction of a long-necked, curly-tailed dragon. Understandably, the dragon is cowering: What beast would not be afraid of such a lusty and dangerous-looking man? In front of the horse is another shield with different heraldic devices. These are the arms of Saer de Quincy, Earl of Winchester, FitzWalter's friend, fellow soldier, and brother-in-arms (who also included a dragon in his armorial bearings). There was no mistaking from his seal die how FitzWalter wished others to think of him. He appeared as the very paragon of early-thirteenth-century valor and nobility, and that vision chimed with the view of the author of the *Histoire des ducs de Normandie et des rois d'Angleterre*, who thought FitzWalter was "one of the greatest men in England, and one of the most powerful."[9]

By inheritance as well as through his marriage to Gunnora, the daughter of a Norman baron, FitzWalter was in possession of ninety-eight knight's fees, a massive landholding that placed him very comfortably in the upper echelons of the noble elite. His seat at Dunmow was on the border between Essex and Suffolk, but FitzWalter held several impressive castles, most notably Hertford, Benington, and Baynard's Castle in the city of London. He had served King Richard and King John in Normandy, and although his incompetent defense of the castle of Vaudreuil in 1198 had resulted in its falling to the French king and FitzWalter's capture, he had managed to pay the ransom and had returned to England midway through John's reign.

For some time FitzWalter had pursued a fairly conventional baronial career. Like the rest of his class, he was interested primarily in attending to his estates and fighting. But his role in the 1212 plot had been extremely damaging. After he fled, FitzWalter had been outlawed in the county courts, his lands had been taken over by the Crown, and his most important castles had been slighted. Even when relations were normalized in the summer of 1213 as a condition of the deal that reconciled John with the Church, it remained clear that the king and FitzWalter regarded each other with suspicion.

During Easter week FitzWalter emerged as the leader of a group of disaffected nobles who had been identified by chroniclers of the time as "the Northerners" because that was where the hostility to King John had first emerged. "Most of them came from the northern parts," wrote the Crowland Chronicler—although this was not strictly true.[10] Many were from Lincolnshire, Nottinghamshire, Derbyshire, and counties farther north, near the Scottish border, but there were also many whose estates lay in other areas of the realm—not least in East Anglia. Barons like de Vesci, who was the lord of the massive coastal fortress at Alnwick, certainly did have substantial interests in the north, as did others who were named in the *Histoire des ducs de Normandie et des rois d'Angleterre* as rebels, including Robert de Ros, Richard de Percy, William de Mowbray, and Roger de Montbegon.[11] But FitzWalter was a man of the south and east, as was his son-in-law Geoffrey de Mandeville and Giles, bishop of Hereford, a son of William and Matilda de Briouze, who had suffered such grisly ends at John's hands.

As they traveled in the direction of Northampton, where John had promised to meet them, this group mustered in arms (and here we can picture FitzWalter as he displayed himself on his seal) at the great tournament field of Stamford in Lincolnshire. They may well have been here when the letters arrived from Innocent instructing them to "appease and reconcile the king by manifest proofs of your loyalty and submission." They did nothing of the sort. According to the chronicler Roger of Wendover, "in their army there were computed to be two thousand knights, besides horse soldiers, attendants, and foot soldiers."[12]

Even if Wendover's numbers are impressionistic rather than

strictly accurate, this was still a large army and it headed en masse
to a second tournament ground at Brackley, a few miles from
Northampton on land held by de Vesci. The barons were now in a
righteous mood and they marched under a righteous banner. Fitz-
Walter had decided to confront the pope's condemnation head-on
and began calling himself "Marshal of the Army of God and the
Holy Church." His men were in Brackley by Monday, April 27, and
together they concocted a list of demands that they were determined John should concede if he were to avoid being violently deposed. This may have been a work in progress since the Bury St
Edmunds gathering the previous autumn. Certainly a written statement of baronial disaffection was now taking shape.

✝

On Monday, April 27, John was a long way from Brackley. He was
traveling from his sprawling, flint-stone hunting lodge of Clarendon, in Wiltshire, to the mighty castle of Corfe in Dorset: a fortress
with a deep moat, huge towers, elegant new Gothic royal apartments, and the most secure dungeons in England. Here, undoubtedly, John felt safe. One hundred and thirty miles northeast the job
of negotiating with the barons was left to two very capable representatives: Archbishop Langton and a loyal earl of even greater status than FitzWalter: William Marshal.

Despite his chastisement by the pope, Stephen Langton was
continuing in his attempts at reconciliation, as was his duty as archbishop. Even if his private sympathies lay with the barons, as they
surely did, he was publicly prepared to play the role of mediator and
peacemaker for as long as he could. The placement of Marshal alongside him was a valuable boon. By his own reckoning—and that of
many others besides—Marshal was the finest knight of his day. His

long life in service to the Plantagenet Crown had seen him rise to the first rank of the aristocracy.

William Marshal was the younger son of a minor baron, born around the time of the civil war known as the Anarchy, and his life was dramatic from the start: As a five-year-old boy he was given by his father as a hostage to King Stephen, who had to be dissuaded from hurling the child from a trebuchet when Marshal's father double-crossed him. Spared this fate, Marshal grew up to excel at horsemanship and earned his fame as a young man on the tournament fields of France, where he fought in teams assembled by John's glamorous and treacherous eldest brother, Henry "the Young King." Marshal visited Jerusalem on the Third Crusade and took secret vows to retire in the future as a Templar Knight. On his return he had become a very useful ally to Richard the Lionheart, fighting at the king's side in the defense of Normandy between 1194 and 1199. Although his relations with John had at times been fraught, Marshal had nevertheless secured for himself marriage to an heiress of the vastly wealthy Clare family and through it the earldom of Pembroke, which brought vast lands in Wales and Ireland. In 1215 he was approaching his seventieth birthday, but he was still one of the most energetic and formidable men in England.

William Marshal had strident views about the way a knight ought to behave, which his thirteenth-century biography, known as the *History of William Marshal*, elucidates in its long accounts of war, bravery, and derring-do. Central to his beliefs was the notion that a chivalrous man ought to display largesse and loyalty. Even the casual phrases and details of his biography burst with colorful examples of the aristocratic culture of the day. A successful mercenary captain has "the luck of the dice" (*a cui si chaïrent li dé*) when he captures a bishop during a siege. Prisoners seen bound together with ropes are "like greyhounds on leashes" (*comme levriers en lesse*). Particularly fine wines are either "clear, soft on the palate [or] sparkling, some with cloves, some spiced," while a dinner is judged excellent because at the end of it "pears, apples and hazel nuts" are served.[13] But what Marshal most admired were feats of physical strength, examples of rough or natural justice, and good old-fashioned war stories.

His best anecdotes, as recounted in the *History*, have the feel of fireside yarns designed to educate as well as entertain young men hoping someday to be chivalric knights. The tale of a siege directed by Richard the Lionheart against the town of Milly in Normandy features Marshal climbing a ladder from a castle's ditch to the top of its battlements (while wearing full battle armor and carrying a sword), before single-handedly fighting off or scaring away every defender present, defeating the constable of the castle in single combat, and sitting on him "to hold him firm" until reinforcements arrived. But perhaps Marshal's best story of all, told at very great length in the pages of the history, was one recounted from his days as a young knight working as a bodyguard for John's mother, Eleanor of Aquitaine.

Attacked by a large group of his French enemies, Marshal fought as fiercely "as a boar does before a pack of dogs" until he was wounded in the leg and hauled away as a captive, roped to the back of an ass. Subsequently Marshal persuaded a "noble-hearted, kind lady" to smuggle some "fine linen bandages" to him inside a loaf of bread. Later his recovery was stalled when he got into a rock-tossing contest with his captors and won but split open the gash on his leg in the process. (Eventually Queen Eleanor paid his ransom and rewarded him with "horses, arms, money and fine clothes . . . for she was," Marshal conceded graciously, "a very worthy and courtly lady."[14])

Queen Eleanor's youngest son had given Marshal a number of reasons to despise and fear him during his sixteen-year reign, threatening and harrying him with the same malicious energy with which he tormented so many of England's other noblemen. (For five years, between 1207 and 1212, Marshal had been more or less exiled to his Irish estates, where he offered assistance to royal enemies like the Briouze family and was periodically attacked by the king's men.) But no man in England prided himself more on being considered a paragon of loyalty. He had been working as the king's proxy in negotiations with the barons throughout the weeks preceding Easter. And while Marshal's task of bringing around the rebels at Brackley was an extremely daunting one, there could have been no more seasoned and dependable man to be negotiating on behalf of his king.

What passed between FitzWalter and Marshal at Brackley during the week commencing Monday, April 27, is not fully known. It is likely that the meeting was tense and probably hostile. According to Roger of Wendover, "the barons delivered to the messengers a paper, containing in great measure the laws and ancient customs of the kingdom, and declared that, unless the king immediately granted them and confirmed them under his own seal, they would, by taking possession of his fortresses, force him to give them sufficient satisfaction."[15] It is not certain what that "paper" was, but several baronial documents drawn up in the spring of 1215 survive and serve as a useful guide to the issues under contention. Among these is a draft schedule of royal concessions produced by someone close to or among the king's enemies, known today as the Unknown Charter.[16] It is not a formal charter: It does not employ the royal "we" and it is not sealed. Rather, the Unknown Charter is better thought of as the articulation of a bargaining position drawn up at some point around Easter 1215.[17]

The Unknown Charter begins by reciting the charter of liberties granted in 1100 by John's great-grandfather Henry I on acceding to the throne, in which Henry had promised to "make the Holy Church of God free," to allow his subjects to inherit on payment of a "lawful and just" relief, to protect widows, to fix the financial penalties for crimes at some (poorly defined) ancient rate, to limit the extent of royal forests, and to keep the peace in the land in accordance with the laws of the last Saxon king, Edward the Confessor. But the Unknown Charter did not solely aim to turn back the clock 115 years. It includes a series of demands—some quite radical—which aimed to reform, or in some cases dismantle, policies that had been pillars of Plantagenet government since the beginning. These demands, written up as though the king has already assented to them, are introduced by a broad and idealistic statement, which would prove to be very close to what would become the famous clauses 39 and 40 of the Magna Carta: "King John concedes that he will arrest no man without judgment nor accept any payment for justice nor commit any unjust act." After this the Unknown Charter includes draft commitments by the king to take only "just reliefs" as payment for inheritance, to protect the rights of widows, to limit military service outside England to Normandy and Brittany "and this properly," to limit scutage, and to return all lands that had been "afforested" (i.e., newly declared to be royal forest) under Henry II, Richard I, and John.

The Unknown Charter thus tells us that the barons who assembled at Stamford were concerned with four key areas of royal government: justice, inheritance law, military service, and the policing of the royal forest. It addressed the most personal features of John's rule—his notorious slipperiness in his dealings with his greatest subjects, the arbitrary fashion in which he treated them, the dubious company he kept, and his dreadful behavior toward families like the Briouzes, who had been hounded to death without anything like fair treatment under the law. The charter set out a policy by which the lands of underage heirs would be managed effectively in trust by "four knights from among the more lawful men" of the realm and stipulated that when the heir reached his majority, the king would not charge an inheritance tax. It also demanded that the king observe men's wills, insisted that he allow widows to remarry according to the wishes of their families, and stated that a widow was entitled to live in her marital home for forty days after her husband's death "and until she has had her proper dower." (This addressed John's deeply unpopular policies of auctioning off brides to the highest bidder, regardless of social status, and charging widows massive sums to avoid forced remarriage, such as he had with Hawise, widow of Baldwin of Béthune.) Heirs were not to be responsible for interest on debts owed to the Jews by their fathers.

Following the statements on widows, two clauses dealt with foreign policy, granting that the king's men "should not serve in the army outside England save in Normandy and Brittany"—and not, therefore, in Poitou, where John had been on campaign at the end of 1214. It also limited the king's right to charge the military tax of scutage to "one mark of silver"—two thirds of a pound, i.e., thirteen shillings and four pence—on each knight's fee held. Together these two clauses amounted to a radical restriction of the king's ability to raise armies and deploy them where he chose or to milk his barons in order to pay for mercenaries to fight in their place. A baron such as FitzWalter, with his ninety-eight knights' fees, would in theory have a maximum liability to scutage of just over £65 rather than the £196 he had been liable for in the scutage that John had demanded in 1213–14 before the Bouvines campaign.*

John had levied scutage on his men eleven times in the sixteen

---

*With the usual caveats, a scutage payment of £65 would today be perhaps the equivalent of a one-off tax of £55,000 ($85,000), whereas £196 might be £165,000 ($255,000). These numbers reflect the historical standard-of-living value of income, as calculated by measuringworth.com.

years of his reign. By comparison, his father and brother, whose territories and tax base had been so much broader than John's, had levied it eleven times between them in forty-five years. For the king to accept such a strict limitation on his ability to levy military taxation effectively meant that he would never be able to afford another war of conquest outside the British Isles.

The rest of the Unknown Charter was taken up with statements on the need to reform the royal forest, an area of perpetual concern throughout the early years of Plantagenet rule. Much of the English countryside was designated as forest land—reserved for the king's hunting and subject to a separate body of law from the rest of the realm. It was a mark of royal favor to permit men the privilege of taking a deer from the forest. Those Englishmen who killed animals in the forest, gathered firewood, or felled trees without such permission were subject to either heavy fines or mutilation, in the case of the poor and socially insignificant. (Forest abuses would become a major trope in the Robin Hood tales, not least when the historical backdrop of those stories shifted from the fourteenth century to the world of King John and Richard the Lionheart.)

It was a bugbear of much of English society that the Plantagenet kings had expanded the boundaries of the forest, because this put men and women at the mercy of a much more stringent code of law with no means of protest. The Unknown Charter aimed to force John to "disafforest all the forests which my father and my brother and I have made." This was not something that John was eager to do.

The Unknown Charter tells us much about the thinking of John's disaffected subjects in the months immediately prior to the drafting of the Magna Carta. They were not only angling to rebel against a king who had treated them roughly and who had failed in war; they were also preparing to challenge a raft of political issues that reached to the very core of the Plantagenet system of government. Whoever drew up the Unknown Charter was reading English history as a succession of perversions and betrayals committed since Henry II's accession in 1154, in which the spirit of the "good old days"—specifically the reigns of Henry I and Edward the Confessor—had been lost. They wished to make a number of specific amendments to policy, setting strict limits to the king's ability to tax and fine his subjects. But they also sought to set out grand and sweeping philosophical statements concerning the king's basic duties to Church and people. It is unlikely that all of the aims were shared by all of John's opponents. No doubt some simply wanted to be revenged on a man who had extorted, bullied, blasphemed, and murdered his way through life and kingship for far too long. But others—and there were many—saw in the immediate crisis of 1215 a chance to change their world in a more fundamental way. It was the alliance of these interests that would make the baronial reform movement of 1215 so irresistible and enduring.

According to Roger of Wendover, when William Marshal and Archbishop Langton relayed to the king the details of the barons' demands, John flew into a rage. "The king . . . derisively said, with the greatest indignation, 'Why, amongst these unjust demands, did not the barons ask for my kingdom also? Their demands are vain and visionary, and are unsupported by any plea of reason whatever.' And at length he angrily declared with an oath, that he would never grant them such liberties as would render him their slave."[18] In the end he calmed down and offered an entirely vague and perhaps deliberately insulting solution: He would abolish evil customs and take the counsel of "faithful men"—which naturally seemed to preclude any involvement of the men who were then mustered in military harness on a tournament field in the midlands.[19] Whatever course they might suggest would be subject in any case to the approval of the pope, whose letters had by now quite comprehensively shown that he was on the side of the king.[20]

Mediation, let alone reconciliation, looked to be impossible.

✝

On the great tournament field in Brackley, Northamptonshire, on May 5, 1215, a group of barons formally renounced their fealty to King John. It had been ten days since John had failed to appear at a scheduled conference at Northampton. By abandoning their oath of duty to the king, the barons were declaring themselves free to make war upon him. It was a position from which they would find it hard to retreat.

That day FitzWalter and the barons sent a messenger (an Augustinian canon, according to the author of the Annals of Southwark and Merton Priory) instructing him to find the king in Reading and deliver news of a final break.[21] There could be no more ambiguity. The barons had unilaterally defied their lord and freed themselves from the feudal oath on which their relationship and the whole of the structure of society depended. They were now outlaws, rebels, and enemies of the realm.

On May 9 and 10 John issued two documents: The first was a charter addressed to "all those faithful in Christ," arguing that it was for the pope (as overlord of England) to arbitrate the dispute between king and barons. Although there was good feudal basis on which to argue this, it led nowhere, for obvious reasons. Nor did the letter issued the following day, in which John promised not to attack his barons by force while they remained in negotiations but instead to proceed by "the law of our realm."[22] Did he really believe that this would be enough to mollify barons who had developed such a detailed and specific critique of his rule? Far more likely he was engaged in cynical posturing, disingenuously framing himself as the penitent son of the Church and the voice of reason. By implied contrast he was setting up the barons as ungodly and seditious. If anyone was taken in, they would not have to wait long for his true colors to show.

On May 12 John sent out orders to his sheriffs commanding them to "take in our possession our enemies' lands ... take for us their things and movables found in those lands."[23] The barons, meanwhile, left Brackley, marched twenty miles to the nearest royal castle—which happened to be in Northampton—and laid it under siege. The war had begun.

8

London

THE SIEGE OF NORTHAMPTON was going badly. The rebellious barons had been camped outside the castle for more than two weeks. They had freed themselves of their oaths of loyalty to the king and now it was essential that they show him they meant business. In the words of the Crowland Chronicler, "After closing the gates and putting guards at the gate and along the wall, they started to attack the garrison that was in the stronghold."[1] Yet it was looking increasingly as if they had chosen the wrong target. After fifteen days in the field, wrote Roger of Wendover, the barons had gained "little or no advantage."[2]

Northampton Castle was a fine, spacious, and extremely well-defended royal fortress, first erected in the aftermath of the Norman Conquest, that stood in the northwest corner of the busy market town.[3] Originally built by Simon de Senlis, the first Earl of Northampton, it had been permanently taken over by the Crown in 1154, when Henry II seized it not long after his accession to the throne. The castle had flourished since then. Its doorways had been topped with elegant arches and decorative stone corbels (Thomas Becket fled through one of those arches following his decisive showdown with Henry in 1164) and no expense had been spared on the castle's upkeep. It was a crucial strategic stronghold—a great stone sentry guarding access to the Midlands. The townsmen advertised their allegiance to the Crown with a seal bearing a Plantagenet lion.[4] The king was a regular visitor to the castle, coming on average twice a year and spending three hundred pounds over the course of his reign to maintain it.*

John had come most recently in late February, hunting the local chases but also putting his mind to the state of the castle's defenses. At that time he had issued careful instructions concerning the guarding of Northampton's prisoners.[5] In the weeks before Easter the king sent further orders, asking that the fabric of the castle be made as secure as possible against potential attack. Northampton castle was surrounded by a moat filled by the river Nene; earthworks protected its main gate and a stout wall encircled a three-acre bailey, or courtyard. To make it safer still, royal foresters were commanded to provide "timber and wood to fortify and wall our castle," while ten thousand crossbow bolts were purchased to fill the armory. As a precaution against possible siege the pantries were stocked with "forty quarters of wheat and twenty-four hog carcasses."† Northampton was thus well prepared to survive more or less anything that was thrown at it. In the first weeks of May the English barons, led by FitzWalter, were finding this out the hard way.

Leading the defense of the castle was Geoffrey de Martigny, a relative of one of John's most trusted lieutenants, the veteran mercenary Gérard d'Athée.[6] Martigny and d'Athée were originally from the Touraine, where the latter had manned the garrison at Loches, the last Plantagenet castle to fall during Philip Augustus's campaign of conquest in 1203–4. Martigny was thus no weak-willed royal flunky but a man who had been brought to England specifically for his ability to

---

*Perhaps £240,000 ($370,000) today. This is the "historic opportunity cost," as calculated by measuringworth.com.

†A quarter was eight bushels—so forty quarters was a great deal of wheat to order. Converting volume to mass is not a precise science when measuring grain, but the 320 bushels the king sent to Northampton in April 1215 might have been as much as twenty thousand pounds of wheat.

serve the king in times of crisis. Yet he could just as well have been an elderly woman with no experience of siegecraft and still have held Northampton Castle, for although FitzWalter and his army had come in numbers, they did not possess a single siege engine. John had spent much of the last three months ordering catapults and large crossbows and sending them to castles up and down the country. His barons had nothing of the sort. There could be no clearer indication of the disparity in resources between a king and even his greatest lords. With no heavy artillery, Northampton's reinforced walls simply could not be breached. The only tactic open to the barons was blockade, with the hope of starving the garrison out—and they were not going to do that without a very long wait.

In fact, the longer they stood outside Northampton, the worse the barons' fortunes grew. Roger of Wendover recorded that several men were slain during the siege. Most embarrassingly, this included FitzWalter's standard-bearer, who was "pierced through the head with a bolt from a crossbow and died, to the grief of many." When word arrived toward the middle of the month that the rebels would receive a warmer welcome if they traveled twenty miles east to Bedford, they hurriedly packed up the siege and left. They arrived in Bedford to be greeted "with all respect" by William de Beauchamp, a sympathetic noble who held the castle in the town.[7]

At this point their fortunes turned dramatically for the better. No sooner had FitzWalter and his men arrived in Bedford than messengers appeared from the City of London, "secretly telling them, if they wished to get into that city, to come there immediately."[8] If they moved fast, the messengers said, the Army of God could leave behind it the second-string castles of the south Midlands and take England's capital. There was no time to lose. They rushed to London, in the words of one writer, "with a view to doing [the king] mischief."[9]

The barons marched through the night and arrived on the out-
skirts of London as the light of a spring morning was spilling over
the city walls. It was Sunday, May 17, 1215. The bells of London's one
hundred churches were pealing, for the "inhabitants were performing divine service."[10] The timing could not have been better. Fitz-
Walter's men had been advised that they would be welcomed into
the city without the need to carry out any further military action,
because "the rich citizens were favorable to the barons, and the poor
ones were afraid to murmur against them."[11] With the city still and
most Londoners at prayer, the rebel barons simply climbed in,
aided by their sympathizers, who helped them scale the walls.
"They placed their own guards in charge of each of the gates, and
then arranged all matters in the city at will," said Roger of Wendover.[12] They had arrived in London ahead of John's half brother William Longuespée, Earl of Salisbury, who had made a vain dash for
the capital with a band of Flemish mercenaries in order to hold it
for the Crown. Longuespée was beaten to the city gates. His failure
was of great importance. Then, as now, holding London was a major step toward controlling England.

✝

The London into which FitzWalter and his allies arrived in 1215
was a thriving city whose population was growing rapidly and
which had long since overtaken Winchester, Norwich, York, and
the other major cities of England in size, influence, and international
recognition. It was a place fit for comparison with Paris or any of
the other burgeoning European capitals. At its thirteenth-century
peak the population would number some eighty thousand souls.[13]
William Marshal's biographer called London *la bone vile* ("that fine
city") and many of his contemporaries would wholeheartedly have
agreed.[14]

William Fitzstephen, a friend and biographer of Thomas Becket, can help us picture London as it might have appeared at the time. The preface to Fitzstephen's *Life of Thomas Becket*, written in 1173–74, took the form of a passionate, rhetorical, romantic paean to the city he called home. Fitzstephen declared that the English capital was chief "among the noble and celebrated cities of the world . . . which extends its glory farther than all the others and sends its wealth and merchandise more widely into distant lands. Higher than all the rest does it lift its head."[15] Forget Paris or Constantinople, Venice or Rome. London was, in Fitzstephen's eyes at least, a paradise of healthy air, Christian belief, military might, topographical good fortune, enlightened citizenship, female virginity, and male sporting prowess. In the streets of this great city students bantered brilliantly, hawkers sold only the finest jewels and furs, and "the matrons . . . are the very Sabines."* It was the new Troy, "the fruitful mother of noble men."

In truth there was more to London than the frolicking of rosy-cheeked men and virtuous maidens. The city, taken together with its suburban satellite towns of Southwark (on the south bank of the Thames) and Westminster (a couple of miles west down the Strand), was the commercial, religious, political, and military hub of the southeast. It was large, wealthy, and sophisticated: a human jumble of merchants and ministers, politicians and tradesmen with a strong sense of its own communal character and a heartfelt wish among its leaders to be free of royal interference. It had its own well-developed systems of internal rule and was in theory (if not in practice) democratic. The

---

*The Sabine women of classical history were famed for their beauty, honor, and feminine wisdom. In 750 B.C. they threw themselves between the lines of their warring fathers (the Sabine men) and husbands (the Romans, who had abducted the Sabine women for the purpose of marriage). Thus, through the imperilment of their own lives, they successfully brokered a peace.

freemen of the city attended courts known as "folkmoots" and "hustings" to hear city business transacted. The city's merchants were members of well-regulated guilds and the city itself was divided geographically into administrative units called "wards." These were run by aldermen, who tended to be appointed from elite wealthy families well practiced in holding office from generation to generation. Sixteen families, all connected by marriage and business, dominated London's political offices between the twelfth and thirteenth centuries.[16]

Every color and smell of human life could be found intermingling within the old Roman walls that curved three miles around from west to east, enclosing a space of about 330 acres, in which palaces and markets jostled up against more modest houses, hospitals, and taverns. The author of *Eustache the Monk*, a romanticized account of a real-life soldier and pirate set around this time, characterized London as a place where magnificent palaces could be built, knocked down, and reerected in even greater finery.[17] Yet this was also a place where, in the popular pseudohistories of King Arthur by Geoffrey of Monmouth, kings had cut down their enemies as they took cover before church altars.[18]

The roads converging on London gave it rapid access to Dover and Canterbury in the southeast, to Colchester, Cambridge, and Norwich in East Anglia, to the corridor between Oxford and Winchester in the west, and to Lincoln and York along the old Roman road known as Ermine Street. By water it was connected upstream to well-to-do royal settlements like Windsor and downstream to the estuary towns in Essex and Kent. Beyond these lay shipping routes to the Continent and thus eventually a connection to every other bustling port of the known world.

The southern boundary of the city was formed by the Thames, deep and wide and dangerously rapid as it rose and fell over the course of the day with the tide. When the city was founded as Londinium in

Roman times, it owed everything to its position as the lowest point downriver where the Thames could safely be crossed. Even so, the river was a broad and occasionally lethal waterway. The huge stone edifice of London Bridge, nearly a thousand feet long and forty wide, was its only foot crossing. The bridge was densely populated, with shops and houses crammed side by side and a chapel dedicated to Thomas Becket. Hundreds of boats thronged the waters below, taking passengers up and down the banks from the mansions on the Strand (the road that linked London with Westminster) to the wharfs and ports that stood farther east, allowing access to the city from the bankside. The stone bridge, begun in 1176 and completed in 1209, had been under near-constant construction for the past four decades, with some of the work overseen by one Isenbert, a master builder known to the king who had previously worked on fine bridges in Saintes and La Rochelle in Aquitaine.[19] A fire had done significant damage to the new bridge in 1212, killing a large number of citizens in the process, so in 1215 further rebuilding was under way.

To the west of the city was another river: the Fleet, which emptied into the Thames at a place that would later be known as Blackfriars. A third waterway, known as the Walbrook, had once partitioned London, but it had silted up long ago, leaving a marsh, or moor, that covered a large area outside the northern walls.

In the center of the city, on Ludgate Hill, stood the cathedral of St. Paul. By 1215 the Norman cathedral had been under construction for more than a century. Although it would not have a steeple for another six years, it nevertheless loomed over the city around it—at least the same size as and perhaps bigger than the great cathedral in England's more ancient capital, Winchester. Inside, a long nave was supported on both sides by huge fluted stone pillars.[20] Outside in the churchyard Londoners gathered to gossip, protest, and witness all manner of political pageantry. Alongside the guildhall, which was the center of London's mercantile and administrative life, St. Paul's was the most important building in the city walls. It marked the geographical midpoint of the city, where the main thoroughfares crossed one another, and was also the spiritual center: Dozens of smaller parish churches dedicated to saints such as Magnus and Margaret clustered around it, with one every few hundred yards at least. There was a small but prominent Jewish population too: Near the guildhall was one of several synagogues and outside the entrance known as the Cripplegate was the oldest Jewish cemetery in England.[21]

Across the river at Lambeth, the archbishops of Canterbury and Rochester had houses, and other churchmen had started to build inns, temples, and mansions outside the walls on the Strand. There was a large Cluniac abbey at Bermondsey and several hospitals both inside and outside the walls, including the great priory and hospital of St. Bartholomew at Smithfield. As the hundreds of church bells all ringing together on the morning of Sunday, May 17, would have suggested, this was a city where the ritual and power of religion were uppermost in the fabric of life.

Yet if London was a spiritual hive, it was also very much a place of commerce. Two large markets dominated the town: the Eastcheap and the Westcheap, where one could barter for life's staples, brought in on carts along the highways that connected London with the countryside and by boat up the Thames estuary. By 1215 London was connected by trade with every corner of the earth. The wool and cloth trade with Flanders boomed, and claret flowed from Bordeaux, whose links with the English crown had been direct since John's mother, Eleanor of Aquitaine, had become queen. In 1138 a papal legate had visited London and been disturbed to see nuns going about in cloaks trimmed with exotic furs such as gris, sable, marten, and ermine, most of which would have originated in the Baltic.[22] Fitzstephen also mentions gold, spices, and incense from the Middle East, arms from Scythia, jewels from the Nile valley, and purple silk from China. Even if he is plainly guilty here of rhetorical exaggeration (the "Scythians" had not ridden the plains of modern Iran for several centuries by this point, so it seems unlikely that they were trading bows and arrows with the English), we know that the trading networks of the capital stretched for thousands of miles.

Yet the barons who piled into the city on May 17 would have known that for all its wealth and glamour the underbelly of London crawled with unpleasantness. Set against Fitzstephen's adoring description of the city is that of Richard of Devizes, who left an account of the city from the perspective of an imaginary, rather stiff-necked Jew who had been to the city and did not like it. "All sorts of men crowd together there from every country under the heavens," he wrote. "No one lives in it without falling into some sort of crime. . . . Whatever evil or malicious thing that can be found in any part of the world, you will find in that city." He went on to list the iniquitous places of the city: crowded eating houses, theaters, and taverns. Of its underclass he wrote: "You will meet more braggarts here than in all France; the number of parasites is infinite. Actors, jesters, smooth-skinned lads, Moors, flatterers, pretty boys, effeminates, pederasts, singing and dancing girls, quacks, belly-dancers, sorceresses, extortioners, night-wanderers, magicians, mimes, beggars, buffoons. . . . If you do not wish to dwell with evil-doers, do not live in London."[23]

Even Fitzstephen admitted that the splendor of urban life was occasionally disrupted, although the worst he would acknowledge was "the immoderate drinking of fools and the frequency of fires."[24] In fact, as recently as July 1212 the terrible fire that had ruined London Bridge had also devastated Southwark and entered the city proper, causing immense damage.[25] And fire was not the only problem facing London's

homeowners in 1215. The Assize of Buildings—a set of detailed planning regulations passed in 1189, at the beginning of Richard I's reign—
laid down the height and position of pavements, gutters, arches, walls,
and doorways and ruled that an unwalled cesspit could not be dug
closer than three and a half feet from the land of a neighbor.[26]

Popular unrest was also frequent. In 1196 William Fitzosbern—a
brilliant and well-educated public speaker famous for his long beard—
had led a rebellion of poor Londoners, imploring them to rise up
against their masters. This ended badly: Having threatened the
Crown, Fitzosbern was trapped in a burning church, stabbed when he
tried to escape, dragged to Tyburn behind a horse, and hanged. (The
spot beneath the gallows where the rebel leader died became a site of
veneration for the poor, who scraped up handfuls of the dirt until
there was a large and unsightly hole in the ground.[27])

One of the richest sources of anecdote concerning London's dark-
est side can be found in the records of royal judges who visited the city
to try criminal cases on a judicial circuit known as the Eyre of 1244.
These hearings date from a generation after the Magna Carta, but the
behavior and the small tragedies they describe are both timeless and
utterly typical of life in a medieval city. In the sad records of the courts,
a world away from tales of skating on the frozen marshes or sniffing
exotic spices, we learn of "Elias le Pourtour, who was carrying a load of
cheese, [when he] fell dead in Bread Street" and John Shep, sergeant of
the sheriff of London, who threw a prisoner "so violently into the
deepest part of the prison that he broke his neck and died."[28] The justices were told that a madman called William de Godeshalve killed
himself with a knife, that William Gambun fell into the Thames
while clambering from one boat to another and drowned, that John de
la Neuwelonde bit Laurence Turpyn's right thumb off, that Robert of
Kingston murdered "Adam, son of Alice" with an ax, and that "a girl
about eight years old was found dead in the churchyard of St. Mary

Somerset. It was believed that she was thrown there by some prosti-
tute" presumed to be her mother.[29]

+

Of everything that could be found in the vast and varied, teeming
city of London, perhaps the most valuable to FitzWalter and his
"Army of God" was its fortifications. There were two significant
castles within the walls of the city: the Tower of London and Baynard's Castle. Both of these sat on the banks of the Thames. The
Tower, which belonged to the king, was a fat, fierce, thick-walled
monster and a potent symbol of royal authority that had loomed
over the city ever since it had been erected by William the Conqueror. (Fitzstephen tells us that the Tower's walls "rise from very
deep foundations and are fixed with mortar tempered with animals' blood."[30]) Baynard's Castle, which controlled access to London from upriver, was Robert FitzWalter's personal power base in
the capital. John had slighted the castle in January 1213 as punishment for FitzWalter's faithlessness and plotting.* But it had been
returned when FitzWalter was pardoned six months later, and its
custody, together with FitzWalter's links in the city to trading interests, meant that from a position of some desperation the baronial party were now transported to a place of great strength.

According to the Crowland Chronicler, FitzWalter's party had
attracted to it a large number of younger men of noble blood: the
"children or grandchildren of magnates," who had come to join the
rebel party in search of adventure and to make their names through

---

*Slighting was a process that consisted of causing considerable damage to the fabric
of a castle: Teams of engineers and laborers pulled down walls and fortifications and
removed valuable timber and stone for use in buildings elsewhere. Less than two
years had passed since Baynard's Castle had been slighted. It had been returned to
FitzWalter in July 1213, so in 1215 it would probably have resembled something of a
building site.

fighting in the war.[31] But this was far from an invading party made up solely of noble interests. For London itself had a long and somewhat fractious history with the Plantagenet kings, and in the last weeks of May 1215 the Londoners saw their opportunity to make a stand against King John and perhaps force him to make concessions in a moment of weakness.

Wringing special privileges from kings was a specialty of London's citizens. In 1130 Henry I had been paid one hundred marks to confirm that the city would be allowed to choose its own sheriffs. When King Stephen was embroiled in the Anarchy, he gave the capital its freedom in return for financial and military support—a relationship that was rewarded in 1141 when Stephen's enemy, the Empress Matilda, was driven out of the city before she could be crowned there. During Richard I's early reign, when the king was absent and his ministers were willing to consider almost any proposal in exchange for silver to pay for his crusading, London even managed to secure permission to elect its first mayor. Henry Fitzailwyn served from 1191 until his death in 1212 and began a long London tradition of independent power wielded by a locally elected leader—a tradition that continues today.[32] John himself had confirmed this right shortly after Fitzailwyn had died, when he had granted to the citizens of London all their ancient liberties. Thus, by 1215, when one Serlo the Mercer had been elected mayor, London was a place that knew how to turn a royal bind to its own advantage. The city would exact a good number of concessions from John in the months that followed the barons' arrival in May.

Once the rebels had secured their position in London, they decided they needed to assure themselves of allies further afield. They did so fiercely. According to Wendover, they "sent letters throughout England to those earls, barons and knights who appeared to be still faithful to the king . . . and advised them with threats, as they regarded the safety of their property and possessions, to abandon a king who was perjured and who warred against his barons, and together with them to stand firm and fight against the king for their rights and for peace; and that, if they refused to do this, they, the barons, would make war against them all, as against open enemies, and would destroy their castles, burn their houses and other buildings and destroy their warrens, parks and orchards."[33] Their actions in the city were just as uncompromising: They attacked houses belonging to the city's Jews, robbed the owners, and stripped stones from their buildings to improve the city's defenses.

The effect of the barons' defiant occupation of the capital was to bring about a stalemate. For all the ordnance, artillery, and men at John's disposal there was no realistic possibility of his besieging London successfully. He had lost access to two of his key sources of wealth: the royal treasury at Westminster and the Tower of London. He remained in control of a number of castles and manors in the nearby area and retained the support of many heavyweight English earls and barons, among them his half brother Longuespée, William Marshal, and the earls of Chester, Cornwall, Warenne, and Albermarle. The king buzzed around the lands between Winchester and Windsor, monitoring his enemies' actions in the capital. Before very long it became clear that, with neither side able to crush the other, the only way to bring some semblance of peace to England would be by negotiation.

Thus, only a week after the fall of London John opened negotiations with the rebels, suggesting that they come to meet him under the protection of letters of safe conduct. One of these was issued to Saer de Quincy, Earl of Winchester, on Monday, May 25. Two days later another safe conduct was issued to Archbishop Stephen Langton, permitting him to come to Staines "to entreat for peace between us and our barons."[34] John was now in direct contact with his enemies, and their negotiations had a mediator in the archbishop.

From late May into the early days of June, messengers traveled back and forth between the king and the rebels holed up in and around Baynard's Castle. Slowly but surely they began to feel out the basis for an agreement—a peace treaty that could be granted by the king in exchange for his enemies' dispersal. Between the king and the rebels—although clearly leaning toward the latter—sat Stephen Langton, the archbishop who had been at the root of so many of John's earlier problems. Langton would be an important mediator, and he would make a profound intellectual contribution to the final charter that appeared in June 1215. By June 10 the outlines of an agreement had taken detailed form, and King John was ready to meet his rebellious barons in person. The stage that was chosen was a broad green meadow alongside the Thames twenty-five miles upstream from London. The Magna Carta would describe it as *in prato quod vocatur Ronimed inter Windlesoram et Stanes:* "the meadow which is called Runnymede between Windsor and Staines."

III

The Rule of Law

9

Runnymede

THE LUSH MEADOW called Runnymede, some twenty-three miles west of London, was a low-lying, damp, green field cut through and watered by the river Thames, lined by trees and rising gently on its western side to form what is now known as Cooper's Hill. Since Saxon times Runnymede had been considered a liminal space: a meeting point where two sides in dispute had traditionally come to work out their differences on neutral ground. This role was etched into its very name, which derived from three old English words: *rūn*, *ēg*, and *mǣd*, referring in turn to the concepts of a place of council and counsel, an island surrounded not by water but by marsh or low hills, and, simply, a meadow.[1] It was quite literally a wetland on which a king might take advice. This was well known in 1215. The Latin term usually used to describe it was *pratum*—a large, grassy meadow, but Matthew Paris wrote that its name was earned because from "ancient times" it was a place for meetings concerning the peace of the kingdom.[2]

Making political deals in liminal spaces like Runnymede was an important tradition in English history. In 1016 the rival kings Cnut and Edmund Ironside had met on Alney Island in the river Severn to swear oaths agreeing to divide the kingdom between them, and it has been argued that the "Hursteshevet," where Edward the Confessor came to meet the thegns (aristocrats) of England in 1041 and cement the terms for his accession to the crown, was the sandy spit at Hurst Head, which sticks out into the sea between Hampshire and the Isle of Wight.[3] The choice of Runnymede could have been a nod to this tradition. Equally, it could simply have been reasoned that Runnymede was a practical place for John to meet the rebel barons, as it was partway between Windsor and rebel-held London. The barons could arrive by way of a town called Staines: Windsor and Staines lay on opposite banks of the Thames, and there were very few means of approaching the meadow from any other direction than those two towns. There could, therefore, be no trickery from either side: no ambushing the meeting spot from an unexpected direction, no surprise attacks on their base camp. The ground at Runnymede itself was in any case too soft to be considered a sensible place to do battle, if either side was thinking of anything so rash.

In the second week of June 1215 the meadow was filled with hundreds of people. The chronicler Ralph of Coggeshall wrote that the barons "gathered with a multitude of most famous knights, armed well at all points."[4] They erected tents across the field. It is likely that many of these would have displayed the arms of the chief baronial rebels: FitzWalter; his brother-in-arms Saer de Quincy, Earl of Winchester; Geoffrey de Mandeville; Eustace de Vesci; and two of the other greatest lords in England, Roger Bigod, Earl of Norfolk, and Richard Earl of Clare, all of them protected by royal letters of safe conduct. The king's party camped on the other side, in large semipermanent pavilions. Above these John might well have displayed the royal banners that he had ordered in the spring: the Plantagenet lions stitched in gold thread.[5]

The king himself did not camp out at Runnymede but spent most of his time in his apartments within the imperious round keep of Windsor Castle, perched high on a chalk cliff overlooking the river.[6] He received visitors at the castle and rode or traveled by barge downriver when his presence was required at Runnymede. His chief advisers were churchmen—Archbishop Langton; Henry, archbishop of

Dublin; William, bishop of London; and others—and a handful of loyal barons, including his half brother Longuespée, William Marshal; the earls of Warenne and Arundel; and others.*

John's private thoughts at the time of the discussions are lost to us. It is unlikely that he was thrilled at having to deal civilly with men who had only recently been plotting to have him murdered, but he did not have much choice. Matthew Paris, although writing later in the century about events that had occurred when he was only fifteen, conjured a vivid image of the king during the negotiations that took place. While John was charming in public, wrote Paris, behind the scenes he "gnashed his teeth, rolled his eyes, grabbed sticks and straws and gnawed them like a madman."[7] And well he might have. The treaty that was being thrashed out in early June would impose devastating new restrictions on every future King of England's ability to govern the realm as he pleased.

✛

The news reaching John from around his realm during the second half of May was not encouraging. Rebellions had broken out in Lincoln and Devon, and the Welsh, under their leader Llywelyn ap Iorwerth, were agitating in the west and moving to take Shrewsbury. Similar foreign opposition could be expected in the north, where Alexander II

---

*John's advisers at Runnymede, as named in the preamble to the Magna Carta, were: "Stephen, archbishop of Canterbury, primate of all England and cardinal of the holy Roman church; Henry, archbishop of Dublin; Bishops William of London, Peter of Winchester, Joscelin of Bath and Glastonbury, Hugh of Lincoln, Walter of Worcester, William of Coventry and Benedict of Rochester; Master Pandulf, subdeacon and confidant of the lord pope, Brother Eymeric, master of the Knights Templar in England; and the noble men William Marshal, earl of Pembroke, William, earl of Salisbury, William, earl of Warenne, William, earl of Arundel, Alan of Galloway, constable of Scotland, Warin fitzGerold, Peter fitzHerbert, Hubert de Burgh, seneschal of Poitou, Hugh de Neville, Matthew fitzHerbert, Thomas Basset, Alan Basset, Philip d'Aubigny, Robert of Ropsley, John Marshal, John fitzHugh, and others of our subjects."

of Scotland was ready to ally with the rebellious barons. It would not
have taken much imagination to see Philip Augustus licking his lips
in France, enjoying every second of his enemy's discomfort.

For the first week and a half of June, messengers rode back and
forth to and through Runnymede, traveling between the king's party
and the barons in London. They were toiling their way toward a solution to the standoff—a means by which the full horror of civil war
could be avoided. And slowly but surely the skeleton of a peace treaty
began to form. The exact sequence of events during the days that led
up to the agreement and production of the Magna Carta and the proc-
lamation of peace between king and barons remains muddied by the
uncertainties of eight hundred years' distance. But we know a great
deal about the process thanks to the many documents and recollec-
tions that have survived.

To start with, John did not give himself wholly over to the idea of
peace and reconciliation. The archbishop of Dublin was instructed to
prepare "two good galleys well equipped and with good crew" for the
use of William Marshal, and William Longuespée was provided with
four hundred Welshmen" to defend Salisbury.[8] In Winchester John
was also amassing a large number of foreign mercenaries brought over
from Poitou. The first week of June marked the lead-in to the festival
of Whitsun,* and John took the opportunity to spend several days in
Winchester inspecting his troops. At the same time he was taking direct and provocative action against his baronial enemies: Manors belonging to Geoffrey de Mandeville and Hugh de Beauchamp (the
castellan of Bedford, who had received the rebel barons in early May)
were stripped and reassigned to John's friends Savaric de Mauléon
and Hasculf de Suligny.[9] Yet for all this, John was beginning to feel

---

*Also known as Pentecost, Whitsun marked the descent of the Holy Spirit to the
disciples following Christ's ascension.

the financial pinch of losing access to his London treasury. A letter sent to Scarborough on June 11 showed the king desperately shuffling money from debtors to creditors in order to pay his servants and crossbowmen back wages.[10] Every day that went by made it more likely that the king would come to terms with the rebels, if only to buy himself time to regroup.

The terms that were being demanded were, by the second week of June, very well fleshed out. We know a surprising amount about the drafting process, because as well as the Unknown Charter, representing baronial demands in the spring of 1215, a remarkable working draft of the charter known as the Articles of the Barons, survives. The parchment on which the articles were written was authenticated with the royal seal and most likely taken for safekeeping by Archbishop Langton, as it ended up in the Canterbury Cathedral archives.

By the time the Articles of the Barons were drawn up, the rebel vision of peace had developed significantly. "These are the articles which the barons ask for and the lord king grants," it began. Unlike the Unknown Charter, it no longer included a copy of Henry I's concessions. But on matters of immediate dispute between king and barons it was much more sophisticated and detailed. It ran to forty-nine clauses, each of which went into considerable technical detail about the rates of reliefs for inheritance; widows' rights; the treatment of debtors to the Crown; levels of scutage, feudal aid, and rents; the extent to which certain writs could be used by the Crown; procedures for dealing with debts to Jewish lenders; and more, down to apparently trivial matters of reform such as weights and measures, the protocol for funding the rebuilding of bridges, and the placement of fish weirs along the rivers Thames and Medway.[11] The king was to exile from the realm his foreign mercenaries and eject from his service a named group of foreign advisers. He was to be forbidden from taking the military tax known as scutage except with public consent "by common counsel of the kingdom." Welsh and Scottish hostages whom John had taken were to be returned.

The very first clause committed the king to setting a limit on payments for heirs to receive inheritances and explained that the precise value "is to be pronounced in the charter" (*exprimendum in carta*). The final clause again referred to "his [the king's] charter" and made reference to a certain period of time "to be determined in the charter" (*determinandum in carta*). The Articles of the Barons were thus drawn up on the understanding that very soon John would be making some larger gesture of conciliation in which all matters of contention outlined in the document would be definitively addressed.

No date was recorded on the parchment itself, but there are grounds for supposing that the version that survives, sealed by John, was drawn up on Wednesday, June 10.[12] Already a long process of negotiations had gone on. Concessions in the articles to Londoners (in the form of a promise that the city was "to have in full its ancient liberties and free customs, both by water and by land"), the Welsh, and the Scots suggest that the list of baronial demands had expanded as they drew new allies into their fold. So too had they begun to account for the interests of the social rank below them: One clause guaranteed that the king would not allow his barons to exploit their feudal obligations; another stated that "no one shall do greater service for a knight's fee than is owed for it." A welter of interests were creeping into the negotiations. There were still some significant gaps in the draft: There is no mention of John's obligations to the Church, which is surprising, as Archbishop Langton was such a prominent figure in negotiations and John had made such a public show of his penitent Christianity and alliance with Rome. Overall, though, the Articles of the Barons show that by the second week of June the king was being pressured into making concessions in which the whole political community of England—indeed, of Britain—might have at least some small claim.

The Articles of the Barons also included the statement that "the body of a free man be not arrested or disseized or outlawed or exiled or in any way victimized, nor shall the king attack or send anyone to attack him by force, except by the judgment of his peers or by the law of the land."* Just as with the Unknown Charter, it is clear that the king's enemies were feeling their way now very closely toward a generalized statement that would commit the king to refraining from tyranny. There was also a recognition, which would come to much greater maturity in the Magna Carta, that the king would need to be compelled to obey the charter's terms: Space was left in the articles for a "security clause," and there was a suggestion that John would have to swear oaths to the English clergy that he would not appeal to the pope against the charter's terms.

On Wednesday, June 10, John came down from Windsor to Runnymede in person and was evidently deep in discussion with his advisers and opponents all day, for when Abbot Hugh of Bury St Edmunds came to try to find him there, he was forced to wait "for a very long time."[13] That night King John had dinner with Hugh in Windsor Castle before sitting on his bed within the royal chamber with the abbot and discussing "many things."[14] The chronicler who recorded the account left it, frustratingly and cryptically, at that. It is not too fanciful to think, however, that at some point the discussions would have turned to events downriver at Runnymede. Hugh had been there waiting on John that very day. He had seen the barons, their knights, their servants, and their clerical staff milling around the meadow, some locked in discussion with the king over the terms of an agreement and others, presumably, hanging around much as he was doing. If he did not know already, then he would have heard directly from John that the Articles of the Barons had

---

*"Disseize" meant to strip someone of his land or property holdings.

been sealed and a fully developed treaty was almost ready to be confirmed, formally granted, and promulgated to the realm. From Windsor on that same day John had extended his grant of safe conduct to the barons for a further four days. They would come back to Runnymede to meet him once again on the following Monday, June 15. Then, in all likelihood, the deal would be done.

This delay probably served two purposes. In the first place it gave time for the interested parties—the king, the various voices within the rebel faction, and the representatives of the Church, led by Stephen Langton—to iron out remaining wrinkles within the terms of the proposed peace. In the second place it allowed time for all to prepare for a gathering that was larger and nobler than the meetings between envoys that had been taking place until that point. This was to be the formal and final creation of the treaty—the document that we now call the Magna Carta.

On June 14 the royal household celebrated Trinity Sunday. At the church service to mark the day they would have heard a lesson read from the fourth chapter of the Revelation of St. John.[15] If any among them—including the king—was looking for portents, he might have found them in the lesson's strange, apocalyptic vision: Twenty-four elders wearing crowns bowed before an enthroned, divine being the color of deep red gemstones whose throne was surrounded by a rainbow that shimmered like an emerald. John's predilection for bright jewels was well known; his interest in the lesson may have been further piqued by its last verses, which described the elders bowing before their master's throne and throwing away their crowns.[16] Was this a metaphor for what was to come? Or would it be John whose crown was cast, as it were, to the floor?

On Monday, June 15, the delegations of king and barons met once again at the usual place. There were still minor disagreements about the details of the deal, but the time had come to make peace or abandon the process. Both sides chose peace. Despite what is often supposed, the Magna Carta was never "signed" in the manner of the great peace treaties of the twentieth century. Rather, a long list of reforms was first sworn to by the king's and the barons' representatives and then—in the words of the agreement itself, voiced in the royal third person—it was "given by our hand" (*datum per manum nostram*). In other words, the terms of a deal were formally granted and sworn to by the king himself before the clerks of his Chancery set to work writing down on sheets of parchment identical copies of the agreement in full. Each copy that was made was called an engrossment. It was made of a single dried, bleached, and scraped piece of sheepskin written upon with quill pens cut from the finest wing feathers of geese, applying ink made from crushed oak galls. Each was certified and given demonstrable legal authority by the attachment of the royal seal: A double-sided piece of colored wax connected to the parchment with a silk cord. Although no one at the time could have foreseen it, the thousands of words that the royal scribes painstakingly copied out would become one of the most famous documents in the history of the world.

The Magna Carta

FOUR PARCHMENT ENGROSSMENTS of the treaty assented to by John on June 15, 1215, at Runnymede survive today. Two are held in the British Library (one of them, originally deposited at Canterbury Cathedral, was badly damaged by a fire in 1731 and a subsequent failed attempt at preservation, although it still has its now-melted seal attached); a third is held in Salisbury Cathedral, and a fourth belongs to Lincoln Cathedral and is kept nearby in the secure environment of Lincoln Castle. There are small variations between the four documents—including an unusual handwriting style used in the Salisbury copy, more typical of books from the period than of government documents. Essentially, though, all are replica agreements, and all would once have carried the solemn royal stamp of authenticity in the form of the royal seal.

There would once have been at least thirteen, and perhaps many more copies of the 1215 Magna Carta—and indeed, dozens of copies and later reissues of the charter survive in archives across the world (including a 1297 edition held in the U.S. National Archives in Washington, D.C.). But precisely how many more of the "original" charters once existed is unknown. It is also hard to say if there was ever one original "master" document sealed in the sort of ceremony that is often romantically imagined, painted, or reenacted. Probably we must abandon altogether the image of King John seated before his great document, quill in hand, and a frown on his brow. No king of John's era would have stooped to such a lowly task as sealing his own documents. (This was a specialized task carried out by a member of the Chancery called a spigurnel.) The Magna Carta was most likely agreed in its terms, symbolically put into action with the renewal of the barons' homage to John on June 19, and then distributed to the counties and towns of England during the last days of the month. The process of making peace and agreeing to constitutional principles was difficult, and it took time.

Ragged as this aspect of the Magna Carta's history and mythology may be, the contents of the charter were still extremely significant, as would have been very obvious to all who read the charter—or, more commonly, heard it read aloud to them. Its words—more than four thousand of them, in Latin—dealt with a vast wealth of political, legal, judicial, ecclesiastical, economic, and feudal matters, often in great detail. The original charter was in continuous Latin prose, though it is now customary to subdivide it clearly into clauses (or chapters), of which there are sixty-three. Read in sequence they feel like a great jumble of issues and statements that at times barely follow one from the other. Taken together, however, they form a critique of almost every aspect of Plantagenet kingship in general and the rule of John in particular.

The Magna Carta begins with a preamble, in which John, still claiming his titles of Duke of Normandy and Aquitaine and Count of Anjou, addresses all the great men of his kingdom—"archbishops, bishops, abbots, earls, barons"—as well as his own servants—"justiciars, foresters, sheriffs, reeves . . . [and] bailiffs." Innocuously but very importantly, the charter is also addressed to *omnibus . . . fidelibus suis*—to all John's "faithful subjects." This faithfulness is crucial. The charter that follows this introduction offers to grant the king's peace and the confirmation of many long-desired liberties. But these two privileges, it is made plain, are only to be enjoyed by those who submit to John's rule, accepting his lordship and—where necessary—seeking reconciliation.

No one could have fooled himself that John was granting these terms to his people with an entirely glad and open heart. All the same, by drawing on the term *fidelus* John was ensuring that this was an agreement that traded some quite serious dents to his royal prerogative for unequivocal submission on the part of his enemies. It is also important to note that five clauses of the charter stressed that its terms could be claimed only by a free man (*liber homo*). This restricted its application yet further.

Next comes a list of those men whom John says have advised him on the document. There are twenty-seven names in total, most of whom were bishops and barons who had remained loyal during the standoff of the preceding weeks. These men are also named in clause 62 as the witnesses to the charter. At the top of the list was Archbishop Stephen Langton, "Primate of all England and Cardinal of the Holy Roman church." Langton had, of course, been the prime mediator at Runnymede and before. He had until this moment not made a definitive move to fold the rights of the Church into the rebel program, but the opening clause of the Magna Carta unmistakably bore his stamp: "Firstly, we have granted to God and confirmed by this, our present charter, for us and our heirs in perpetuity that the English Church shall be free."

These first words are of immense importance, for here was an attempt by Langton to settle for good the argument that had raged between Plantagenet kings and their archbishops ever since Henry II and Thomas Becket first clashed in the 1160s. Generally speaking, the reference to the Church and its liberties echoed the opening remarks of Henry I's coronation charter, a formative influence on the Magna Carta. More specifically, Langton was securing from the king a promise to avoid interfering in Church elections—and clearly Langton's personal experience gave him ample cause for this. Yet just as important is the fact that at the end of this clause, once his vows to refrain from meddling with the Church have been made, John effectively reintroduces the charter, stating, "We have also granted to all the free men of our realm . . . all the liberties written below." John's promises to the Church are therefore placed above all others—awarded preeminence and perhaps even special protection.

In the earlier Articles of the Barons there had been no mention anywhere of Church freedom, despite the fact that England was, in theory, a vassal state whose overlord since 1213 had been the pope. In the Magna Carta, by contrast, the issue is elevated above all others. Langton's hand, late in the negotiations, had lifted his own concerns directly to the top of the list. And for the avoidance of any doubt, the sixty-third and final clause restates the fact: "We wish and firmly command that the English Church shall be free and that men in our kingdom have and hold all the aforesaid liberties." The Magna Carta is often thought to be a document concerned with the secular rights of subjects or citizens—yet in 1215 its religious considerations were given pride of place.

Next the charter addresses one of the biggest issues of dispute between John and his barons: that of relief from inheritance taxes. Here John agrees to limit his demands for allowing earls, barons, and other great men to inherit to "£100 for the whole barony" or one hundred marks in the case of a knight. No longer would men like William FitzAlan be charged outlandish sums like ten thousand marks to come into their inheritance. No longer, equally, would John be able to force his great men into effective bankruptcy as a means of political control. John's bailiffs would not be allowed to "seize any land . . . for any debt, so long as the debtor's chattels [i.e., possessions] are sufficient to pay the debt" (clause 9). The process for assessing the wealth of the freshly dead—and therefore the inheritance tax due to the king—was spelled out in an attempt to blunt the teeth of aggressive royal officials (clauses 26 and 27). In other words, the power of the

Exchequer—which had grown markedly under Henry, Richard, and John—to extort, bully, and ruin anyone whom the king happened merely to dislike was now placed under strict supervision.

Other major political issues can be traced throughout the document. The county "farm"—the fixed tax taken by royal sheriffs—was to be held at its "ancient" (*antiquas*) rates, although what these rates were is not defined (clause 25). The occasions on which the king could take scutage—the military tax John had levied eleven times during his relatively short reign—were limited to paying a ransom for his person, "the knighting of our first-born son, or the first marriage of our first-born daughter" (clause 12). Much more important, in terms of England's later constitutional development at least, was the promise that the king would take scutage only at a "reasonable" rate and after taking "the common counsel of our realm" (*per commune consilium regni nostri*)—counsel that was to be summoned according to a newly defined protocol in clause 14. During the later thirteenth and fourteenth centuries, the notion that tax was to be taken only when the kingdom had agreed on it—in Parliament, as the formal meetings between king and subjects became known—would emerge as one of the most sacred ideas in English political thought and practice (and in turn would have profound implications for the inhabitants of the English colonies in the New World, as the American Revolution would attest).

Other clauses in the charter dealt with different aspects of the law and custom of inheritance. Widows were to have their "marriage portion and inheritance straight away and without difficulty" and without being forced to pay the king a fine for the privilege, and they would not be forced to marry against their will (clauses 7 and 8). (The Magna Carta was not wholly liberal minded with regard to women, however—clause 54 stated that "no man shall be arrested or imprisoned because of the appeal of a woman for the death of anyone but her husband.") Young men who were under the legal age of majority at the time that they inherited their lands were not to be charged fees to come into their inheritance when they grew up (clause 3), and the king agreed not to seize young men and claim them as his wards without good feudal reason (clause 37). Men who were granted the wardship of such young heirs were to treat their parks, woods, and farmland with respect and diligence, preserving the inheritance rather than simply milking the land for quick profit (clauses 4 and 5).

Other issues touched upon debt to Jewish moneylenders. The king was forbidden from taking over high-interest loans and pursuing the interest on them with his own officials (clauses 10 and 11). London—whose citizens had played such an important role in bringing John to the point of negotiation with his enemies—had its ancient liberties confirmed "both on land and on water" (clause 13) and the city's merchants were granted freedom of movement and an exemption from "evil tolls" (*malis totis*) in clauses 41 and 42.

The Welsh were promised justice for any "lands or liberties or other things" that had been taken from them "without lawful judgment of their peers" (clause 56). Prince Llywelyn himself was named: He would have hostages returned (clause 58). So was Alexander, King of Scots, since the death of his father in late 1214, whose sisters were being held at John's court: They would be returned, along with other hostages. In the case of any of Alexander's liberties and rights that had been affronted, John promised to act "in accordance with the way we deal with our other barons of England" (clause 59).

The Court of Common Pleas—the highest court in the land—was to have a fixed home rather than requiring people seeking justice to find John wherever his caravan court might then be resting. County courts were also to be held at fixed times and in fixed places throughout the year (clauses 17–19) and the fines (known as "amercements") that they imposed for offenses were to be reasonable (clauses 20–22).

Clause 23 regulated bridge building, while clause 33 banned fish traps—the wooden contraptions that blighted river transport—from the Thames and Medway. In clause 35 weights and measures were regulated for the most important things in life: corn, cloth, and ale. The Magna Carta forbade the hated practice of purveyance—by which royal officials, and particularly the garrisons of the king's many castles up and down the land, took goods, crops, horses, and carts for the king's use without paying (or intending to pay) for them (clauses 28, 30, and 31). And it touched briefly upon the contentious laws of the English forest, pledging not to use forest judges to try men who lived outside forest land (clause 44), to investigate corruption among forest officials (clause 48), and to reverse the creep of forest boundaries that had taken place during John's reign (clause 47)—although, crucially, not that which had taken place under Henry II and Richard I.

As well as these specific reforms, the document dealt, of course, in grand ideas. Indeed, it is thanks to its broadest—and in some ways least politically successful—clauses that the Magna Carta has remained famous for eight centuries. Judges, sheriffs, and other royal officials were to be competent (clause 45). Earls and barons were to be "amerced" (fined) only "by their peers" and "in accordance with the nature of the offence" (clause 21). Later, in clause 39, the charter expands the principle of judgment by equals yet further, in what is perhaps one of most enduring clauses of any major constitutional document in the last thousand years: "No free man is to be arrested or imprisoned or disseized, or outlawed, or exiled, or in any other way ruined, nor will we go or send against him, except by the legal judgment of his peers or by the law of the land" (*nisi per legale judicium parium suorum*).

In 1215 this statement was designed to stop John's highly personal and arbitrary pursuit of his greatest men. Over the years, however, clause 39—in tandem with the next clause, which simply states: "to no one will we sell, to no one will we deny or delay right or justice"—has been taken to enshrine the principle of trial by jury, the right of habeas corpus, and the basic idea that justice should always restrain the power of government.

Yet for everything that was grand and far-reaching in the Magna Carta, there was much that remained vague, woolly, or fudged. In places the document feels like frustratingly unfinished business. Clauses such as "no one is to be distrained to do more service for a knight's fee . . . than is owed for it" (clause 16) were clearly pushing toward much more complex political issues: In this case the issue at stake was John's practice of demanding military service or payment from those who were not, in fact, required by feudal law to give it. But—perhaps due to the pressures of time or the intractability of negotiators—such issues were diplomatically abandoned, the bones of an idea left unfleshed. The king promised to "immediately restore all hostages and charters that have been given over to us by Englishmen as security for peace and faithful service" (clause 49) and to expel both named individuals and "all foreign knights, crossbowmen, serjeants and mercenaries" (clauses 50 and 51)—although how or where this de-commissioning process was to take place was left unspoken.

In other places King John's manifest duplicity fairly leaps from the ancient parchment: The king promised to restore "lands, castles, liberties [and] rights" to those whom he had maltreated (clause 52), whether in England or Wales (clause 56), yet in the case of dispute or of complaints from his subjects that dated back to the reigns of Henry II and Richard I (clauses 53 and 57) the cases were to be adjourned for the duration of John's crusade. Whether or not John really intended to leave England to torment the infidel instead of his own subjects we may doubt. Surely many at the time did. Nevertheless, the king was protected as much as he was obligated by the crusader's cross he had taken up in March 1215.

John's capacity for wriggling had escaped no one, and it was for this

reason that the most important clause of all was added to the agreement. Attention is often lavished on clauses 39 and 40 by those seeking in the Magna Carta the foundation stones of Western democracy.
But equally significant is clause 61, for it is with this, known as the
"security" clause, that the men of 1215 sought to find some way to hold
the king to his word. For quite clearly all the fine efforts in bringing
the king to Runnymede, persuading him to grant the charter, and
having it sent far and wide across the country would come to nothing
if John decided simply to break his promises and return to the mode
of kingship he preferred: overbearing, extortionate, and cruel.

The security clause sets up what must have seemed like a sensible
enough scheme to tie the king to his word. If John were to "transgress
against any of the articles of peace," a panel of twenty-five specially
elected barons was entitled under the terms of the charter to "distrain and distress us in all ways possible, by taking castles, lands and
possessions and in any other ways they can . . . saving our person and
the persons of our queen and children." If the king backslid, he would
find himself under attack by his own subjects. Or to put it more simply, the treaty allowed for licensed civil war.

Here lay the great contradiction at the heart of the Magna Carta.
The barons had attempted, for the first time in English history, to
create a mechanism that would allow the community of the realm to
override the king's authority when that authority was abused. This
would be the aim of many generations of rebels after them—in
England, in America, and around the world. Yet as they found, this
was no easy task. And so it was that a document that was intended
as a peace treaty ended up sanctioning a return to war. Indeed, it
may be said that the Magna Carta made war more and not less likely,
for its explicit mechanism of enforcement was to invoke a large-scale
baronial revolt of the sort that the charter was designed to halt.
How could this possibly be a recipe for peace?

Taken in the round the Magna Carta was an extraordinary agreement. It was much longer, more detailed, more comprehensive, and more sophisticated than any other statement of English law or custom that had ever been demanded from a King of England. Its scope ran from the minute to the massive and from the profound to the particular. It did not employ the same crude hankering for past laws that had been the basis for the Unknown Charter. It looked to the past—by demanding ancient customs and payments at their "ancient" levels—but represented reform as well as retrenchment, and it was not wholly conservative.

Pulsing beneath the host of details and specificities were two simple ideas. The first was that the English barons could conceive of themselves as a community of the realm—a group with collective rights that pertained to them en masse rather than individually. The second was that the king was explicitly expected to recognize in himself two duties. He was still the man who made the law, but now he had to obey it as well. This was the same thought that had been expressed by the theologian John of Salisbury in his *Policraticus*, composed almost six decades earlier: Salisbury compared a prince with a tyrant and concluded that the essential difference between the two was that while both made and enforced laws, the prince also subjected himself to the law. In searching for a way to restrain a powerful monarch, King John's enemies had begun to seek an answer to a basic and enduring constitutional question, with far-reaching consequences.

✝

In the days following Monday, June 15, several attempts were made to reopen negotiations on certain points in the charter. Some barons were not happy that the rate for inheritance reliefs was one hundred pounds rather than one hundred marks. There was an attempt to harden the language of the security clause.[1] John was forced, outside the terms of the charter, to dismiss his justiciar, Peter des Roches, bishop of Winchester—a man wildly unpopular in the country. A secondary agreement was made with the rebel barons, including Fitz-Walter, about London: In it John accepted that his enemies (still calling themselves the Army of God) could continue to hold the city for two months, until August 15, with the Tower of London being supervised by Archbishop Langton.[2] This had the outrageous and to John very inconvenient effect of keeping the king cut off from his capital and his best sources of revenue. Yet for some barons this was still not enough to compel them to trust John. According to the Crowland Chronicler, during the days that followed the charter's granting "some of the magnates from beyond the river Humber" left Runnymede "and under the pretext that they did not attend [the granting of Magna Carta], they resumed hostilities."[3]

For those who remained, Friday, June 19, was a day of ceremony and reconciliation. The rebel barons were received by the king and granted the kiss of peace. They made their homage anew and then ate and drank with John at a feast to mark the occasion.[4] Some—including Eustace de Vesci—were persuaded to witness official documents, which was a clear sign of royal favor. John's clerks, meanwhile, continued to copy out the agreement, and his sheriffs were instructed to make its terms known far and wide about the country. Those who were not busy with that laborious task were put to work writing letters to John's castellans, sheriffs, and constables, ordering them to restore possessions that had been taken unlawfully either during or before the outbreak of hostilities. A typical letter was sent to William Longuespée on June 19, when the king was back at Windsor following the reunification banquet: "You must know that peace has been re-established between our Barons and us and that we give back immediately all the lands, castles and properties we seized from someone without a trial and unjustly."[5] On June 23 he even ordered the return of some of his foreign soldiers to Poitou.[6] John was on his best behavior. Yet beneath it all he was scheming. Matthew Paris's image of him frothing at the mouth and gnawing sticks during negotiations may have been fanciful, but a wide gap certainly existed between John's public and private demeanors.

The weeks that followed the breakup of the conference at Runnymede were messy and marked by increasing distrust. Although FitzWalter had extracted from the king a promise to keep London in baronial hands for two months, he was loath to leave the capital for fear that it would fall in his absence. He tried to encourage as many of his allies as possible to remain in the south and in the saddle by organizing a summer tournament not far from Runnymede at which the grand prize was a bear.[7]

John, meanwhile, had far more to concern himself with than tournaments and bears. In the immediate aftermath of the charter's confirmation he received a flood of demands from all over the country, insisting that he give back lands, castles, and privileges that he had confiscated in the previous years. In the ten days that followed the feast of June 19 he was forced to make fifty restorations to the rebels. FitzWalter, Saer de Quincy, and Eustace de Vesci all directly profited, receiving in turn Hertford Castle, Mountsorrel Castle (in Leicestershire), and the right to run dogs in the forests of Northumberland.[8]

John kept this up for about four weeks. But before long the effort or humiliation became intolerable. A meeting was held at Oxford between July 16 and July 23 at which the king and his enemies came together to address issues arising from the enforcement of their agreement. Six freshly drawn-up engrossments were handed out and a few more concessions were made, but at this point John embarked on a political maneuver that swiftly eroded the peace. Through

Archbishop Langton and a group of other high-ranking churchmen he issued an open letter to his barons, asking them to supply *him* with a charter acknowledging the fact that they were "bound by oath" to defend him and his heirs "in life and limb."[9] They refused. Indeed, on one day of the conference, when John was laid up in bed with painful feet, likely caused by gout, they refused even to obey his orders to meet him in his chamber.[10] According to Matthew Paris, John's own mercenaries now mocked him, sniggering that there were twenty-five other monarchs in England and that John was a disgrace to kingship.[11] From that point on, what little trust existed between the two sides evaporated. As the Oxford conference broke up in rancor, John made a move that would flush all remaining goodwill away forever. He wrote to Pope Innocent III, explaining what had happened in his realm and asking him to annul the charter and release him from his oath to obey it.

The fragile peace of Runnymede had lasted, wrote the Dunstable annalist, "only for a little time."[12] This was quite an understatement. In late August Pope Innocent III wrote back in a state of righteous anger that he could summon better than any man in Europe. The situation in England, he wrote, was the work of the devil:

> Although our well beloved son in Christ, John illustrious king of the English, grievously offended God and the Church . . . the king at length returned to his senses. . . . But the enemy of the human race [i.e., Satan], who always hates good impulses, by his cunning wiles stirred up the barons of England so that, with a wicked inconstancy, the men who supported him when injuring the Church rebelled against him when he turned away from his sin.[13]

The pope went on to rehearse his prior instructions to the English barons, noting that he had explicitly told them "to strive to conciliate the king by manifest proofs of loyalty and submission." They had ignored him, he noted. "And so by such violence and fear as might affect the most courageous of men he was forced to accept an agreement which is not only shameful and demeaning but also illegal and unjust, thereby lessening unduly and impairing his royal rights and dignities.

"We refuse to ignore such shameless presumption," thundered the pope. "For thereby the Apostolic See would be dishonoured, the king's rights injured, the English nation shamed, and the whole plan for a Crusade seriously endangered."

What came next left little room for interpretation: "We utterly reject and condemn this settlement, and under threat of excommunication we order that the king should not dare to observe it and that the barons and their associates should not require it to be observed. . . . We declare it null, and void of all validity forever."

The letter was dated August 24, 1215, at Innocent's hometown of Anagni, near Rome. The minute it left the pope's secretariat, the Magna Carta was certifiably dead. In practice, by then it was dead already. On September 5 Peter des Roches, John's loyal bishop of Winchester, and Pandulf Verraccio, the papal legate, excommunicated the baronial leaders by name. In response, in early September the barons wrote to Louis, the heir to the crown of France, inviting him to come and take John's place as the new ruler of England. Two weeks later John sent an order to his men to start seizing FitzWalter's lands. The arrival of Innocent's letters in England toward the end of September merely confirmed what everyone knew.

The country erupted into war.

II

England Under Siege

THE FIRST the English knew of the shipwreck was when the soldiers' bodies washed up on the beaches. The men came first: Knights and their companions who had until recently been living in Flanders were now thrown up on a foreign shore by the cold lap of the North Sea, which carried them to Great Yarmouth, the formidable walled town famous for its herring trade, a few miles to the east of Norwich. Behind them came the corpses of their families: Women and children had been piled onto the boats with the promise of a new life and fortune. Their hopes had been violently dashed.

The soldiers had been recruited by Hugh de Boves, one of John's most experienced military contractors. Described by the incorrigibly judgmental Roger of Wendover as "a brave knight but a proud and unjust man" (and loathed by at least one other chronicler, the Dunstable annalist), Boves had been sent to northwest Europe to help raise an army with which John could strike back against his rebel barons.[1] For the most part the recruiters had succeeded: Convoys of troop carriers had been arriving in Dover from the Continent for days, and John had been present in the town to watch his hired swords disembark. But as all sailors knew, an autumn crossing of the Channel carried risks. On calm seas and with a good wind, the crossing should have taken a day. But gales blew up from September onward, and when they did, the lurch of the waves could easily overwhelm vessels better suited to hugging the coastline than to venturing into open water.

That was precisely what had happened. A storm had risen during

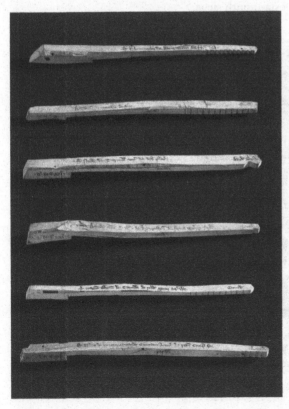

This miniature from a medieval legal treatise shows Henry II remonstrating with Thomas Becket while knights ominously finger their swords. Henry developed an intense and efficient system of government to rule his expanding empire, but he fell into dispute with the English Church, as did his son John.

A collection of tally sticks, used for accounting by the Exchequer. Each stick was split in two and one half was given to the debtor. The notches aligned, showing the status of loans and payments. The king's Exchequer could ruin barons in a single day by calling in debts that were owed to the Crown, and John's exploitation of this power would earn him the hatred of many of his subjects.

The distinctive remains of Château Gaillard, set in an imposing position overlooking the Seine in Normandy. It was constructed under Richard in 1196–98 and was supposed to be unconquerable—but within a decade, John would lose it to the French after a six-month siege.

King John, as drawn by the great St. Alban's chronicler Matthew Paris for his *Historia Anglorum*, composed in the 1250s. John is bottom left in a royal quartet featuring his father, brother Richard, and son Henry III. John was capable of being a flexible administrator but he was also deceitful, rash, bullying, and unlucky. For the most part, he was loathed.

Perhaps the greatest medieval pope, Innocent III, shown here in a fresco at the Monastery of St. Benedict in Subiaco, was a crusader, a reformer, and a tireless defender of the rights of the Church. John crossed him and was punished with an interdict and excommunication, until he engineered a cunning, strategically timed rapprochement.

A silver penny, from 1205–7 minted in Winchester. It bears the name "Henricus," as all pennies did up to the reign of Edward I, but it shows the goggle-eyed King John. John loved money. During the decade leading up to 1215 he stockpiled vast wealth, particularly in the form of silver pennies held in his castles. He was richer, for a time, than any English king before him.

The Battle of Bouvines on July 27, 1214, as depicted in a detail from the fourteenth-century manuscript of the *Grandes Chroniques de France*. In this scene, John's ally Count Ferrand of Flanders is captured. Other allies fled the battlefield. John effectively bet a decade's worth of accumulated wealth on a campaign to reconquer his lost French lands and lost.

The seal die and an example of the resulting seal belonging to Robert Fitz-Walter; beneath the mounted knight and shield bearing his arms is a *dragon retardant*. One of John's chief enemies in the years leading up to 1215, FitzWalter was a powerful East Anglian baron who was implicated in a plot to kill John. Later, he awarded himself the title Marshal of the Army of God and held London against the king.

The undated Articles of the Barons, a working draft of the Magna Carta. They do not contain the clauses about protecting the freedom of the Church— most likely later added at the insistence of Archbishop Langton—but are clearly the product of advanced negotiations between the king and his barons.

An eighteenth-century engraving in which John signs the Magna Carta at Runnymede as Archbishop Langton looks on. The quill pen alone tells us that things were not quite like this. Medieval kings did not sign charters—they granted them and their officials subsequently made written copies, called engrossments, which were then sealed.

A number of copies were issued in 1215 as the charter was distributed across England. This is one of the two held at the British Library; the two other surviving copies are owned by Salisbury and Lincoln cathedrals. Written in closely scripted Latin on parchment, many of its words are abbreviated.

The great seal of King John. Once the Magna Carta was granted, the royal seal would have been applied to the various copies then produced by industrious scribes. Only one of the four surviving copies still has remnants of its seal.

It was in a meadow called Runnymede, beside the Thames, that the Magna Carta was negotiated and subsequently granted by King John. This memorial, commissioned by the American Bar Association, is a testament to the profound impact of the Magna Carta in the founding of the United States.

King John's effigy surmounting his tomb in Worcester Cathedral. Had he lived longer and continued to alienate a dwindling group of loyal barons, the rebels and Prince Louis of France might have proved strong enough to topple the Plantagenet dynasty.

The great lawyer Sir Edward Coke as painted by Gilbert Jackson in 1615. A thorn in the side of both James I and Charles I, Coke was almost single-handedly responsible for the "rediscovery" of the Magna Carta during the years preceding the English civil wars in the 1640s. After centuries of decline, the Magna Carta was once again at the heart of politics.

THE PATRIOTIC AMERICAN FARMER.
J-N D-K-NS——N Esqr BARRISTER at LAW:
Who with Attic Eloquence and Roman Spirit hath Asserted,
The Liberties of the BRITISH Colonies in America.

'Tis nobly done, to Stem Taxations Rage,
And raise, the thoughts of a degen'rate Age,
For Happiness and Joy, from Freedom Spring;
But Life in Bondage, is a worthless Thing.

Printed for & Sold by R. Bell. Bookseller

A testament to the power of the Magna Carta in America, this illustration from 1772 depicts John Dickinson, author of *Letters from a Farmer in Pennsylvania* and the man who became known as the Penman of the Revolution. His writings were instrumental in building dissent against British rule in the years before the American Revolution. While his hand clasps a manuscript of his own writings, he leans on a book titled *Magna Charta*, as the document was often referred to by the founding fathers.

the crossing, smashing Boves's boats to pieces, and everyone aboard had been lost. Boves was one of the many who washed up, wet and dead, at Yarmouth. According to Wendover, "at each of the ports on that part of the sea coast there was found such a multitude of bodies of men and women that the very air was tainted by their stench." He wrote of children who had been drowned as they slept in their cradles; once cast into the ocean, the flesh had been nibbled from their little bones by "the beasts of the sea and the birds of the air."[2]

When John learned of Boves's death, he was said to have flown into one of his temper tantrums. "He was dreadfully enraged and took no food that day but remained until the evening as if he were possessed by madness," wrote Wendover.[3] Still, this was a king quite used to seeing men around him perish, and he had more pressing concerns than a few boatloads of dead Flemings. Those who had survived the crossing composed the core of a formidable army, bolstered further by the presence of fighters from Poitou and Gascony in the south, Louvain and Brabant in the north. By the end of September the time had come for this fierce body of men to mobilize.

The key to controlling England remained the possession of London. Thanks to the continued support of Mayor Serlo, the capital was still in rebel hands, but it was certain John would march on the city as soon as he felt strong enough to do so. The king's mercenary army was growing larger and more dangerous every day. By the end of September the barons had decided to stall him on his path by occupying the best-defended stronghold on the road between London and Dover: Rochester Castle. The battle for control of this imposing fortress would be remembered as one of the most famous sieges of the Middle Ages.

✛

Castles had been erupting like great, craggy molehills across the English landscape ever since the conquering Normans had imported the science of castle building in 1066. For more than 150 years the castle had been the most important piece of military technology in existence in England. Strict laws set out who could and could not build castles and laid down the conditions governing which buildings could be crenellated and turned into fortresses. This had been the case since at least the days of Henry I, whose law code, the *Leges Henrici Primi*, stated that the king had "jurisdictional rights ... in his land solely and over all men ... [over] fortifications consisting of three walls" and that "construction of fortifications without permission" was an offense that would "place a man in the king's mercy."[4] Kings and barons paid dizzying amounts to erect and maintain these castles: Dover Castle, one of the finest and most formidable in the realm, had gobbled up seven thousand pounds of royal expenditure over the eleven years it took to build.*

Men who knew how to put up a strong castle were highly valued by the crown: They are known in the records as *ingeniator*, or "engineer," but were likely to have combined the roles of architect and foreman. Maurice the Engineer—also known as Maurice the Mason—was paid a shilling a day to oversee work on Dover Castle and the keep at Newcastle upon Tyne in the 1170s. Fortinus the Engineer was paid in clothes: He earned a robe in 1203–4 for helping to repair Colchester Castle for the king. The best engineers could—and did—remain in royal service for generations. John had inherited from his father and brother the services of Master Elias of Oxford, who had built or renovated everything from royal houses and hunting lodges to the Tower of London. Castles were an indispensible tool of kingship, and the men who made them were highly prized.[5]

Ever since Henry II, successive Plantagenet kings had sought to

---

*Spending £7,000 on a public capital project like Dover Castle in the thirteenth century would be the equivalent of spending at least £1.7 billion on one today. This value represents the "relative economic cost," according to measuringworth.com.

increase the number and strength of the castles under royal control. Some were built from scratch. Others were repaired or refortified. Many more were simply seized from their owners. From the time of the great war of 1173–74, when large numbers of castles were taken into the king's possession as punishment for rebellion, around 50 percent of the fortresses in England were held by the Crown.

John controlled well over one hundred castles in England. They ranged from relatively modest and simple military bases to the huge edifices of Dover, Corfe, Odiham, Kenilworth, and the Tower of London. He spent vast sums on improving his castles, particularly in the frontier regions of the southeast, the Welsh Marches, and the northern borders with Scotland. He invested two thousand pounds on Scarborough and more than one thousand pounds on each of Kenilworth, Knaresborough, and Odiham. Castle building was at times the greatest single cost that the Crown's revenues had to bear.[6] To John, as to his brother and father, the massive expense was more than just a matter of bravado and status. Castles were the hard currency of politics. They served as royal houses, prisons, treasure stores, garrisons, and centers of local government. To possess a castle was to control the area around it, and to hold a castle with the king's permission was a mark of royal favor. To hold a castle against the king was an outright declaration of war.

Who exactly had the right to keep Rochester Castle was a matter of some disagreement. It had been erected for the king by Gundulf, bishop of Rochester, between 1087 and 1089 in lieu of payment of a debt, and it consisted, like most castles of its age, of a huge, squat, rectangular stone keep surrounded by powerful walls and an "outer bailey": a well-defended area containing outhouses, workshops, servants' quarters, and animal sheds. The walls were built from the local hard, blue gray Kentish limestone known as ragstone. Like any good castle, Rochester was well situated: set inside a curve of the river Medway and further protected to the south by a hill and to the north and east by a ditch.

More significant than any of this, however, was the matter of Rochester's custody. In 1127 Henry I had granted it to the archbishop of Canterbury, William de Corbeil, and a condition of the gift was that it would remain in the custody of his official successors in perpetuity.[7] Thus it had come into the keeping of Archbishop Stephen Langton, who had arranged for it to be maintained day to day by Reginald de Cornhill, sheriff of Kent. Since August 9 John had been trying to arrange for the castle's transfer to one of his own followers, Peter des Roches, bishop of Winchester. But Langton, increasingly unable to hold his neutrality in the war between king and country, had resisted, and the matter was unresolved when the archbishop left England for Rome in mid-September, heading for the Fourth Lateran Council, Innocent III's grand ecumenical gathering to which almost every major churchman in Christendom had been summoned. The matter of the castle therefore rested with Sheriff Cornhill, and by the early autumn Cornhill had decided to throw his lot—and Rochester Castle—in with the rebels.

In the second week of October a force estimated between 90 and 140 knights had poured out of London heading in the direction of Rochester. They were led by William d'Aubigny, Lord of Belvoir (pronounced "Beaver"), in Leicestershire, one of the council of twenty-five barons that had been named to enforce the Magna Carta, who was also, according to Wendover, "a man bold and tried in war."[8] They could scarcely have hoped for a better commander. D'Aubigny knew castles inside out. His own power base at Belvoir Castle was one of the strongest and most dominant in the Midlands, and he was highly conversant with the conventions and craft of holding a fortress against an attacking force. Over the weeks that followed he would exhaust every ounce of his skill and bravery trying to resist the waves of troops sent by the indignant king of England to reduce Rochester Castle.

✦

Besieging a castle was an undertaking theoretically weighted in favor of the besieged. By the early thirteenth century, most English castles were built in stone, not from timber (as had been the case before the Norman Conquest) and could therefore easily resist attack by fire, arrows, crossbow bolts, stones, spears, axes, and almost every other small arm known to the Christian mind. Once a large and well-maintained castle was secured, it could be held by a relatively limited number of men for a considerable length of time. Even if the outer walls were breached—itself no easy task—the towering stone keeps that were characteristic of Plantagenet castles were themselves very difficult to assail successfully, defended as they were by ditches, thick-walled towers, and tiny, slitted windows from which missiles and arrows could easily be aimed but through which they could seldom be successfully returned. The lowest doors on castle keeps were usually on the first floor rather than at ground level. When a castle came under attack, its defenders would simply haul up or even burn the wooden ladder that gave access to the door, so that it could be neither stormed nor battered down with a ram.[9] Stones, arrows, boiling liquid, and red-hot sand could be tipped onto the heads of attackers, making any attempt to scale a castle's defenses using ladders or scaffolds very dangerous. All of this meant that, more often than not, a castle would fall to a siege not because its defenses failed but because the will, the health, or the stomachs of the defenders gave out first.

In autumn 1215 Rochester Castle was garrisoned by a relatively large number of knights, accompanied by their attendants and retinues.[10] This was a far greater defending force than the thirteen men who would manage the following year to hold off for eight days an attack on Odiham Castle in Hampshire. Yet the number of men in-side Rochester was not necessarily helpful to its defense. When d'Au-bigny and his men dashed into the castle, they found it "destitute not only of arms and provisions, but also of every kind of property." Wen-dover, who clearly admired d'Aubigny, wrote that the rebels immedi-ately lost heart and wanted to abandon the castle but were dissuaded by their leader, who warned them of the chivalric humiliation that they would bring down upon themselves if they were to be thought of as "knights-deserters."[11] A scramble for supplies took place in which the town of Rochester was thoroughly plundered, but there was "no time left for them to collect booty in the country around." There were, in other words, many mouths inside the great square-towered keep of the castle and perilously little with which to feed them. And John, with his army of mercenaries, was on his way.

The road between Dover, where John was based, and Roches-ter, where the rebels were frantically rounding up food and provi-sions, was known as Watling Street and had originally been built to move Roman armies about the realm. According to Wendover, it took John's army—now an "immense multitude of knights and sol-diers, [which struck] all who beheld them with fear and dismay"—just three days to decamp from the south coast and lay Rochester Castle under siege.[12] It was a daunting sight. Besides a large number of trained soldiers, including crossbowmen "who thirsted for nothing more than human blood," the royal army brought with it large siege engines including what Wendover called *petrarias*, or stone throwers: large catapults for hurling rocks.* These were set up within range of

*Terms for medieval catapults were varied and vague, but there seem to have been several types in use. A trebuchet had a pivoted hurling arm that was powered by a counterweight: Modern tests have shown that a trebuchet with a one-ton counterweight could sling a fifteen-kilogram lump of rubble between 120 meters and 180 meters with the accuracy of a mortar. (See Hansen, "Reconstructing a Medieval Trebuchet,"in *Military History Illus-trated Past and Present* 27 (1990). A ballista was a giant crossbow powered by a winch. A the castle and went to work; John "severely annoyed the besieged by incessant showers of stones and other weapons."[13] The dust and the noise generated as lumps of rubble smashed into the sides of the fortress would have been mightily impressive.

Siege warfare was the most important form of conflict in the Middle Ages, from western Europe to China and Mongolia, when in 1215 the dreaded warlord Temüjin, better known as Genghis Khan, had successfully besieged and massacred the population of Zhongdu (modern Beijing). Whereas pitched battles were dreadfully uncertain affairs, as John had found to his cost at Bouvines in July of the previous year, sieges were regular and somewhat more predictable. They proceeded according to centuries of military science and were governed (or semigoverned, at any rate) by a code of chivalric conduct under which deals could be struck between besiegers and besieged to determine the terms of engagement. Presiege agreements would typically state the length of time that a siege would be held in hope of relief before the garrison either formally surrendered, to be treated with mercy, or held out until it was stormed and slaughtered. The wisdom that informed the conduct of siege warfare in Europe dated from classical times, and the writings of men like the fourth-century A.D. Roman military writer Vegetius and the first-century B.C. military engineer Vitruvius were collected and studied in the courts and royal libraries of medieval Europe.*

---

mangonel threw stones, which were released from a fixed wooden throwing arm when it was hauled back and then released to hit a crossbeam. These catapults were often given scary names, such as "God's Stone Thrower," "Malcousin," "The Furious," and—in the case of the infamous catapult owned by John's grandson Edward I, "Warwolf." They had changed little in design since Roman times, as a glance at Vegetius shows: Flavius Vegetius Renatus, *De Re Militari* (Driffield, UK: Leonaur Press, 2012), 66.

*The Bibliothèque Nationale in Paris contains twenty manuscript editions of Vegetius's writings made in the eleventh and twelfth centuries: That there was a direct intellectual link between Roman and medieval siege warfare is beyond doubt. See J. Bradbury, *The Medieval Siege* (Woodbridge, UK: Boydell & Brewer, 1992), 3–4.

The fact that sieges were scientific and partially rule bound, how-ever, did not mean that they were civilized. Fierce and ingenious tools and tactics were employed on both sides, and famous sieges tended to produce infamous tales of the ghastly privations inflicted on attackers and defenders alike. It was said that at the siege of Con-stantinople in 717–18, the Arab besiegers had been in such a sorry condition that they had been forced to eat human flesh and human feces pounded together into patties and cooked.[14] Perhaps this was a symbolic exaggeration designed to invoke the horror rather than the actuality of the siege, but similarly vile stories abounded elsewhere in history. Vikings besieging Chester in 918 had been driven back when defenders dropped boiling ale and water on the attackers and threw live beehives at them, so that their skin blistered and peeled from their flesh and their hands and feet swelled up with painful stings. John's grandfather Geoffrey Plantagenet, Count of Anjou, was said to have created the legendary potion known as Greek fire by mixing together nut oil and hemp flax, which he blasted from a catapult when he was attacking a castle at Montreuil-Bellay on the frontiers between Anjou and Maine. The great twelfth-century Holy Roman Emperor Frederick Barbarossa was especially adept at siege terror tactics: His troops were said to have played football with their enemies' severed heads and tortured captured defenders by scalping them or cutting off their hands and feet to provide amuse-ment and relief from the boredom that naturally accompanied such an attritional method of warfare.

Cruel and unusual devices were deployed to try to break sieges: Beyond the conventional siege engines such as ladders, scaling towers, belfries, battering rams, and catapults, there was a degree of biological and psychological warfare that could sink to great depravity. Rotting corpses—animal and human—were flung into castles to cause dis-gust or dunked into water sources to spread disease. During sieges in which noncombatants had been ejected from the castle or town in order to reduce the number of hungry mouths among the defenders, it was deemed perfectly acceptable under the rules of war for the besieging army to trap the unarmed civilians in no-man's-land, within view of the castle, and allow them to starve to death. Taunting, torment, and creative displays of despicable cruelty were all used to grind down the minds and wills of those behind the walls and encourage them to give up as quickly as possible.

Even when the violence was not grotesque, siege sites were awful and deadly places for both sides, cursed by sickness and starvation. After all, John's brother Richard had died from gangrene at the siege of Châlus-Chabrol in 1199. Both John's men and the barons barricaded inside Rochester would have known that what lay ahead was a dangerous and potentially deadly encounter.

"Our age has not known a siege so hard-pressed nor so strongly resisted," wrote the Crowland Chronicler.[15] For several days John's catapults pounded the walls of the castle while archers and crossbowmen sent up a hail of arrows and bolts; but it soon became obvious that the fortifications were too strong simply to be smashed down with missiles. (There was a small irony here: John himself had provided £115 early in his reign to improve Rochester's defenses when it had briefly been in royal hands.) On October 14 the king sent a writ to the nearby town of Canterbury demanding that his officials there see to the production "by day and night of as many picks [i.e., pickaxes] as you are able." If the walls could not be knocked down, then they would have to be reduced from below. This was bad news for d'Aubigny and the garrison. Undermining—tunneling under the walls of a fortress—was not likely to be a swift process, no matter how many picks the reeves of Canterbury managed to send. The defenders' best hope for a rapid end to the siege was going to be relief from outside.

On October 26 an armed band of barons rode out of London in the direction of Rochester intending to distract John's forces. The sortie included seven hundred horses—a substantial relieving party—but they got no farther than Deptford before they heard that John, whose numbers were far greater, was preparing to head them off. It was not a battle that the rebel leadership was inclined to fight, so—despite the fact that they had apparently sworn an oath to assist the garrison—they turned tail, scuttled back to London, and hoped for the best. To Roger of Wendover this was nothing short of cowardice. "They turned their backs on the besieged William and his followers and returned to their old haunt," he wrote. Safe in London, the chronicler continued (probably fancifully), "amusing themselves with the dangerous game of dice, drinking the best wines which they chose at their own option, and practising all other vices, they left their besieged companions at Rochester exposed to the danger of death, and enduring all kinds of misery."[16] John worked his crossbowmen and catapult operators in shifts to keep up the bombardment around the clock, while d'Aubigny's followers defiantly threw back the rocks with which they were being assailed from the top of the castle walls. Beneath the clatter of rubble against masonry, one could have heard the quieter but deadlier sound of picks and shovels cutting through the Kentish soil, inching their way beneath the fortress.

Sapping was a potent, if perilous, means of breaking a siege. It required men to dig tunnels below the walls of the castle, weakening the defenses at the foundations. When the tunnel was big enough it was deliberately collapsed, in the hope that it would bring down a portion of the fortress with it. This could be an effective technique, even if it carried the risk of the tunnel collapsing prematurely and crushing or burying the miners alive. Indeed, John himself had experienced the unwelcome results of skilled sapping in 1203–4, when

Château Gaillard—the greatest Plantagenet castle on the banks of the Seine in Normandy, built by his brother Richard to be impervious to attack—had partially collapsed and ultimately been lost to the French thanks to the efforts of miners working close to the base of the walls, protected from bombardment by a large, movable wooden shield known as a sow.* During the course of the Middle Ages mining and countermining would become fine arts, and castle defenses would stretch below the ground to include tunnels built to intercept offensive sappers, who could be fought off hand to hand if necessary.† At Rochester in 1215, however, the defenders had no way of keeping King John's tunnelers at bay.

The area of the castle that both artillery and diggers were targeting was the southeast corner, where the keep was positioned close by the castle's long surrounding curtain wall. At some point, probably at the very end of October or the start of November, the relentless assault from above and below succeeded in punching a hole through that wall. This was a significant achievement, testament to the effort and manpower John had devoted to the task. It meant that the royal forces now had access to the bailey. Still, there remained the matter of the keep itself, into which the garrison was now firmly backed. One hundred and fifty feet high, rugged and thick, there was still plenty of work for John's men to do before they could hope to break in. Yet if there was one thing that the King of England never lacked, it was determination. He commanded his miners to keep digging.

And so they dug. Evidently they moved at a good rate too, because on November 25 John sent a writ to Hubert de Burgh, his

---

*The image intended was of a large mother pig protecting her piglets, the miners, beneath her belly as they suckled. Sows were also known as cats or weasels.

†Visitors to the medieval tunnels beneath Dover Castle can still see evidence of this aspect of subterranean warfare.

justiciar and loyal servant, asking him for a rather unusual service. He demanded that Hubert "send to us with all speed by day and night forty of the fattest pigs of the sort least good for eating to bring fire underneath the tower."[17] This could only mean one thing: The tunnel below the southeast corner of the keep was considered to be deep enough to do its job. The shaft—and by extension, John hoped, one of the four towers—was now held up only by the wooden struts inserted by the sappers and was ready to fall.

Pig fat melts at around 45°C, smokes at around 120°C, and ignites spontaneously when its temperature climbs up near 300°C. With forty pigs' fat smeared all over the wooden struts of John's mine, it would have been a fairly straightforward matter to create a blistering fire beneath the southeast corner of Rochester's keep. When the fire began to burn, it must have been a peculiarly disquieting experience for the hungry garrison inside, who by this point, according to Wendover, had been reduced to eating the flesh of their warhorses.[18] The scent of woodsmoke, mixed first with the fragrance of roasting bacon, was followed soon after by the acrid tang of burning lard. This would presumably have been followed by a pause in the bombardment as the attackers watched eagerly to see whether their many weeks of mining had been successful; and finally, fatefully, there would have been the awful thundering sound of falling masonry. For when John's infernal mine collapsed, it took down a large chunk of the southeast tower. The attackers rushed the hole in the wall, and d'Aubigny's men were forced to scramble a retreat to the very last possible place of safety left to them.

The structure of Rochester's keep was such that a strong internal wall divided the building in two, which made it possible to seal off half of the rooms. Now a small rear guard from among the garrison took cover behind this wall. There was not room for everyone, however, so those who were thought to be the weakest were thrown out to the mercy of the king's men, who apparently treated them very badly indeed, cutting off their arms and legs for sport. Everyone soon realized that this was the end: According to Wendover, the garrison knew that their choice was either to come out, gambling that the king would spare their lives, or remain where they were, secure behind a stone wall but certain to run out of food. Within days—or possibly hours—of the southeast wall's falling, the remainder of the rebels packed behind the dividing wall made their decision. On November 30 they held council, where they agreed "it would be a disgrace . . . to die of hunger when they could not be conquered in battle."[19] Thus resolved, they came out from their final bolt-hole, bedraggled and undernourished, and surrendered themselves and what remained of their broken hideout to a triumphant but extremely angry King John.

The siege of Rochester Castle had lasted nearly two months. That it had gone on as long as it did was a testament to the fortitude of the rebel barons who had held the castle, allowing London and other strategically important parts of the southeast to be secured against the king. That it had been broken so comprehensively was a testament to the fixity of purpose that drove John as he fought to recover from his humiliations. The king was sufficiently riled by the difficulty to which he had been put that he wanted "all the nobles strung up on the gibbet."[20] In the end, however, calmer voices convinced him that this would increase the chances of his own garrisons' being dealt with badly when circumstances were reversed. In any case, the rules of war frowned upon massacring a force that had surrendered rather than being taken by storm, and even if John's men had mined their way to the heart of the donjon, it had still been the choice of d'Aubigny's garrison to surrender, in the expectation of being shown mercy. Presumably somewhat let down by this anticlimax, John allowed his enemies to live—although he did not stretch to granting them freedom. D'Aubigny and his fellow noblemen were packed off to be locked up "in close custody" in the king's notorious dungeons at Corfe Castle. A few others—Wendover names them as Robert de Chaurn, Richard Giffard, and Thomas of Lincoln—were kept by John's side.[21] They joined the royal court as it finally moved away from the smoldering ruins of Rochester, heading north to the Midlands, where the king would celebrate Christmas at Nottingham.

Endgame

I T HAD BEEN EXPENSIVE and frustrating to keep an army of foreign troops and mercenaries in front of Rochester Castle for nearly two months, and in the weeks that followed the castle's collapse, John let his soldiers off the leash. They went plundering. Plenty of damage had been done to the area around Rochester during the siege. Now, as Christmas approached, the king gave his troops permission to expand their locus of terror far across the country.

This was bold. Then again, things certainly seemed to be going John's way. Bringing down Rochester was a huge military achievement, and the barons' attempts to entice Louis to offer himself as a rival king had thus far come to little. Although Saer de Quincy and Henry de Bohun had gone to France to urge the prince to make haste, Louis had sent only 140 knights to London and otherwise seemed very far from coming to lead a full invasion in person.

Meanwhile, in Rome, John's political case against the rebel barons was growing stronger. By an unholy coincidence, on the very day that Rochester's walls had fallen—November 30—Pope Innocent III had heaped opprobrium on those who dared to oppose the English king. Innocent had spent the whole of November chairing his massive ecumenical gathering known as the Fourth Lateran Council, attended by the highest-ranking churchmen in Christendom. It had been convoked to rally the Church behind his proposed Fifth Crusade, though its decrees would ultimately penetrate much deeper into the fabric of Christian life. The council gave Innocent a chance to remain personally involved in the affairs of England, as all but four of the English bishops were in attendance.

The seventy decrees, or canons, of the Fourth Lateran Council—preceded by a statement on the creation, the fall of man, and the redeeming promise of belief in the Holy Trinity—offered up a wide-ranging reform of Church life. A council of this kind was at most a once-in-a-generation gathering: The Third Lateran Council had taken place in 1189 and the fifth would not convene for nearly three hundred years, until 1512. Innocent had summoned more than a thousand churchmen, including two of the four Church patriarchs, to lend approval to his muscular vision of Christian rejuvenation and to take back to their homelands the message that it was time to muster up a new crusade.

The issues touched upon were many and varied.[1] The pope's long-running concern with heresy and irregular doctrines was at the fore: The council condemned "every heresy setting itself up against this holy, orthodox and catholic faith" and threatened excommunication and anathema on "all heretics whatever names they go under." Uppermost in Innocent's mind were the Cathar heretics of southern France, against whom he had launched such a ferocious campaign, but heresy and heretical sects were not unknown among the English either. Walter Map recorded one particularly salacious account of Cathars engaging in bestial orgies at the behest of a master who took the form of a giant black cat before going on to say: "To England . . . there have come no more than sixteen, who by order of King Henry II, were branded and beaten with rods and have disappeared."[2] This had taken place in the 1160s, and since then organized English heresy had been notable mainly by its absence. There was, however, a degree of popular skepticism about matters of doctrine. Around 1200 the London-based monk Peter of Cornwall had written that "there are many people who do not believe that God exists. They consider that the universe . . . is ruled by chance rather than Providence . . . nor do they think that the human soul lives on after the death of the body."[3] If John had been considering slackening his watch over heresy, the decrees of the Lateran Council might have given him pause: "If a temporal lord . . . neglects to purge his land of this heretical filth he shall be bound," the document boomed, "with the bond of excommunication."

The Fourth Lateran took rigorous action to improve the quality and education of the clergy and had little patience for churchmen who fell into lust, drink, or other frivolities. One sternly worded article banned churchmen from keeping their own furniture in holy buildings and condemned "altar-cloths and communion-cloths so dirty that at times they horrify some people." Clergy were forbidden to hunt or hawk or to own hunting dogs or falcons. They were "not to watch mimes, entertainers and actors," nor to "indulge in red or green clothes, long sleeves or shoes with embroidery or curved toes." Nor were priests to wear "cloaks with sleeves," "spurs that are gilded" or "buckles or belts ornamented with gold or silver." Sexual impropriety among the clergy was to be punished "according to the rules of canon law" while drunkenness was now to be grounds for suspension from office. The council was especially concerned with drinking games, "whereby in certain parts drinkers bind each other to drink measure of measure and he in their judgment is most praised who has made most people drunk and drained the deepest cups."

It is arguable, of course, whether any of this fundamentally changed the reality or perception of a louche clergy: These same sins of pride and wantonness would underpin much of the anticlericalism that lay behind the sixteenth-century Reformation. In other areas of life, however, the Fourth Lateran would have a profound and long-lasting effect. Canon 18 stated that "no clerk may decree or pronounce a sentence of death; nor may he carry out a punishment which involves blood or be there when it is carried out ... nor shall any clerk write or dictate letters requiring a punishment which involves blood ... Also let no clerk be put in command of mercenaries, crossbowmen or suchlike men of blood ... and none is to bestow any blessing or consecration on a purgation by ordeal of boiling water or of cold water or of the red-hot iron."

This brief decree redrew the boundaries between churchmen and the secular powers they served. For generations bishops had been able to ride into battle; now the days of the warrior bishop were numbered. The clergy would still attend battles and sieges—but in the centuries that followed their weapons were to be crucifixes, relics, and prayer rather than clubs and maces.

Even more far-reaching in its implication was the new prohibition on clerical involvement in what was then known as "trial by ordeal." The ordeals of water and fire were fearsome physical ways of taking God's measure of a crime. The ordeal had a long history in England—dating back long before the Norman Conquest—and was regarded as an acceptable way of settling an accusation that could not be proven by producing clear and unambiguous human evidence. (Other methods included the judicial duel and the swearing of oaths by supporters of the accused and the accuser.) Henry II's legal reforms had begun the process of shifting such cases to juries, but in 1214 trial by ordeal was still very common.

The ordeal by water was conducted according to a complex ritual rooted in communion with the Almighty—who was, after all, supposed to be taking as keen an interest in the proceedings as the participants. According to a twelfth-century account, a typical experience went like this: On a Tuesday evening the condemned would go to vespers barefoot and dressed in woolen clothes. There he would remain for a three-day fast, eating only unleavened bread, watercress, and salt and drinking only water. On Friday he was stripped of his clothes, given a small loincloth and a cloak, then led in solemn religious procession to a specially dug water pit measuring twelve by twenty feet, filled to the brim with water and overlaid with a wooden platform on which a priest could stand in order to bless the water. Around the pool would be standing the judges and the defendant's accuser. Both the accused and his accuser swore oaths, then the former's hands were tied tightly behind his bent knees and a length of rope attached to his waist. A knot in the rope marked "the length of his longest hair"—in other words, a depth of perhaps a foot or so above his head. Slowly, so as not to disturb the water's surface, the accused would be lowered into the pit. He would either sink or float. To sink to the knot in the rope was a sign of innocence; to float was a mark of guilt. The accused would in that instance be hanged. It has been argued by modern academics, who have simulated the experience of the trial by ordeal, that it should have been possible for about four out of five men in the Middle Ages to pass the ordeal by water, assuming that they were not grossly overweight, fasted sufficiently in the buildup to the ordeal, and made sure to blow as much of the air out of their lungs as possible before they took the plunge.[4] The ordeal by fire proceeded by similar means, with the accused holding a red-hot ingot of metal for a prescribed period of time and waiting to see if the burn that was caused became infected—a sign of guilt.

Once it was stripped by the Lateran Council of its essential sanctification, the trial by ordeal fell into disuse. When taken alongside the provisions in the Magna Carta that placed the onus for judgment on a man's peers, this meant that the ancient, purgative methods of determining guilt were replaced in England with a reliance on the word of the community, as spoken by a jury. Trial by ordeal would return—not least during the frenzy of witch-hunting in the seventeenth century. But for medieval England 1215 was the point at which the chilling process of deciding a man or woman's culpability based on whether he or she drowned or could hold a burning ingot in his or her hand without consequences were eclipsed by a less supernatural approach to justice.

If the Fourth Lateran began a process by which the Church withdrew from its central role in determining and administering secular justice, in other areas it pushed Christian doctrine deeper into the lives of ordinary men and women. "Every Christian of either sex after reaching the years of discretion shall confess all his sins at least once a year privately to his own priest," read canon 21. After this all should "receive with reverence the sacrament of the eucharist at least at Easter." Confession had become an increasingly important part of popular religious life during the twelfth century and was encouraged on Maundy Thursday, which was known as the "day of absolution." Its inclusion in the decrees of Fourth Lateran emphasized its now-central place among the sacraments of the Church. It also bound it closely to the Eucharist. This rite, which joined every single member of Christendom in the miracle of bread and wine becoming the flesh and blood of Christ, was one of the central pillars of popular religious culture in the Middle Ages.[5] A generation after the Fourth Lateran, the celebration of the Eucharist gave birth to a new Church festival: Corpus Christi. By the fourteenth century Corpus Christi was one of the most important popular and raucous occasions in the Church calendar, celebrated on the Thursday after Trinity Sunday (a movable feast falling between mid-May and mid-June) with parades, mystery plays, and (ironically) the same orgies of gluttony, drunkenness, and vice that the Fourth Lateran had taken such care to condemn.

When its conclusions were promulgated across Christendom in December 1215, the full implications of the Fourth Lateran Council were far from understood. According to Roger of Wendover, its articles seemed "agreeable to some and tedious to others."[6] But if anyone had been moved to speculate what agreement of the previous year would have the most long-lasting effect on English society, it is doubtful they would have thought of the short-lived and inconclusive treaty between John and his rebel barons. The peace of Runnymede had rapidly dissolved. Innocent's canons, compiled at comparable length, would have seemed to promise far more important changes.

In immediate political context too events at Fourth Lateran had a sharp effect on England. At the opening of the conference on November 4, Innocent confirmed the suspension of Archbishop Stephen Langton from his ecclesiastical duties as punishment for his failure to bring the rebel barons into line over the course of the previous nine months.[7] During the final session the pope confirmed the excommunication of all the barons of England "and all who aided them" and sent his verdict back to England to be publicly declared in churches all over the realm on every Sunday and feast day. The sentence was to be accompanied by the ringing of bells. This was only a confirmation of the decisions that the papal legate had promulgated two months earlier, but news that the pope remained squarely behind him must have been encouraging to John, who could now approach Christmas with confidence that his realm would soon be once more under his control.

✝

On Friday, December 18, King John and his retinue arrived at the monastery of St. Albans in Hertfordshire to thrash out the next phase in his war against the barons. On Sunday he assembled his followers in the chapter house of the massive, sprawling monastery, and the monks were in attendance as the pope's letters about the suspension of Archbishop Langton and the excommunication of the barons were read aloud. After this the king withdrew, along with his closest advisers, into the abbey cloisters, where, in Roger of Wendover's words, they "devised plans for overthrowing his enemies, and arranged as to the payment of the foreigners who were fighting under him."[8]

The plan with which they emerged was strategically simple and tactically pitiless. The royal army would split into two. John would take half his men north. William Longuespée, Fulk de Breauté, and Savaric de Mauléon would remain in the south. Both halves of the army would "ravage the whole country with fire and sword."[9] Despite the counsel of loyalists like William Marshal, who remained with the king but who claimed to be "sorely grieved by the outrages committed by both sides," this was total war, waged largely by professional soldiers from another land.[10] The prospects for anyone who stood in the way of the royal army were dire.

As word spread that John was about to let his army loose, spirits dipped among the rebels. "They were downcast," wrote the Crowland Chronicler. "And struck with terror they gathered in London or in religious houses. Few now believed in fortresses."[11] This was hardly surprising: Rochester Castle had been one of the solidest strongholds in England; what hope could there be for anywhere less stoutly defended should the king appear with his forest of catapults and hordes of sappers bearing pickaxes and pig fat?

No one relished the prospect of facing an army composed predominantly of mercenaries given free rein to do their worst. A generation earlier Walter Map had written that mercenaries were as depraved as heretics who avoided the Mass. Map called them "routiers," but they were also referred to as Brabançons, because the most bloodthirsty of them were popularly supposed to come from the Low Countries and particularly from the region of Brabant. (Other good places from which to hire soldiers included Aragon, Navarre, Basque, and Wales.) A mercenary was a soldier who fought for profit before loyalty and operated generally outside his country of origin: Such a person was assumed to have little regard for the well-being of anyone he came across or the customs of the territory he plagued.[12] Walter Map described routiers as "armed from head to toe with leather, iron, clubs, and swords" and accused them of leaving "monasteries, villages, and towns in ashes, and practicing indiscriminate adulteries with force, saying with all their heart, 'There is no God.'"[13]

A church council of 1179 had sentenced mercenaries and all who maintained them to excommunication, for "they respect neither churches nor monasteries, and spare neither widows, orphans, old or young nor any age or sex, but like pagans destroy and lay everything waste." This view was shared by many of England's most honored knights. William Marshal looked very dimly upon John's mercenaries. Not only were they dishonorable men, he thought, they were poor allies too. His biography states that in the autumn and winter of 1215 the king's "foreign knights and soldiers, who every day were set on pillage . . . spared hardly a moment's thought on how to advance his cause in war, being bent instead on laying waste his land."[14]

John instructed his sheriffs and military captains to confiscate lands from rebels and give them to loyalists, first doing "what should be done to the land of a King's enemy and traitor."[15] Scores of these ominous orders sped from the king's Chancery, licensing his followers all over the country to start helping themselves to enemy land. From St. Albans he then began his journey north to the heart of rebel country. Roger of Wendover provided a vivid description of the damage in his wake. The king, he said

> spread his troops abroad, burnt the houses and buildings of the barons, robbing them of their goods and cattle, and thus destroying everything that came in his way, he gave a miserable spectacle to all who beheld it. And if the day did not satisfy the malice of the king for the destruction of property, he ordered his incendiaries to set

fire to the hedges and towns on his march, that he might refresh his sight with the damage done to his enemies, and by robbery might support the wicked agents of his iniquity.

All the inhabitants of every condition and rank who did not take refuge in a church-yard, were made prisoners, and, after being tortured, were compelled to pay a heavy ransom. The castellans who were in charge of the fortresses of the barons, when they heard of the king's approach, left their castles untenanted and fled to places of secrecy, leaving their provisions and various stores as booty for their approaching enemies; the king placed his own followers in these empty castles, and in this manner marched with his wicked followers to Nottingham.[16]

John reached Nottingham in time for Christmas and spent several days in the area. According to the Crowland Chronicler, he celebrated the festival "not in the usual manner, but as one on the warpath." His concerted effort to terrorize his realm showed no sign of abating. England was now in the grip of a war that bore down just as heavily on the ordinary men and women who made up the majority of its population as on the barons who had sparked it. These people were not touched by the promises of the Magna Carta, but they were certainly harmed by its failure.

+

Most thirteenth-century Englishmen and women were peasants: rural smallholders for whom life was seldom easy. A minority were free men, at liberty to live and work where they chose, permitted to plead in royal courts, and perhaps even fortunate enough to accrue enough land to rent some out or to employ their neighbors at busy times of the year. Most, however, were serfs—also known as rustics, villeins, or neifs. These people effectively belonged to the lord of their land. As a condition of being allowed to live, eat, farm, marry, raise a family, and eventually die in peace, they owed the lord months of unpaid manual labor every year. They could not move away from his estate and were at the mercy of his estate officials. When a father died, his surviving family had to pay heriot—a tax that consisted of the best ox, cow, or horse that they possessed. When a daughter married, they had to pay the lord a fine called the merchet, and other arbitrary taxes known as tallages might be levied as the lord saw fit throughout the year. Serfs could be bought and sold along with the land on which they lived. They were, effectively, chattel.

Before the Norman Conquest England maintained a good trade in slaving—the practice of purchasing or kidnapping villagers and transporting them for sale elsewhere in the realm, particularly to Ireland. This had ceased in the early twelfth century, largely thanks to pressure from the Church. There was a significant difference between the condition of an eleventh-century slave and that of a thirteenth-century villein—in that a villein was at least associated with a plot of land and had a limited scope to live his life as he wished, even if there were major restrictions placed on his freedom. Serfs could not be killed or maimed simply because the lord willed it and were not sold out of their families. All the same, the difference between villeinage and slavery may not always have felt obvious to the persons concerned.

Peasants typically lived in small but sprawling villages, which could be found throughout the length and breadth of England. Villages were highly dependent on the interaction of neighbors, the benevolence and protection of the lords from whom they held their land, and the vagaries of the weather. Within them one could find a relatively wide range of prosperity. The best-off freemen might hold up to fifty acres. But for most serfs the amount of land they could cultivate varied between five and thirty acres.[17] Below this level families might even scratch by on a couple of acres, perhaps even

less, being otherwise totally reliant on the charity of and employment by their neighbors.

Families dwelled in timber-frame buildings of twenty-five to fifty
feet in length and twelve to sixteen feet in width. The best of these
were built with walls of stone, clay, or cob (a mixture of clay, straw,
and water) and shared with family members and animals. What the
peasant family did to support themselves depended somewhat on the
area of the country in which they lived. In much of the country sheep
farming was big business. Otherwise, peasants raised crops, both for
themselves and on their lord's land, working large fields by digging
them in long strips with plows drawn behind teams of oxen, and sow-
ing corn, wheat, oats, or barley in the spring for harvest at the end of
the summer. Pigs and cows grazed pasture held in common, while
gardens near peasant houses yielded useful domestic crops like on-
ions, leeks, cabbages, peas, beans, parsnips, celery, garlic, parsley, apples, pears, plums, cherries, and walnuts. In southern parts there were
still occasionally grape vines; English wine was more common then
than it is today. For peasants, however, the staple drink was not wine
but beer. Thus the job of brewing was a vital one and bad brewers
were harshly punished. (In Chester they were forced to sit in the "shit-
seat"—presumably a form of stocks.[18]) Brewing was not the only spe-
cialist trade into which a peasant might enter: Surnames found in
early-thirteenth-century legal records also tell us that in England there
were Bakers, Butlers, Carpenters, Cooks, Dyers, Fishers, Porters, Mill-
ers, Smiths, Tanners, and Weavers.[19]

A remarkable document written a generation or so after 1215
characterizes life for the English peasant in the thirteenth century.
It is a letter designed as a formulary to teach students basic compo-
sition, but it reveals how life for the majority of the English population was viewed. There is, no doubt, an element of exaggeration or
caricature for rhetorical effect, but this suggests a life a world away

from that of the Magna Carta, whose provisions were shaped by barons, bishops, and knights.

"A peasant to a peasant, greetings," begins the letter. "You have seen well we have a harsh lord, a sly serjeant, a wicked reeve, and almost barren land, and all these are adverse beyond measure. We almost entirely lack intervals of rest ... nor is there on earth anything while we live that revives our spirits. ... And since men of free condition abhor both common manners and common people, were it not for our rational souls we would be held but as rabid dogs among them. In these things the ability to endure hardship is necessary for us, because if, complaining, we resist, our misery will be cut short for us. We have but one solace: we shall die, and at our death our servitudes will end."[20]

What, then, did the war that erupted in the aftermath of the Magna Carta mean for a peasant family? The months of deliberation and unraveling would not for them have represented a great turning of the wheel in English justice. Rather, the trouble between John and his barons meant the outbreak of misery of the sort that came around once in every generation. England in the twelfth and early thirteenth centuries was a more peaceful realm than France— where most of England's wars took place.[21] But when trouble did erupt, it was terrifying.

The twelfth-century Norman poet Robert Wace had written a dark description of the common experience of warfare in the age of marauding armies. "What sorrow and what injury they did to the fine folk and the good land," he wrote, recalling soldiers

burning houses and destroying towns, knights and villeins, clerics, monks and nuns they hunted, beat and murdered ... You might see many lands devastated, women violated, men speared, babies disemboweled in their cradles, riches seized, flocks led off, towers brought low and towns burnt.[22]

This was more than just gloomy war poetry. "The powerful shall suffer powerful torments" went the old saying from the Book of Wisdom.[23] But in truth the powerful never suffered in isolation.

+

On New Year's Day 1216, traditionally a day for giving presents, John's men raided the abbey of Coggeshall and stole twenty-two horses.[24] It was an appropriately grim start to the year. Things did not get better after that. The first target of John's wrath was the north and specifically the ginger-haired Alexander, King of Scots, who had chosen to capitalize on his rival's distress by entering into a deal with his enemies. During the siege of Rochester Castle the northern barons, led by Eustace de Vesci, had agreed to recognize Alexander as overlord of the three northern counties of Northumberland, Westmorland, and Cumbria. This expressly defied the terms of the 1209 Treaty of Norham, under which Alexander's father had been brought to heel. In mid-January 1216 John marched north with the intention, as he put it, of chasing "the red Scottish fox from his lair." Just as the Scots had rampaged through England, so now John's mercenaries cut a swath as far as the banks of the river Forth, pillaging from village to village. Then John turned back south and led a violent assault on East Anglia. For a few months it seemed that he was battling his way back to supremacy, forcing his defeated enemies to swear an oath against obeying the Magna Carta. But as spring came, the tide began to turn. According to Marshal's biography, the king was nearly broke.[25] Worse, John's enemies were buoyed by news from across the Channel. Having dallied for months, Louis the Lion, heir to the crown of France, had finally decided to cross the sea and join in the fighting on the barons' side.

On May 21, 1216, Louis made landfall in England, arriving at Sandwich on the Isle of Thanet in Kent with a considerable army behind him. And now the John of old—the man mocked as John

Softsword—returned. Faced with the threat of aggression from a French royal house that he had confronted in Normandy and Poitou with such disastrous consequences, he fell back. Between 1200 and 1204 this attitude had cost him most of his French lands: Now it seemed likely that it would cost him his crown. Louis swept through Kent into London, and as news of his arrival spread, the men who had clung to John's side started melting away. Some who had been listed as his advisers in the Magna Carta, like the Earls of Warenne and Arundel, abandoned his cause. Seventeen of his household knights slunk away and, most hurtful of all, John's own half brother, William Longuespée, now defected to Louis. Fewer and fewer men remained at the king's side—except, of course, that paragon of Plantagenet loyalty William Marshal. ("A man of loyal and noble heart, [Marshal] stayed with him in hard and difficult circumstances," recorded Marshal's biography proudly. "He never changed that steadfast heart of his."[26]) To everyone else John was a lost cause. The would-be King Louis I held the future of England in his hands.

London rejoiced at Louis's arrival. The Welsh rallied against John's forces in the west and Alexander II regained some pride by sailing in person to Dover to pay homage to Louis for the Scots' gains in the north of England. Late in the summer the vexing news arrived that on July 16 Pope Innocent III had died suddenly at Perugia, aged around fifty-six. John had lost his one remaining hope. He continued to move back and forth across his country, tamping down fires wherever he could, but by now the effort was starting to tell and his luck was running out.

On October 11 John found himself passing through King's Lynn, a town in the far north of East Anglia on the edge of a large estuary, where several rivers empty into the North Sea. This could be treacherous terrain. John skirted around the estuary, called the Wash, and set off in the direction of Swineshead on the other side, but as his baggage train followed, his servants misjudged the tide. Many of John's carts, animals, and men were soon sucked into quicksand. According to Ralph of Coggeshall, John "lost his chapel with his relics, and some of his packhorses with divers household effects." Roger of Wendover claimed the loss was more devastating still: By his account John lost "treasures, precious vessels, and all the other things which he cherished with special care. . . . Not a single foot-soldier got away to bear tidings of the disaster."[27] At the very least this was inconvenient and embarrassing. But worse was to follow.

As his bags vanished into the heavy sands of the North Sea, John was himself deteriorating. He was forty-eight years old but in poor health: Gout had hobbled him the previous year and now he was attacked by dysentery. Without his relics or the effects of his chapel the sickness was an even more severe business than it would have otherwise been, since divine intervention, which was an important part of medical treatment at the time, was now much harder to request. As his condition grew worse over the course of the next few days, John finally despaired of his life. At this point, unexpectedly, he turned his mind to atonement for his sins and granted land for a monastery to be founded in Hertfordshire in memory of Matilda de Briouze and her eldest son, whom he had starved to death. On October 15 he wrote miserably to the new pope, Honorius III, begging for absolution for his sins and hoping that God "will look on us with the eye of his mercy, and deem us worthy to be placed in the number of the elect."[28] Three days later he was on his deathbed; he died in Newark during a violent storm on the night of October 18. William Marshal was at his side and described to his biographer a penitent king who apologized for his misdeeds before "death that great harrier, that wicked, harsh creature, took him under her control and never let him go."[29]

John had ruled for seventeen and a half years, and his time on earth had ended in misery and failure. The king died with thunder booming in his ears and scant hope that his kingdom or his dynasty would survive his passing. His two sons by Isabella of Angoulême were perilously young: Henry was nine and Richard seven. (Their three girls, Joan, Isabella, and Eleanor, were younger still.) In 1209 John had demanded that his barons swear allegiance to a then-two-year-old Henry as his successor, and since 1212 the boy had been under the academic tutelage of John's staunch ally Peter des Roches, bishop of Winchester. But this hardly seemed a strong prospect on which to peg the future of the Plantagenet royal family or through whom to rebuild the shredded political stability of the realm.

John was not buried at Beaulieu Abbey, which he had founded at the beginning of his reign, for it was under enemy control. Instead John's entrails were removed from his corpse and taken for preservation by the abbot of Croxton, while his body was carried by a cortege composed of mercenaries to Worcester Cathedral. There he was buried next to the tomb of St. Wulfstan, a tenth-century bishop known for his miracles, prolific church building, and campaigns against the slave trade.[30] John's legs and torso were covered in a crimson-embroidered robe, his left hand held a sword in a leather scabbard, and his crownless head was strapped into a monk's cowl.[31] Less than two years had passed since he had sat in much the same spot at Christmastime 1214, enjoying a personal performance of "Christus Vincit." How things had changed. When the chronicler Matthew Paris reflected on the fate of John's soul twenty years after his death, he famously declared that "England reeks with John's filthy deeds; the foulness of Hell is defiled by John."[32] Surely, though, even John could not have plunged hell into a very much worse state than the earthly realm he left behind.

IV
Afterlife

The Magna Carta Reborn

KING JOHN'S ELDEST SON was crowned Henry III on October 28 at Gloucester Abbey, with a small corps of long-suffering loyalists, William Marshal foremost among them. A new papal legate, Guala Bicchieri, was also at his side. Louis's forces still controlled London and the southeast, and it was far from clear that the nine-year-old Henry would ever be accepted by his countrymen as king, let alone recover the formidable power that had been enjoyed by his father, uncle, and grandfather. Aside from the immediate military necessity of waging a war against the rebels and the French invaders, it was now vital that the men around the young king offer their enemies some grounds for reconciliation—some gesture that would allow them to believe that with King John dead and buried, the greatest obstacle to peace had been removed.

As John lay dying he had begged those around him to see to it that Marshal be given command of the kingdom in the name of his son. This was not controversial: Although he was around seventy years old, Marshal was one of the most respected figures in England and the only earl who had remained loyal until the end. He accepted the post of regent with some reluctance, but once ensconced in his new role he began drawing back to the royal cause those who had abandoned it. He received invaluable support from Guala, who excommunicated all those who followed Louis. No bishop would crown a king who was exiled from the spiritual community of the Church. This bought time and gave a slender thread of hope to the

loyalist cause. And Marshal's deft handling of the regency's difficult politics slowly began to bring John's enemies back around.

Letters went out to barons offering recompense and restitution
to any who would come over to the new king's side. More important,
it was not long before the treaty John had begrudgingly agreed with
his barons was dusted off and offered up as an emollient to bring
back into the fold those who might be wavering. The Magna Carta
was reissued for the first time on November 12, 1216, under the seals
of William Marshal and Guala Bicchieri. This was an extraordinarily bold move. After all, the late pope had condemned the Magna
Carta as "null and void of all validity forever"—hardly words that
left a lot of room for interpretation. John had died fighting a war
against everything the charter stood for. But both Innocent and
John were now dead, and new circumstances dictated new thinking.
It is to Marshal's and Guala's credit that they were flexible enough to
see that with some small but significant amends (which included re-
moving the troublesome "security" clause) the charter did not have
to be a stick with which the Plantagenet Crown could be beaten. It
could stand as a promise of good conduct and the foundation of a
new monarchy.

The effects of this new Magna Carta were encouraging but not
immediate. We can see from its list of witnesses—most of the
English bishops and now three earls besides Marshal—that it had
persuaded a few men to turn. Plenty, however, fought on. The war
dragged into 1217, heaping further misery on both sides: William
Marshal's biographer reported having seen a hundred dead French-
men lying slain on the ground between Winchester and Romsey
with hungry dogs ripping the flesh from their bones.[1] Yet eventually
the resolve and resources of the French began to weaken. Louis left
England to attend to business across the Channel for eight weeks in
the early spring, and although he came back, his absence saw a

trickle of further defections from the rebel camp. Fighting for an uncrowned French prince against a crowned English king whose government was committed to reform started to look less and less reasonable. The chronicler Roger Wendover believed that for many of the rebels by now the only difficulty in switching sides was the shame of being thought a turncoat.[2]

Yet for all the flagging enthusiasm of the opposition and the growing confidence of the men around Henry, several months would pass before a decisive moment was reached in the war. This came at the Battle of Lincoln, on May 20, 1217, when a powerful and impressively armed force led by William Marshal descended on the castle, routing the rebels who were camped there and capturing a large number of their leaders. It was a crushing defeat for Louis from which his cause would never recover.

In August 1217 Hubert de Burgh destroyed a French fleet off the Kentish coast at the Battle of Sandwich, and almost immediately a downcast Louis sought terms on which he could depart England without losing too much face. Peace was made in the Treaty of Lambeth on September 20, and Louis departed the country with a massive bribe of ten thousand marks (a quarter of England's royal annual revenue) to salve his wounded pride. Once he was gone, the business of restoring some normality to government after two years of exhausting civil war began. The charter wrung from a reluctant King John at Runnymede was once again reissued.

This time it was accompanied by a new grant: the Charter of the Forest. This reversed the Plantagenet policy begun under Henry II of expanding the territories classed as forest land and subject to the burdensome system of forest law. The charter reduced the size of the royal forest and severely restricted the purview of forest justice. The extent of forest land was to be as it had stood on the day of Henry II's coronation in 1154. Free men were to be allowed to let their pigs forage in the forest; they were to be allowed to build mills, dig ponds, and gather firewood without being prosecuted. "Any archbishop, bishop, earl or baron whatever who passes through our forest shall be allowed to take one or two beasts under the supervision of the forester," ran one clause, and another promised that "no one shall henceforth lose life or limb" for poaching venison, although men found taking royal deer without permission could still be fined heavily, thrown in jail for a year and a day, and exiled from England.[3] It was from 1217 that the Magna Carta earned its famous name—in order to differentiate it from the Charter of the Forest.

The 1216 and 1217 reissues of the Magna Carta contained some important variations from the text of the original. Strongly worded statements on foreign ministers, which had featured in the 1215 version, were quietly dropped, because many of the men who surrounded Henry III in his minority—such as Peter des Roches, bishop of Winchester—were themselves of alien birth. The clauses regulating purveyance were redrawn, and there were substantial tweaks made to provision for widows' rights and the procedures for recovering debts, both to the Crown and to Jewish moneylenders. A clause was introduced in 1217 ordering the destruction of castles that had been erected during the war. New restrictions limited the frequency with which sheriffs could hold their courts, and the commitment to investigate historical abuses dating back to Henry II and Richard I's reigns disappeared.

It is telling that both the 1216 and 1217 reissues of the Magna Carta were presented without the "security clause." The question of how to restrain an out-of-control king would remain alive for the duration of the Middle Ages and beyond, but in 1216 and 1217 it was shelved. Partly this was because its openly bellicose methods had justified civil war instead of promoting peace. More important, however, was the fact that in just two years the Magna Carta had shifted in purpose. Although reissued on both occasions from the jaws of civil war, it was now no longer a peace treaty imposed by the king's enemies. This time it was an offering by the king's friends, designed to demonstrate voluntarily the commitment of the new regime to govern by principles on which the whole realm could agree. The Magna Carta had mutated from a begrudgingly acceded text of compromise into an assurance of good faith. As it was copied out by clerks and distributed to the shires of England to be read aloud in the sheriffs' courts, the charter had taken on a new purpose.

William Marshal died in May 1219, and on his deathbed he warned the young Henry not to "follow in the footsteps of some wicked ancestor."[4] Stephen Langton, who returned to England in 1218 with his sentence of suspension lifted by the new pope, worked until his death in July 1228 to ensure that the charter remained alive. For the rest of Henry's reign—indeed, for the rest of the thirteenth century—the Magna Carta would be reconfirmed and reissued at moments of political instability or crisis.

In 1225 Henry III turned eighteen and another revamped version of the charter was published, given by the king—according to the preamble—"of our own spontaneous goodwill" (*spontanea et bona voluntate nostra*).[5] This was slightly disingenuous. As clause 37 of the 1225 edition of the Magna Carta made clear, the charters were in fact reissued as one side of a political bargain. The king promised to observe and uphold the customs of the realm, and in return "all of our realm have given us a fifteenth part of all their movables." In other words, the king swapped a concession of liberties for tax revenue.

This would become an enduring practice. Over the course of the thirteenth and fourteenth centuries English government would become anchored by the principle that the king exercised his right to tax his subjects only if he agreed to remedy grievances and reform his realm. In the 1225 edition of the Magna Carta that idea was actually made explicit for the first time. (The 1225 charter was also notable for its bestowal, in the preamble, of its liberties upon "all of our realm"; specific clauses were still, however, restricted to "free men.")

Further reissues followed. In January 1237 both the Magna Carta and the Charter of the Forest were again confirmed in binding and perpetual form, protected by a third "small charter," whose witnesses included a few old men who had been at Runnymede in 1215. Once again a tax was granted. By this time something of a myth had started to grow. The charter was widely circulated with each revision and reissue. The Magna Carta was referred to frequently in legal cases. Barons began to offer charters of liberties to their own tenants that were clearly modeled on the form and content of the Magna Carta.

The charter was still protected explicitly by the Church. English parish churches were the venues for readings of the Magna Carta in the vernacular. Excommunication was pronounced as the penalty for disobedience in both 1225 and 1237: On May 13, 1253, a confirmation of both the Magna Carta and the Charter of the Forest took place in Westminster Abbey, in which the archbishop of Canterbury and thirteen bishops passed the familiar sentence of excommunication on those who ignored the Magna Carta's provisions. (The saints called upon to observe the sentence included Edward the Confessor and Thomas Becket, both of whom had played their own small roles in the history of opposition to John and his Plantagenet relatives.) When the sentence was passed, the bishops all threw down the lit candles they had been holding and said together: "Thus are extinguished and reek in Hell all those who attack this sentence." The king promised to guard the Magna Carta in all its terms, which he declared was his duty as a "man, a Christian, a knight and an anointed king."[6]

In the century that followed John's promulgation of the charter at

Runnymede, the collapse into civil war, and the king's death, the Magna Carta was probably copied out, in its various editions, more than a thousand times. There remain in existence more than a hundred medieval copies, ranging from those official exemplifications of the Magna Carta 1215 held in London, Salisbury, and Lincoln to privately made copies held in abbeys and archives. One of the latter is the elegantly scripted copy that exists among the records of Cerne Abbey in Dorset—a hybrid of the 1217 and 1225 editions, with the Charter of the Forest bolted directly on as though it were part of the same treaty.[7] These were not merely documents of antiquarian interest. The importance of the charter was clearly and regularly stated. Even where its clauses grew irrelevant and obsolete, much importance was still attached to the idea of the Magna Carta as a bargaining chip, particularly in relation to taxation.

In 1242, at one of the earliest recorded parliaments in English history, Henry III requested financial aid from the realm to pay for a military expedition to France. He was refused on the grounds that previous grants of taxation had not resulted in good governance, "because the king had never, after the granting of the thirtieth [i.e., his requested tax], abided by his charter of liberties, nay had since then oppressed [his subjects] more than usual."[8] When Henry and his eldest son Edward found themselves embroiled in a long war against Simon de Montfort, Earl of Leicester, during the 1250s and 1260s, the Magna Carta was again at the heart of the political wrangling. When de Montfort was at the peak of his powers during the first half of 1265, he not only forced Henry and Edward to swear an oath to obey his own constitution, which de Montfort had established the previous year but also required the king to reconfirm the Magna Carta and the Charter of the Forest. In a sense this took the charter back to its original state—the weapon of a radical, rebellious faction in English politics seeking to extract promises from a king by intimidation. But de Montfort's insistence on reconfirming the charters in 1265 was also an illustration of just how symbolically potent the mere name of the Magna Carta had become for anyone seeking to put his mark on English government. De Montfort sought legitimacy. He found it by wearing the badge of the Magna Carta.[9]

Henry III confirmed or reissued the Magna Carta on average about once every five years during his reign—and increasingly the charter was promulgated in French and English as well as the Latin in which it had first been written. It was known in Normandy, where it became a model for charters of liberties negotiated there. By Henry's death in 1272 the Magna Carta had become a political commonplace whose significance, if not its precise detail, was etched deep into the minds of Englishmen of almost every literate rank. But the final and in some ways definitive version of the charter was produced not under Henry III but during the reign of Edward I (1272–1307).

The reign of this tall, imposing, warmongering king was—although broadly more successful than those of his father and grandfather—still troubled by moments of crisis. The worst came in 1297, when the crippling costs of Edward's wars of conquest (in Wales and Scotland) and resistance to French Continental advances (in Gascony) were rejected by a coalition of barons and bishops, who revolted en masse against his heavy-handed rule and relentless financial demands. The compromise that was thrashed out included the *Confirmatio cartarum* (Confirmation of the Charters) of October 10, 1297, by which the Magna Carta and the Charter of the Forest were reissued once more, accompanied by other concessions and guarantees of good government. Not all of these would be kept by the king or his descendants—in fact, the history of the Magna Carta is largely the history of kings failing to stick to its terms. All the same, by the end of the thirteenth century a peace treaty that had lasted just a few weeks more than eight decades earlier had become, in many ways, the founding stone of the whole system of English law and government.

Edward confirmed and reissued the Magna Carta and the Charter of the Forest one final time in 1300.* Subsequent medieval kings confirmed the charters' terms many times over, but the Magna Carta was never again to be copied out and distributed in the same formal fashion as had first occurred in June 1215. Nevertheless, it was appealed to dozens of times in parliamentary petitions and private legislation. It also gave a model for the baronial opposition movements that sprang up during the reigns of Edward II (1307–27) and Richard II (1377–99), both of which attempted to restrain the king by drawing up ordinances and contracts that restricted his behavior and attempted to force him to rule by cooperation with his leading subjects. Inevitably, time stripped the Magna Carta of legal relevance. But its influence—and its legend—survived.

---

*One of these 1300 editions came to light in February 2015 in the archives of the British seaside town of Sandwich, where it had been tucked away in a Victorian scrapbook. It is quite badly damaged but has still been estimated to be worth around $15 million.

Then and Now

B Y THE SIXTEENTH CENTURY the Magna Carta was a legal antique. Parliaments still made occasional reference to it: In 1497, for example, a parliament of Henry VII passed a weights and measures act that aimed "to prevent the great deceptions involving weights and measures practised for a long time within this his [sic] realm contrary to the statute of Magna Carta and other statutes."[1] The charter was preserved in the wider public memory thanks to the arrival of the printing press: The first printed edition was issued by Richard Pynson in 1508, and the full text was subsequently included in a prominent position in legal handbooks and collections of statutes, which reinforced the idea that it was the primal law of the land.[2] But the Magna Carta could scarcely be said to have dominated constitutional discourse as it had in the thirteenth century—not least, perhaps, because its basic content was so much at odds with the political mood of the times.

King John's submission to the pope in 1214 and the charter's explicit protection of the rights of the English Church would come to sit rather uneasily with the Tudor Royal Supremacy, created by acts of Parliament in the 1530s. Indeed, King John became a hero to those who admired his defiance of the pope during the interdict. In 1528 William Tyndale, a radical antipapist best known for translating the Bible into English, exhorted readers of his *Obedience of a Christian Man* to "read the story of King John, and of other kings" in order to understand the damage that the Catholic Church had done in earlier times to the authority of English monarchs. According to Tyndale's contemporary Simon Fish, John was "a righteous king" who suffered "for no other cause but for his righteousness."[3]

A notebook of Henry VIII's first minister, Thomas Cromwell, shows the suspicion with which he, at least, regarded the charter: In a list of "remembrances" or daily tasks, Cromwell instructs himself to "remember the ancient chronicle of Magna Carta."[4] It is thought that this undated note was made around the time of the trial of Sir Thomas More in 1535. If so, it shows the legally minded Cromwell wrestling with the task of defending his king's wish to rule the Church with the Magna Carta's long-standing statement that the same Church should be free. Certainly Cromwell was well versed in the history of John's reign and enjoyed bending its truth to fit his own political ends. Those in his circle disapproved of popular plays about Robin Hood, which they believed taught the ordinary people to be insubordinate. In response Cromwell encouraged the seditious playwright John Bale to produce dramas like the execrable *King John*, which was performed at Christmas in 1538 in the house of Thomas Cranmer, archbishop of Canterbury. Here John is a virtuous ruler eager to protect the rights of a widow (unlikely, this!) who is being pillaged by the Church. Tragically, he dies after being poisoned by a monk, but he manages to croak out with his final breath the risible statement "My pleasure was to help such as were needy."[5]

The Magna Carta is nowhere here. Nor was it later in the century, for when William Shakespeare wrote his own history play *King John*, probably in the mid-1590s, there was no mention of a charter whose relevance was clearly thought to escape the minds of London's theater-going public. For more than a century the Magna Carta was ignored, if not forgotten.

It was not until the seventeenth century that the charter returned to real prominence in England and beyond. For this was an age when the basic relationship between Crown and subjects would once again come under intense examination. First there were the civil wars that broke out under Charles I, in large part because the king had determined to govern by autocratic, arbitrary, and absolute means, attempting to revive feudal aspects of the monarchy that had long been abandoned and using his own will to override English laws and customs. Charles's opponents searched for historical precedent and parallel through which to state their case against tyranny—and they alighted upon the Magna Carta, a seemingly perfect example of an out-of-control king from centuries past being brought into line. Thus under the Stuarts the great charter designed to restrain the Plantagenets was reborn. It was taken cheerfully out of its historical context and held up as an "original" constitution—proof that Charles I was betraying not only his own people but also English history writ large.*

At this time the Magna Carta was championed most fiercely by the lawyer Sir Edward Coke, who since the days of James I had been convinced not only of this ancient treaty's usefulness as a bulwark against Stuart tyranny but also of its monumental, totemic importance in the broader landscape of English history. In 1619, while condemning abuses in royal government on the grounds that they contravened clauses of the Magna Carta, Coke told the House of Commons that the charter had earned its name "not for the largeness but for the weight."[6] He cleaved to the idea that the king had no right to tax his subjects without their consent, and he grounded that belief in the historical struggles that had produced the Magna Carta.[7] Coke

---

*The comparison was not entirely misguided. In many ways Charles I acted and suffered just as John did. He was willful, obstinate, and autocratic. His own misdeeds—which were ample—were compounded by those committed by his predecessors. And in the end he died during the course of a war largely of his own making against his own people.

drafted the Petition of Right, passed in 1628 by both houses of Parliament in defiance of Charles I's attempts to collect forced loans and arbitrarily imprison his enemies: This was a very conscious attempt to bind Charles to certain principles of government in precisely the same way that John had been bound by the barons in 1215. Thereafter the Magna Carta was cited at the other moments of tumult and crisis during Charles's reign, including the trials of royal allies the Earl of Strafford (1641) and Archbishop Laud (1645).

The revival of the Magna Carta—or at least the *idea* of the Magna Carta—during these years of chaos and civil war added to the mythical status of the document itself, and as a result it began to occupy a cherished place in the story of the English constitution. The realm emerged from the seventeenth century with a sense of the sequential history of English liberty: a history (later associated with the "Whig" approach) that began with King John at Runnymede and culminated in the passing of the Bill of Rights in 1689. There was, admittedly, tempting ground for believing this to be so at the time. The Bill of Rights was not just loosely modeled on the Magna Carta; it sprang out of an age that offered very obvious historical parallels with the early thirteenth century. In 1215 English rebels had secured a charter of rights and attempted to bring a foreign prince to the throne in place of a tyrant. In 1688–89 English rebels actually succeeded in doing something similar, albeit in a different order, by chasing the Catholic James II from the realm, inviting James's Protestant son-in-law William of Orange to rule in his place, and then securing a broad-ranging statement of English law and custom that would be revered for generations afterward.

Yet it was not only in England that the Magna Carta was to have a profound influence on constitutional development. The second way in which the charter bore down upon the seventeenth century was in its adoption as the basis for the emerging constitutions of the New World. The principles of founding charters had been taken across the Atlantic with the first English colonists, and communities of settlers up and down the eastern seaboard, from Massachusetts to Georgia, established their governments from the outset according to ideas that they—following Coke—believed to have originated with the Magna Carta. The colonists saw themselves as English freemen whose rights were to be afforded precisely the same protection as those in the old country.

In the eighteenth century this attitude would become a matter of literally world-changing importance. No taxation without representation; no imprisonment without due process. These were the issues that lay beneath the Declaration of Independence and the revolution that followed as the American colonies wrenched themselves free from British rule. The Magna Carta had been published in the colonies as early as 1687, and just under a century later, as revolution swept through North America, it was to the Magna Carta that men turned once again for their inspiration. In October 1774 the delegates to the First Continental Congress of the thirteen discontented colonies explicitly justified their gathering to express grievances by claiming that the colonies were acting simply "as Englishmen, their ancestors in like cases have usually done."[8]

When independence had been won, and the newly formed United States of America was busily writing itself into constitutional existence, the Magna Carta was again a model. The Declaration of Independence, as drafted by Thomas Jefferson and ratified by Congress in 1776, condemned King George III for (among other things) obstructing the administration of justice, "for imposing Taxes on us without our Consent; For depriving us in many cases, of the benefits of Trial by Jury," and for "transporting large Armies of foreign Mercenaries to complete the works of death, desolation and tyranny." All of these followed near-identical complaints made against King John in the Magna Carta 561 years earlier. In concluding that "a Prince, whose character is . . . marked in every act which may define a tyrant, is unfit to be the Ruler of a free people," the declaration expressed with beautiful clarity what the Magna Carta had been feeling its way toward in its unsatisfactory security clause.

The Magna Carta's influence was thereafter felt throughout the process of independence and state building in revolutionary America. Article III of the Constitution states that "the Trial of all Crimes, except in Cases of Impeachment, shall be by Jury." The Bill of Rights, ratified in 1791 and consisting of the first ten of James Madison's list of constitutional amendments designed to limit the powers of the state over its citizens, also echoes the Magna Carta in several places. The Fifth Amendment states that no person should be "deprived of life, liberty, or property, without due process of law; nor shall private property be taken for public use, without just compensation." Compare the first half of this with clause 39 of the original Magna Carta: "No free man is to be arrested, or imprisoned, or disseized, or outlawed, or exiled, or in any other way ruined, nor will we go or send against him, except by the legal judgment of his peers or by the law of the land." Then compare the second half with clause 30: "No sheriff or bailiff of ours, or anyone else may take any free man's horses or carts for transporting things, except with the free man's agreement."

The similarities are striking. So too with the Sixth Amendment of the American Bill of Rights: "In all criminal prosecutions, the accused shall enjoy the right to a speedy and public trial, by an impartial jury." What is this if not a reformulation of clause 40 of the Magna Carta: "To no one will we sell, to no one will we deny or delay, right or justice"? It is perhaps no surprise that since the earliest years of the United States' existence citizens have looked upon the Magna

Carta with an almost Coke-ian enthusiasm, which was marked in 1957 by the erection of the only permanent monument to the Magna Carta at Runnymede—paid for by the American Bar Association.

By the nineteenth century the Magna Carta was enshrined in Western political thought as a document of great and formative importance to modern ideas of freedom. It has remained so ever since— and small parts of the charter can still be found embedded in the constitutions of nations connected with the former British Empire, from Canada to Australia (where a 1297 edition of the charter is on display in Parliament House in Canberra) and New Zealand. Original editions of the charter are highly prized and extremely valuable: During the Second World War the Lincoln copy of the 1215 Magna Carta was kept safe in Fort Knox and there was great consideration given in Britain to gifting it permanently to the nation as a token of gratitude for American assistance in the war in the form of the lend-lease agreement. This was decided against only when it came to light that the Lincoln Magna Carta was not the property of the British government to give away! But the United States has a fine copy of the charter all the same: In December 2007 a copy of the 1297 Magna Carta, complete with the seal of Edward I, was bought at auction in New York for an astonishing $21.3 million and put on display at the National Archives in Washington, D.C.

It is true that the majority of the Magna Carta's clauses and the circumstances of its creation have long ceased to be politically or legally important or have been superseded by more recent legislation. Certainly those clauses that were most important to the handful of English barons who rebelled against King John in 1215 have no bearing at all on life on either side of the Atlantic in the twenty-first century. No one in England still concerns themselves with feudal dues or forest laws; and even the grander catchall phrases concerning life and liberty have been superseded in English and Scottish law by newer legislation, including the European Human Rights Act.

All the same, other of the charter's phrases continue to exert influence across the world, and particularly in the United States, where it occupies a hallowed position as the starting point for the principles on which the nation is founded. This is more than just a matter of language, evolved from the contracted and dense Latin of the Magna Carta to the elegant English of the Constitution and the Bill of Rights. It is a matter of principles: The insistence on freedom from harassment and annoyance by the state and the hatred of excessive taxation remain formidable, mobilizing political causes. There are many people today who would find common cause with John's subjects in the shared will to limit the power and size of government and to reduce its capacity to meddle in the business of everyday life. The sting of raising taxes to pay for expensive overseas wars is still keenly felt in twenty-first-century America—just as it was by barons in thirteenth-century England, who were so unwilling to fund John's adventures in France.

So too has the influence of the Magna Carta been felt on the widest global stage. It is still striking to see, when we look at the European Human Rights Act or the United Nations' Universal Declaration of Human Rights, how closely the language of the Magna Carta continues to inform basic legal protections across the world. Here is article 9 of the Universal Declaration of Human Rights, a document that was described at the time of its conception by its champion, Eleanor Roosevelt, as "the international Magna Carta for all men everywhere": "No one shall be subjected to arbitrary arrest, detention or exile." Once again these are echoes of the famous clause 39 of Magna Carta 1215. It is not only impossible but also probably fatuous to imagine that the men who stood in Runnymede in June 1215 imagined that the text they were thrashing out might, in eight hundred years' time, be employed in the defense of the rights of the poorest and meanest citizens in countries in every corner of the world. But that is the way it turned out.

✦

One of the great paradoxes of the Magna Carta is the fact that the less relevant most of its words become to modern life, the greater the reverence attached to its name. "Magna Carta" is today used as a byword for all types of aspiration to freedom, liberty, and (quite erroneously) democracy. When Nelson Mandela made the case for his commitment to democratic ideals during his Rivonia trial in 1964, he told the court: "The Magna Carta, the Petition of Rights, and the Bill of Rights are documents which are held in veneration by democrats throughout the world."[9] Mandela's cause was noble but in truth the link between the Magna Carta and democracy is no more than assumed and associative. No clause of the charter mentions or was intended to promote anything that we would today consider "democratic"; indeed, the idea of democracy was alien and would quite possibly have been offensive to the wealthy, oligarchical, and largely self-interested barons who opposed King John in 1215. The Magna Carta protected the Church and the City of London; it gave the privileges to the aristocracy and limited the basic rights of women and Jews. This was not in the modern sense a "liberal" or egalitarian document.

Nevertheless, men and women all over the world continue to venerate the Magna Carta as a founding text of Western liberal democracy, not always with completely convincing results. In 2014, for example, the British prime minister David Cameron promised, in a speech, to make every schoolchild in the United Kingdom study the Magna Carta, saying that "the remaining copies of that charter may have faded, but its principles shine as brightly as ever, and they paved the way for the democracy, the equality, the respect and the laws that make Britain."[10] In fact precisely the opposite is true: Many of the remaining copies of the charter are in good condition, while most of their principles are now obsolete, and the clauses have nothing to do with democracy, equality, or respect.* But this sort of political platitude is commonplace, and it speaks to the myth of the Magna Carta that has developed during the last eight hundred years. At times that myth can have great political potency: The Magna Carta's ancient proclamations against detention without trial were instrumental, in 2008, in opposition to the British government's Counter-Terrorism Act, which sought to extend the period for which a person could be imprisoned without charges from twenty-eight to forty-two days. At other times it is used in ways that are rather confused.

This confusion tends to be greatest when the Magna Carta is invoked for causes besides the more general ideals of liberal democracy or freedom from tyranny. A "Magna Carta for the Web" is regularly called for now, to challenge both official (and often covert) monitoring and surveillance of online communications and also the rising power of new supranational organizations—Google, Facebook, Apple, and so on—that are thought to be exercising new and unchecked control over private data, freedom of information, and personal reputations.[11] There have been calls in recent years for a Magna Carta for disabled people, for medical banking, for American coal miners, and for Filipino call-center workers.[12] In 2013 the Magna Carta even found its way into mainstream popular culture in the title of one of Jay-Z's hip-hop albums, *Magna Carta Holy Grail*, which sold more than two million copies in the United States during the months following its release. Quite what the phrase "Magna

---

*David Cameron would have done better to follow one of his predecessors as prime minister, Winston Churchill, who wrote that the Magna Carta was "the foundation of principles and systems of government of which neither King John nor his nobles dreamed."

Carta Holy Grail" really means is not very easy to discern—perhaps the artist's desire to rewrite the rules of commercial activity in the music industry. But look past the bathos, and we can reflect that it is extraordinary that the phrase "Magna Carta" has gained such popular currency across the world that it can be co-opted with apparent seriousness into the posturing and sloganeering of mainstream American pop music.

This, then, is where we stand. The second decade of the twenty-first century, accompanied by loud and vigorous discussion, marks the eight hundredth anniversary of a document that was born out of two generations of opposition to the excesses of early Plantagenet government during the late twelfth and early thirteenth centuries; that document came to define nearly a hundred years of political conflict between English kings and their noblemen and has since passed into the realm of myth and legend, its name called on in support of all manner of movements in which authority is challenged or restrained by the people.

As time goes by, the Magna Carta's name will undoubtedly continue to be hitched to causes both noble and absurd. One thing, however, is certain: The fame and the symbolic importance of this hard-born charter are as great now as at any time in its history. Few other documents can claim such revered status, and few will again. Certainly this would have come as a surprise to the men who stood at Runnymede in June 1215 and thrashed out an unsatisfactory peace treaty. But it is a fitting testament to their struggle.

Acknowledgments

Thanks to my agent, Georgina Capel, for her brilliance and support. Anthony Cheetham first suggested this book and I owe him my thanks for (another) very good idea. Joy de Menil is my inspirational editor in the United States and has for some time been telling me to write about the Magna Carta. I am pleased finally to have done so and thrilled to be working with Joy and the rest of the team at Viking on this, our third book together. At Head of Zeus in the UK Richard Milbank and Mark Hawkins-Dady offered many crucial notes on an early version of the text. I was greatly assisted by the staff at the National Archives in London and Washington, D.C., the British Library, and the London Library. A number of brilliant scholars have offered me their time, thoughts, and comments during the time I have been working on this book. Thanks to Julian Harrison and Dr. Claire Breay at the British Library; Dr. Nick Barratt at the National Archives; Professor Elizabeth Eva Leach at the University of Oxford; Dr. Eleanor Giraud at Lincoln College, Oxford; Professor Miri Rubin and Dr. Thomas Asbridge at Queen Mary, University of London; Professor David Carpenter at King's College London; Professor Louise Wilkinson at Canterbury Christ Church University; Dr. Kate Wiles; and Dr. Helen Castor. Marta Musso and Chiara Zanforlini helped with aspects of the research. Last, the biggest thanks of all are to my girls: Jo, Violet, and Ivy Jones. With love, as always.

Appendix A
The Text of the Magna Carta, 1215

JOHN, BY THE GRACE OF GOD King of England, Lord of Ireland, Duke of Normandy and Aquitaine, Count of Anjou, to his archbishops, bishops, abbots, earls, barons, justices, foresters, sheriffs, reeves, officers and all his bailiffs and faithful subjects, greetings. Know that, for the sake of God and for the salvation of our soul and the souls of all our ancestors and heirs, to the honour of God and the exaltation of the holy Church, and for the reform of our realm, by the advice of our venerable fathers Stephen, Archbishop of Canterbury, Primate of All England and Cardinal of the Holy Roman Church; Henry, Archbishop of Dublin; William, Bishop of London; Peter, Bishop of Winchester; Jocelin, Bishop of Bath and Glastonbury; Hugh, Bishop of Lincoln; Walter, Bishop of Worcester; William, Bishop of Coventry; and Benedict, Bishop of Rochester; Master Pandulf, subdeacon and confidant of the lord pope; Brother Aymeric, Master of the Knights Templar in England; and the noble men William Marshal, Earl of Pembroke; William, Earl of Salisbury; William, Earl Warenne; William, Earl of Arundel; Alan of Galloway, Constable of Scotland; Warin FitzGerald; Peter FitzHerbert; Hubert de Burgh, Seneschal of Poitou; Hugh de Neville; Matthew FitzHerbert; Thomas Basset; Alan Basset; Philip d'Aubigny; Robert de Roppel; John Marshal; John FitzHugh and other of our faithful subjects:

1. Firstly, we have granted to God and confirmed by this, our present charter, for us and our heirs in perpetuity, that the English

Church shall be free, and shall have its rights in full and its liberties intact; and we wish this to be thus observed, which is clear from the fact that, before the discord with our barons began, we granted and confirmed by our charter free elections, which are considered to be of the utmost importance and necessity to the English Church, and we obtained confirmation of this from our lord Pope Innocent III; which we shall observe and which we wish our heirs to observe in good faith in perpetuity. We have also granted to all the free men of our realm, for ourselves and our heirs in perpetuity, all the liberties written below, for them and their heirs to have and to hold of us and our heirs.

2. If any of our earls or barons, or others holding in chief* of us by knight service, dies, and at his death his heir is of full age and owes relief, he shall have his inheritance by paying the ancient relief: that is, for the heir or heirs of an earl, £100 for the whole earl's barony; for the heir or heirs of a baron, £100 for the whole barony; for the heir or heirs of a knight, 100 marks at most for the whole knight's fee; and anyone who owes less gives less, according to the ancient custom of fees.

3. If, on the other hand, the heir of any such person has been underage and has been in wardship, when he comes of age he is to have his inheritance without paying relief and without a fine.

4. The guardian of the land of such an heir who is underage, shall not take from the heir's land any more than reasonable revenues, reasonable customs and reasonable services, and this shall be done without the destruction or waste of men or goods; and if we have committed the wardship of any such land to a sheriff or anyone else who answers to us for its revenues, and he destroys or wastes the lands,

---

*"Holding in chief" meant holding as tenant-in-chief—holding land directly from the Crown.

we will take amends from him, and the land shall be committed to two law-abiding and discreet men of the fee,* who will answer to us or the person we have assigned them, and if we give or sell the wardship of any such land to anyone, and he destroys or wastes it, he shall lose the wardship, and it shall be handed over to two law-abiding and discreet men of the fee who shall answer to us as previously said.

5. Moreover, so long as the guardian has wardship of the land, he shall maintain out of the revenues of the land the buildings, parks, fishponds, pools, mills, and other things pertaining to the land; and when the heir comes of age he shall restore to him all his land stocked with ploughs and growing crops, such as the agricultural season requires and the revenues of the land can reasonably sustain.

6. Heirs shall be married without disparagement, provided that before a marriage is contracted, the heir's closest relatives are informed.

7. After the death of her husband a widow shall have her marriage portion and inheritance straightaway and without difficulty, nor shall she pay anything for her dower, her marriage portion or her inheritance which she and her husband held on the day of his death. She may remain in her marital home for forty days after his death, during which period her dower will be assigned to her.

8. No widow shall be forced to marry for as long as she wishes to live without a husband, provided that she gives security that she will not marry without our consent, if she holds of us, or without the consent of her lord of whom she holds, if she holds of someone else.

9. Neither we nor our bailiffs will seize any land or any rent for any debt, so long as the debtor's chattels are sufficient to pay the debt; nor

*"Men of the fee" were men connected to the land in question.

are the pledges of the debtor to be distrained so long as the principal debtor has enough to pay the debt. And if the principal debtor defaults on the debt, not having the means to pay it, the pledges are to answer for it. And if they wish, they may have the debtor's lands and rents until they have had satisfaction for the debt they have settled for him, unless the principal debtor demonstrates that he is quit with regard to the pledges.

10. If anyone has taken any sort of loan from the Jews, great or small, and dies before the debt is settled, the debt shall not carry interest for as long as the heir is underage, whoever he holds from; and if that debt should fall into our hands, we will take nothing but the principal sum recorded in the charter.

11. And if anyone should die owing a debt to the Jews, his wife shall have her dower and pay nothing of that debt. And he leaves surviving children who are underage, their needs are to be provided for according to the holding of the deceased, and the debt shall be paid from what remains, saving the service owed to the lords. Debts owed to others besides the Jews are to be dealt with in the same way.

12. No scutage or other aid is to be levied in our realm, except by the common counsel of our realm, unless it is to pay for the ransoming of our person, the knighting of our first-born son or the first marriage of our first-born daughter; and for these only a reasonable aid is to be taken. Aids taken from the city of London will be treated in the same way.

13. And the city of London shall have all its ancient liberties and free customs both on land and on water. Furthermore we wish and grant that all other cities, boroughs, towns and ports shall have all their liberties and free customs.

14. And for us to have common counsel of the realm for the levying of an aid (other than in the three cases previously mentioned) or for the levying of a scutage, we will have archbishops, bishops,

abbots, earls and greater barons summoned individually by our letters; and furthermore we will have a general summons made by our sheriffs and bailiffs, of all of those who hold from us in chief; for a fixed day, at least forty days away, and at a fixed place; and in all our letters we will explain the cause of the summons. And when the summons has thus been made, the business shall proceed on the agreed day according to the counsel of those present, even if not all of those summoned have come.

15. In future we will not grant to anyone that he may take an aid from his free men, except to pay a ransom on his person, or on the knighting of his first-born son, or on the first marriage of his first-born daughter; and for these there is only to be a reasonable aid.

16. No one is to be distrained to do more service for a knight's fee, or for any other free tenement, than is owed for it.

17. Common pleas are not to follow our court, but are to be held in some fixed place.

18. Recognizances of novel disseisin, mort d'ancestor and darrein presentment* are not to be held except in their proper county court, and in this way: We, or, if we are out of the realm, our chief justiciar, shall send two justices to each county four times a year, who, with four knights of each county chosen by the county court, shall hold the said assizes in the county court, on the day and in the meeting place of the county court.

19. And if on the day of the county court the said assizes cannot be held, as many knights and free tenants [as are required] out of those who were present in the county court on that day will remain for the sufficient making of judgments, according to whether the business is great or small.

---

*Novel disseisin, mort d'ancestor, and darrein presentment were common legal procedures initiated by writs of Chancery, all connected with ownership of property.

20. A free man may not be amerced [i.e., fined] for a small offence, except according to the nature of the offence; and for a great offence he shall be amerced according to the magnitude of the offence, saving his livelihood; and a merchant in the same way, saving his merchandise; and a villein shall be amerced in the same way, saving his growing crops, if they fall into our mercy. And none of the said amercements may be made, except upon the oaths of honest men of the neighbourhood.

21. Earls and barons are not to be amerced except by their peers, and only in accordance with the nature of the offence.

22. No clergyman is to be amerced on his lay tenement, except in accordance with the nature of his offence, in the way of others mentioned previously, and not in accordance with the size of his ecclesiastical benefice.

23. Neither town nor man shall be forced to build bridges over rivers, except those who are obliged to do so by custom and right.

24. No sheriff, constable, coroner or other of our bailiffs shall hold the pleas of our crown.

25. All counties, hundreds, wapentakes and ridings shall be at their ancient farms, without any increment, except for our demesne manors.*

26. If anyone holding a lay fee of us dies, and our sheriff or bailiff shows our letters patent of a summons for a debt which the deceased owed us, it is to be lawful for our sheriff or bailiff to attach and record the chattels of the deceased found on the lay fee, to the value of the debt, in the view of law-abiding men, so that nothing is to be removed from there, until the clear debt is paid to us; and the residue is to be relinquished by the executors to carry out the will of

---

*Hundreds, wapentakes, and ridings were administrative subdivisions of counties or shires with their origins in Anglo-Saxon times; "farms" meant fixed sums of money due annually in taxes from an area of land.

the deceased; and, if nothing is owed to us by him, all the chattels shall go to the deceased, saving reasonable portions for his wife and children.

27. If any free man dies intestate, his chattels are to be distributed by his closest kinsmen and friends, under the supervision of the Church, saving to everyone the debts that the dead man owed them.

28. No constable, or any of our bailiffs, shall take anyone's corn or any other chattels, unless he immediately pays for them in cash, or else he can agree with the seller to postpone payment.

29. No constable may compel any knight to give money instead of performing castle guard, if he is willing to perform that guard in person, or, if he is for some good reason unable to do it himself, through another reliable man. And if we have led or sent him in the army, he shall be relieved of guard duty, in accordance with the amount of time he spent in our military service.

30. No sheriff or bailiff of ours, or anyone else may take any free man's horses or carts for transporting things, except with the free man's agreement.

31. Neither we nor our bailiffs may take anyone's timber to a castle, or to any other business of ours, except with the agreement of the timber's owner.

32. We will not hold the lands of convicted felons for more than a year and a day, and then the lands will be returned to the lord of the fee.

33. In future, all fish-weirs will be completely removed from the Thames and the Medway and throughout the whole of England, except on the sea-coast.

34. The writ called Praecipe will not, in future, be issued to anyone for any holding in respect of which a free man could lose his court.

35. There shall be one measure of wine in the whole of our realm, and one measure of ale, and one measure of corn, namely, the quarter

of London, and one width of dyed, russet and haberget cloths, namely two ells within the borders. Let it be the same for weights as it is for measures.

36. Nothing shall in future be given or taken for the writ of inquisition of life and limb, but it shall be freely given and not refused.

37. If anyone holds of us by fee-farm, socage or burgage,* and holds land of someone else by military service, we will not, by reason of the fee-farm, socage or burgage, have wardship of his heir or of his lands belonging to another man's fee. Nor will we have custody of that fee-farm, socage or burgage, except if the fee-farm, socage or burgage owes military service. We will not have custody of anyone's heir or anyone's lands which he holds of someone else by military service, by virtue of some petty serjeantry by which he holds of us by the service of rendering us knives or arrows, or suchlike.

38. No bailiff is in future to put anyone to law by his accusation alone, without trustworthy witnesses being brought forward.

39. No free man is to be arrested, or imprisoned, or disseized, or outlawed, or exiled, or in any other way ruined, nor will we go or send against him, except by the legal judgment of his peers or by the law of the land.

40. To no one will we sell, to no one will we deny or delay, right or justice.

41. All merchants are to be safe and secure in leaving and coming to England, and in staying and travelling in England, both by land and by water, to buy and sell without any evil tolls, but only by the ancient and rightful customs, save in time of war if they come from an enemy country. And if such are found in our land at the beginning of war, they will be detained without damage to their persons or

---

*Fee-farm, socage, and burgage were different forms of feudal tenure, where payments or military services were owed to the king in return for possession of land.

goods, until it is clear to us or our chief justiciar how the merchants of our land are treated in the enemy country; and if ours are safe there, the others shall be safe in our land.

42. In future it is lawful for anyone, saving his allegiance to us, and except for a short period during time of war, to leave our realm and return, safe and secure by land and water, for the sake of the general good of the realm; except for those imprisoned or outlawed according to the law of the land, and people from the enemy country, and merchants—who shall be treated as previously described.

43. If anyone dies who held of any escheat, such as the honours of Wallingford, Nottingham, Boulogne, Lancaster, or of other escheats which are in our hand and our baronies, his heir will not pay any relief or do us any other service than he would have done to the baron if the barony was in the baron's hand; and we will hold it in the same manner as the baron held it.*

44. From now on men who reside outside the forest will not come before our justices of the forest on a general summons, unless they are impleaded, or they are pledges for any person or persons who are attached for forest business.

45. We will not appoint justices, constables, sheriffs or bailiffs, other than those who know the laws of the realm and intend to keep it well.

46. All barons who have founded abbeys, for which they have charters of the kings of England, or ancient tenure, shall have custody of the abbeys when they are vacant, as they should have.

47. All forests which have been afforested in our time shall be immediately disafforested, and let the same be done for riverbanks which have been fenced off during our time.

48. All evil customs of forests and warrens, foresters and warreners, sheriffs and their officers, riverbanks and their keepers are

*Escheat was land that reverted to its lord if the tenant were to die without an heir.

immediately to be investigated in each and every county by twelve sworn knights of the same county, who are to be chosen by upright men of their county, and within forty days of the inquiry [the evil customs] are to be entirely abolished, provided that we, or our justiciar if we are not in England, know about it first.

49. We will immediately restore all hostages and charters that have been given to us by Englishmen as security for peace and faithful service.

50. We will completely remove from their offices the relations of Gérard d'Athée, so that from now on they shall have no office in England: Engelard de Cigogné, Peter and Guy and Andrew de Chanceaux, Guy de Cigogné, Geoffrey de Martini and his brothers, Philip Mark and his brothers, and his nephew Geoffrey, and all their followers.*

51. And immediately after the restoration of peace we will remove from the realm all foreign knights, crossbowmen, serjeants and mercenaries, who have come with horses and arms to the detriment of the kingdom.

52. If anyone has been disseized or dispossessed by us of lands, castles, liberties or of his rights, without lawful judgment of his peers, it shall immediately be restored to him. And if dispute should arise over this, then let it be settled by judgment of the twenty-five barons, as mentioned below in the security clause. For all those things of which anyone was disseized or dispossessed during the reign of King Henry our father or King Richard our brother, which we hold in our hand or which others hold, which we ought to warrant, we will have respite during the crusaders' term; excepting those cases when a plea was begun or an inquest made on our order

---

*This group represented the only people to be condemned specifically by name in the Magna Carta: The foreign mercenary captain Gérard d'Athée and his relatives had been rewarded for their service to John with high office in England and favor at court.

before we took the cross. But when we have returned from our pilgrimage, or if by chance we do not go on our pilgrimage, we will immediately do full justice.

53. We shall have the same respite, and in the same manner, in doing justice on disafforesting or retaining those forests that Henry our father or Richard our brother afforested, and concerning wardships of lands which are part of another fee, wardships which we have held by reason of a fee which someone held of us by knight service, and of abbeys which were founded on a fee other than ours, in which the lord of the fee has claimed his right. And when we return, or if we do not go on our pilgrimage, we will immediately do full justice to those complaining about these things.

54. No man shall be arrested or imprisoned because of the appeal of a woman for the death of anyone other than her husband.

55. All fines which were made with us unjustly and contrary to the law of the land and all amercements made unjustly and contrary to the law of the land shall be completely remitted, or shall be settled by the twenty-five barons mentioned below in the security clause, or by the judgment of the majority of them, together with the aforementioned Stephen, Archbishop of Canterbury, if he can be present, and others such as he may wish to bring with him for this purpose. And if it is not possible for him to attend, let the business proceed without him, provided that if any one or more of the twenty-five barons are in such a suit, they shall be removed from this particular judgment, and shall be replaced in this case only by others chosen and sworn in by the twenty-five.

56. If we have disseized or deprived Welshmen of lands or liberties or other things without lawful judgment of their peers, in England or in Wales, they are to be returned to them immediately. And if a dispute arises about this, then it is to be settled in the March by judgment of their peers, for English tenements according

to the law of England, for Welsh tenements according to the law of Wales, for tenements of the March according to the laws of the March. And the Welsh will do the same to us and ours.

57. However, with regard to all of the possessions of which any Welshman has been disseized or dispossessed without the lawful judgment of his peers, by King Henry our father, or King Richard our brother, and which we have in our hand, or which others hold which we ought to warrant, we will have respite for the common crusaders' term, except in cases where a plea was started or an inquest held by our instruction before we took the cross; however, when we return, or if by chance we do not go on crusade, then we will immediately do justice according to the laws of Wales and the parts previously mentioned.

58. We will immediately restore the son of Llywelyn and all the hostages from Wales, and charters that were delivered to us as security for peace.

59. We will deal with Alexander, King of the Scots, regarding the return of his sisters and hostages and his liberties and rights in accordance with the way we deal with our other barons of England, unless it should be otherwise under the charters which we have from his father, William, former King of Scots. And this will be by judgment of his peers in our court.

60. All the previously mentioned customs and liberties which we have granted in our kingdom as far as we are concerned with regard to our own men, shall be observed by all men of our realm, both clergy and laity, as far as they are concerned with regard to their own men.

61. Since we have granted all these things for God and for the correction of our kingdom, and for the better settlement of the discord that has arisen between us and our barons, wishing these things to

be enjoyed with full and firm stability in perpetuity, we make and
grant them the following security: namely, that the barons are to
choose twenty-five barons of the realm, whoever they wish, who
with all their strength should observe, uphold and cause to be observed the peace and liberties which we have granted to them and
confirmed to them in this present charter, so that if we or our justiciar, or our bailiffs, or any other of our officers shall in any way of-
fend against anyone, or transgress against any of the articles of
peace or security, and the offence has been shown to four of the said
twenty-five barons, those four are to go to us, or our justiciar if we
are out of the kingdom, setting forth the offence and demand that
it be set right without delay. And if within the space of forty days of
being shown the offence, we do not set right or if we are out of the
realm, our justiciar does not set it right, the said four barons are to
refer the case to the rest of the twenty-five barons, and those twenty-
five barons, with the community of the whole realm shall distrain
and distress us in all ways possible, by taking castles, lands and possessions and in any other ways they can, until it has been put right
in accordance with their judgment, saving our person and the persons of our queen and children. And once redress has been made let
them obey us as they did before. And whoever of the land wishes
may swear that he will obey the orders of the said twenty-five barons and with them distress us as much as he can, and we publicly
and freely give permission to swear to whoever wishes to do so, and
we will never prohibit anyone from swearing. Furthermore we will
compel all those of the land who do not wish to swear with the
twenty-five barons to distrain and distress us with them to swear as
has been said. And if any of the twenty-five barons should die, or
leave the land, or is in any other way prevented from doing his duties as previously mentioned, the remainder of the aforementioned

twenty-five barons are to elect another in his place, by their own discretion, who will be sworn in the same manner as the rest. Furthermore, in everything that has been entrusted to the twenty-five barons to undertake, if it should happen that the twenty-five are present and disagree among themselves on anything, or if any of them, having been summoned, will not or cannot attend, whatever the majority of those present shall provide or command shall be considered as fixed and binding, as if all the twenty-five had agreed to it. And the aforementioned twenty-five swear that they will faithfully observe all the aforesaid and cause it to be observed to their fullest ability. And we will ask nothing of anyone, either ourselves or through anyone else, through which any of these grants and liberties shall be revoked or diminished. And if any such thing shall be obtained, let it be null and void and we will never make use of it, through ourselves or through anyone else.

62. And we have fully remitted [to] all ill-will, indignation and rancor that has arisen between us and our men, clergy and laity, during the time of discord. Moreover, we have fully remitted to all men, clergy and laity, all the transgressions committed as the result of that discord between Easter in the sixteenth year of our reign until the establishment of peace, and as far as we are concerned, they are completely forgiven. And in addition we have had letters patent made by Lord Stephen, Archbishop of Canterbury, Lord Henry, Archbishop of Dublin, and the aforesaid bishops, and Master Pandulf testifying to this security and the aforesaid grants.

63. Wherefore we wish and firmly command that the English Church shall be free and that men in our kingdom have and hold all the aforesaid liberties, rights and grants, well and in peace, freely and quietly, fully and completely, for themselves and their heirs of us and our heirs, in all things and in all places, in perpetuity as has been said.

This has been sworn to both on our behalf and on behalf of the barons, that all the previously mentioned things shall be observed in good faith and without evil intent. Witnessed by the above-mentioned and many others. Given by our hand in the meadow called Runnymede, between Windsor and Staines, on the fifteenth day of June, in the seventeenth year of our reign.

Appendix B
The Enforcers of the Magna Carta

Matthew Paris (c. 1200–59), in his *Chronica Majora*, lists (in this order) the twenty-five barons who were appointed to enforce the Magna Carta of 1215. Under the terms of clause 61, these men were empowered to "distrain and distress [the king] in all ways possible" if he or his officials broke the terms of the charter and did not provide remedy within forty days. Another copy of this list, now held in Lambeth Palace, included the number of knights that each of the twenty-five barons (with the exception of the mayor of London) was expected to bring to war in the event of the security clause's being activated.

Richard, Earl of Clare (d. 1217)

Otherwise known as Richard de Clare, Earl of Hertford, a title he held from 1173, Richard was present at the coronations of both Richard I and John, although he enjoyed a closer relationship with the older brother than with the younger. His power base was at Tonbridge Castle in Kent, and Richard was among the rebellious East Anglian barons; he may have been involved in the plot to kill John in 1212. His lands were seized during the First Barons' War of 1215–17, and he was excommunicated by the pope. Richard died in November 1217, leaving as his heir a son, Gilbert, who was also named among the twenty-five.

William de Forz, Count of Aumale (c. 1190s–1241)

Aumale was a small town in Normandy, so in theory William's English title should have become obsolete when Philip Augustus reconquered the duchy. But it was obstinately maintained under King John and linked with the lordship of Holderness in Yorkshire. William's mother, Hawise, suffered the opposite blunt force of John's feudal extortion: When her husband (William's stepfather) died in 1212, she had to pay five thousand marks to avoid being forced to remarry. Although raised mostly outside England, William came to the realm to claim his inheritance on Hawise's death in 1214 and immediately found reason to join the baronial opposition. However, he switched to John's side in late summer 1215 and profited mightily from grants of confiscated rebel lands. William was a witness to the reissues of the Magna Carta under Henry III in 1216 and 1225 but also caused significant political trouble during Henry's minority. He lived a relatively long and very active life before dying on his way to Jerusalem on pilgrimage.

Geoffrey de Mandeville, Earl of Essex, Earl of Gloucester (d. 1216)

De Mandeville was a wealthy baron whose responsibilities included being custodian of the Tower of London. He was driven to rebellion in 1214 when, after marrying the king's divorced first wife, Isabel, Countess of Gloucester, he was browbeaten into agreeing to pay the monstrous sum of twenty thousand marks for the privilege—by some distance the most outlandish of all John's feudal extortions. The debt was simply unpayable, and it was probably set at an impossible level so that John could seize back Gloucester lands that he had forfeited by separating from Isabel. De Mandeville was expected to bring two hundred knights to oppose the king if the "council of twenty-five" went to war to enforce the Magna Carta—the only other baron contracted for so many was William Marshal the Younger. De

Mandeville's was a brief rebellion: He was killed at a tournament in London in February 1216.

Saer de Quincy, Earl of Winchester (d. 1219)

A major landowner on the Scottish borders, de Quincy was also an experienced soldier who fought with Richard the Lionheart and John in Normandy and who was captured by the French at Vaudreuil in 1203. Later he served John in Scotland, Ireland, and Germany, worked as a royal justice, and was heavily involved in the work of the Exchequer. De Quincy witnessed both John's legal deposition against William de Briouze in 1210 and the king's submission to the pope in 1213. He took the cross with the king in March 1215 but turned on him weeks later, traveling to Scotland to stir up Alexander II for an invasion of England's north. A great friend and brother-in-arms of Robert FitzWalter, de Quincy allowed the rebels to use his lands at Brackley to renounce their homage before the march on London in May 1215. Later he was among the party of barons who invited Prince Louis to invade England. Captured at the Battle of Lincoln (1217), de Quincy returned to loyalty and was present during the council that granted the Magna Carta of 1217, but he left the realm on crusade eighteen months later and died in Damietta, to be buried in Acre.

Henry de Bohun, Earl of Hereford (c. 1175–1220)

Hereditary Constable of England, de Bohun was the nephew of William I (the Lion), King of Scots, to whom he was sent on diplomatic business shortly after John's coronation. Disputes with John, stemming in part from an argument with the king's half brother William Longuespée over Trowbridge Castle in Wiltshire, caused de Bohun to side with the rebels, and all his lands were confiscated by the king. He went back to John's side late in 1215, then switched once again to support Prince Louis against Henry III. Captured at the Battle of Lincoln in 1217, he made peace with the new regime and died on pilgrimage to the Holy Land in 1220.

Roger Bigod, Earl of Norfolk (c. 1143–1221)

The Bigod family had a history of conflict with Plantagenet kings dating back to Roger's father, Hugh Bigod, and his involvement in the "Great War" against Henry II of 1173–74. Despite this, Roger was close to Richard I and very active in the service of King John, taking part in campaigns in Poitou, Scotland, Ireland, and Wales. It may have been John's grinding financial demands that lay behind Roger's decision to join the rebels as part of the bloc of East Anglian barons. Whatever his reasons, Bigod remained unreconciled with John at the king's death and returned to loyalty only in 1217, once it was clear that William Marshal, Earl of Pembroke, and the supporters of Henry III had won the war. His heir was Hugh Bigod. The Bigod earls remained vastly powerful for several generations before dying out in the early fourteenth century.

Robert de Vere, Earl of Oxford (d. 1221)

Another eastern rebel, de Vere was named by Roger of Wendover as one of the prime movers of dissent against John's regime. His actions seem to have been inspired more by pragmatism than by deep rebellious commitment—he was one of the barons who wavered back and forth between John and Prince Louis in 1216 and was active as a royal judge following the victory of the Plantagenet loyalists.

William Marshal the Younger (c. 1190–1231)

William experienced the rough end of John's kingship as a young man when he was kept as a hostage at court for seven years to guarantee the good behavior of his father, the illustrious William Marshal, Earl of Pembroke. Unlike the elder Marshal, the young man sided with the opposition in 1215–16 and was appointed the marshal of Prince Louis's army. But he switched sides early in the war and fought under his father at the Battle of Lincoln (1217). After his father's death early in Henry III's reign, Marshal set about expanding his family's possessions in Wales, Ireland, and southern England. He died suddenly and without offspring in 1231, leaving his brothers—Richard, Gilbert, Walter, and Anselm—as his successive heirs. None produced legitimate children, and in 1245 the Marshal estates were broken up among their sisters and heiresses.

Robert FitzWalter (d. 1235)

FitzWalter was one of the rebel ringleaders in 1212, when he plotted with Eustace de Vesci to have John murdered. A rich and powerful East Anglian, he had particularly close links to Saer de Quincy, whom he considered a brother and whose arms he bore on his seal. Argumentative and easily stirred to violence, FitzWalter led the widespread baronial refusal to fight alongside John during the Poitou and Bouvines campaigns of 1213–14. In May 1215 he declared himself marshal of the Army of God and led the march on London. Despite his riches and his large following, FitzWalter failed to relieve the siege of Rochester Castle during the fighting in autumn 1215 and was captured during the Battle of Lincoln in 1217. After the war he traveled with Saer de Quincy to Damietta on the Fifth Crusade. Unlike his friend, he survived, returning to England a much-changed man: He served Henry III's regime loyally until his death.

Gilbert de Clare (c. 1180–1230)

The son and heir of Richard, Earl of Clare, Gilbert was around thirty-five years old in 1215 and had been guided by his rebellious father in his political activity during the preceding years. He sided with Prince Louis during the war following John's death but switched sides to ally with William Marshal, Earl of Pembroke, following the Battle of Lincoln (1217). Gilbert inherited the great earldom of Gloucester from his mother, Amicia, but was never a very active political figure. Present at the reissue of the Magna Carta by Henry III in 1225, he died in Brittany on campaign with the king five years later.

Eustace de Vesci (1169/70–1216)

De Vesci was a northerner of considerable status, thanks to his marriage to an illegitimate daughter of William I (the Lion), King of Scots. One of the ringleaders of baronial rebellion from the very start, he was implicated deeply in the plot to assassinate John in 1212. Chroniclers from William of Newburgh onward suggested that the root of such long-standing opposition was the king's lecherous designs on de Vesci's wife. Whether this was true, de Vesci was committed to rebellion early. He supported Prince Louis's invasion and was killed during the siege of Barnard Castle in County Durham when an arrow was shot through his brain.

Hugh Bigod (d. 1225)

The son and heir of Roger Bigod, Earl of Norfolk, Hugh inherited the earldom when his father died in 1221. He married Matilda, a daughter of William Marshal, Earl of Pembroke. Bigod survived long enough to witness the reissue of the Magna Carta in 1225 but died shortly afterward.

William de Mowbray (c. 1173–c. 1224)

Although physically tiny, apparently no larger than a dwarf, de Mowbray was respected for his courage and generosity. He was an active warrior in the service of the king until 1215, when he joined with his fellow northerners in rebellion. He remained in opposition until the Battle of Lincoln (1217), where he was captured, but he later made peace with the new regime.

The "Mayor of London": Serlo the Mercer (dates unknown)

At the time of the Magna Carta, the mayoralty was held by the textile dealer and property owner Serlo the Mercer, who kept houses across the city, including in the parish of St Mary-le-Bow. Serlo served as mayor in 1215 and again from 1216 to 1221. His support for the baronial opposition was crucial, because holding London was vital leverage in obtaining the charter of liberties from John. The only member of the twenty-five not expected to raise knights, Serlo was instead required to give the City of London over to baronial control if John contravened the Magna Carta.

William de Lanvallei (d. 1217)

De Lanvallei was connected to Robert FitzWalter by virtue of having married his niece. He was also governor of Colchester Castle, over which he tussled with the Crown between 1214 and 1217, when he died while still in rebellion.

Robert de Ros (c. 1182–1226/7)

A staunch northerner with estates in Yorkshire and Northumberland, de Ros was a regular companion of the king in the early years of John's reign, when he was even to be found at the royal gambling table. He witnessed John's submission to the pope and was still enjoying royal favor and holding royal office in April 1215. Dragged into opposition very late in the day, de Ros remained estranged until the autumn of 1217. He witnessed the 1225 reissue of the Magna Carta and then retired to live out the last months of his life as a monk.

John de Lacy, Constable of Chester (c. 1192–1240)

A young man at the time of the Magna Carta, de Lacy inherited his father's massive estates in northern England only in return for an enormous levy of seven thousand marks. He took the cross with John on March 4, 1215, for which he was granted a substantial reduction in his debts to the Crown. Rebelling only in the final three weeks before the Magna Carta was granted, de Lacy never seemed greatly convinced by the cause, flitting back and forth between king and rebels. After reconciliation with Henry III's regime in 1217, he went to Damietta on crusade before returning to play a full part in the new reign. He was one of the few men of 1215 (Richard de Montfichet was another) who also went on to witness both the 1225 and 1237 reissues of the Magna Carta.

Richard de Percy (d. 1244)

A young northerner who refused to serve on John's Bouvines campaign in 1214, de Percy entered active opposition during the summer of 1215. He brought Yorkshire under the obedience of Prince Louis in 1216 and was reconciled to the Crown only relatively late, in November 1217. Apparently one of the less wealthy barons, he was expected to bring only ten knights in the event that the council of twenty-five declared war on John. Toward the end of his life, de Percy was witness to the 1237 reconfirmation of the Magna Carta.

John FitzRobert (d. 1244)

Both a northern baron and a man of substance in East Anglia, FitzRobert had landholdings reaching from Warkworth and Rothbury in Northumberland to Clavering in Essex. His cousin John de Lacy was a fellow member of the twenty-five. Given that he had served as a royal sheriff, FitzRobert is a good example of a rebel knitted into the ranks of the opposition by a number of parallel links of territory and family connection.

William Malet (c. 1175–1215)

A crusading companion of Richard the Lionheart, Malet was a significant landholder in Somerset, far from the main geographical centers of rebellion in the north and east of England. He found himself in serious debt to the Crown in the years before the Magna Carta, owing two thousand marks in 1214, which he attempted to have canceled in return for military service in France. This tension probably explains his decision to join the rebels in the summer of 1215, although the fact that he had previously served as a sheriff and had not shirked his military duties suggests that he may have been one of the more moderate barons among the twenty-five.

Geoffrey de Say (c. 1155–1230)

Geoffrey de Say took part in military campaigns for the king in Ireland. He subsequently inherited his father's lands across southeast England and the home counties, for which he paid only a moderate fine. However, he joined the baronial opposition nonetheless and was briefly deprived of his lands in October 1215. De Say made peace with Henry III's regime in 1217 and subsequently went twice on pilgrimage, to the Holy Land and then to Santiago de Compostela in Spain.

Roger de Montbegon (d. 1226)

A landowner in Lincolnshire and Lancashire and at one point the keeper of Nottingham Castle, de Montbegon refused to pay scutage to the king or do military service in the years leading up to the Magna Carta. Erroneously named Roger de Mowbray by Matthew Paris and in the Lambeth Palace Library manuscript, de Montbegon was expected to bring just ten knights to any punitive military action taken by the twenty-five in the case of John's breaking the terms of the charter.

William de Huntingfield (d. c. 1225)

With lands scattered from Essex and Suffolk to Lincolnshire and Lancaster, de Huntingfield was an active supporter of King John until the defeat at Bouvines in 1214: He served as a justice in the eyre in 1208–9 and as sheriff of Norfolk and Suffolk the following year. In spring 1215, however, he went into opposition and was active in East Anglia during the First Barons' War of 1215–17, taking control of the region on behalf of Prince Louis. Seemingly a bird lover, he appears in the records early in John's reign seeking favor from the king with gifts of a falcon and six "beautiful Norwegian hawks."

Richard de Montfichet (c. 1190–1267)

One of the few men to live through both the Barons' Wars of the thirteenth century (1215–17 and 1264–7), de Montfichet came of age just in time to travel with King John to Poitou in 1214. His family was hereditary custodians of royal forest land in Essex, which de Montfichet secured during the Magna Carta negotiations but which was withdrawn during the subsequent fighting, only to be restored to him in 1217 by the young Henry III's government. Like John de Lacy, he witnessed both the 1225 and 1237 reissues of the Magna Carta. Perhaps having learned his lesson during the troubles of his early days, he remained neutral during the wars between Henry III and Simon de Montfort, Earl of Leicester, in the 1260s.

William d'Aubigny (d. 1236)

William d'Aubigny was Lord of Belvoir in Leicestershire, and he served as a sheriff in three different counties. Despite being critical of the Crown, he remained neutral for a long time during the rebellion against John, eventually joining the rebels in time to be among the twenty-five barons. He subsequently led the defense of Rochester Castle during its siege (October–November 1215), where he was said to have dissuaded a crossbowman from assassinating John from the castle's battlements. D'Aubigny was imprisoned in Corfe Castle following the fall of Rochester Castle, but he was released on John's death. He joined Henry III's side and was a commander at the Battle of Lincoln in 1217.

Appendix C
Eight Hundred Years of the Magna Carta

1100

King Henry I, on becoming King of England, grants a charter of liberties promising, among other matters, freedom for the Church and to keep peace in the land.

1154

Henry II accedes to the English throne and grants a charter of liberties to mark his coronation.

1166

The Assize of Clarendon extends royal law deep into local areas, with crimes investigated via the General Eyre.

1170

Archbishop Thomas Becket is murdered in Canterbury Cathedral, the culmination of a dispute with Henry II over royal attempts to bring secular law to bear on churchmen.

1173–74

The "Great War," a baronial rebellion, ends in Henry II's favor. There is a massive program of castle demolition and seizure, and the Treaty of Falaise subjects Scots to English overlordship.

1189–90

Henry II dies, to be succeeded by his son Richard I "the Lionheart." By the end of the year Richard departs on crusade, paid for by heavy taxation and the sale of public offices.

1192

Richard I is captured while returning from the Holy Land and imprisoned by the Holy Roman Emperor Henry VI until 1194, only to be released on payment of a massive 150,000 mark ransom.

1199

April 11: Richard I dies while commanding the siege of the castle at Châlus-Chabrol.

May 27: Richard's brother John, who had fomented rebellion in the Plantagenet empire during Richard's absence and imprisonment, is crowned King of England.

1200

John agrees to unfavorable terms with Philip II (Augustus) of France in the Treaty of Le Goulet, earning him the demeaning nickname of "Softsword."

1202

John loses Anjou, Maine, Touraine, and other Plantagenet lands on the continent to Philip Augustus and his allies.

1203

c. April: Arthur of Brittany, John's nephew and a rival for the throne backed by Philip Augustus of France, disappears while in John's captivity, probably murdered.

December: John leaves Normandy for England while the duchy is threatened by Philip Augustus.

1204

Normandy falls to Philip Augustus, a severe blow to John.

The French invasion of Gascony reduces the Plantagenet "empire" to a small strip of Aquitaine.

1205

July 13: Hubert Walter, archbishop of Canterbury, dies; John refuses to accept Pope Innocent III's election of Stephen Langton as his replacement.

John launches an abortive invasion of Poitou, which ends in stalemate and a two-year truce with France.

1207

John intensifies the financial expropriations from his barons, through taxation, feudal dues, and the proceeds of legal processes.

1208

March: England is placed under interdict by Pope Innocent III in the escalating dispute with John over Langton's appointment; churches fall silent, and John takes the opportunity to seize Church wealth. John also begins pursuit of William de Briouze for nonpayment of debt.

1209

August: William I (the Lion), King of Scots, submits to John at the Treaty of Norham; the hostages include his two daughters.

November: In the continuing royal–papal stand-off, John is excommunicated by Pope Innocent III.

1210

John leads a military campaign in Ireland in pursuit of William de Briouze.

De Briouze's wife, Matilda, and son are starved to death in prison after attempting to negotiate with John on his behalf.

1211

March–July: John invades Wales and forces Llywelyn ap Iorwerth "the Great" of Gwynedd to recognize him as overlord.

September: William de Briouze dies in exile in France.

1212

August: A plot to murder John is led by two disgruntled barons, Eustace de Vesci and Robert FitzWalter, who flee abroad and are declared outlaws. John aborts attempts to muster an army to regain his continental empire.

1213

April: Philip Augustus of France and his son, Prince Louis, plan an invasion of England to topple the excommunicated John.

May 15: In the face of the French threat, John publicly backs down in the dispute with Pope Innocent III, submitting and accepting papal overlordship in return for the lifting of the interdict.

May 30: English ships burn the French fleet in the river Zwin, and the invasion of England is abandoned.

November 2: John meets the still-intractable northern barons in an attempt to gain support for Continental war.

1214

January: John demands from Geoffrey de Mandeville, Earl of Essex, twenty thousand marks for the right to marry the king's former wife, Isabel of Gloucester.

February: John sails for La Rochelle to join a two-pronged attack on Philip Augustus.

July 27: The coalition of John's allies is soundly beaten by Philip Augustus at the Battle of Bouvines.

October 13: The defeated John leaves France for England, where baronial unrest, especially in the north, is reaching breaking point.

Between October and late spring 1215, the so-called Unknown Charter, demanding reforms, is compiled.

1215

January: A conference between John and the barons in London breaks up with the latter demanding reconfirmation of Henry I's coronation charter.

March 4: John takes the cross, hoping that crusader status with the pope will strengthen his hand domestically and internationally.

April 25: John fails to meet barons at Northampton to respond to their demands (perhaps those contained in the Unknown Charter).

May 5: Baronial opponents formally renounce their feudal loyalty to King John at Brackley, Northamptonshire.

May 12: John orders the besieging of rebel castles.

May 17: London is captured by rebels under Robert FitzWalter, who styles himself "Marshal of the Army of God."

June 10: Negotiations between royal and rebel parties begin at Runnymede. John accepts a draft document, the Articles of the Barons, as terms for negotiation of a peace.

June 15: John grants the Magna Carta at Runnymede. It contains a range of royal promises, breach of which is liable to enforcement (by military means) by a named group of twenty-five barons.

June 19: Formerly rebellious barons signal their acceptance of the Magna Carta by renewing their homage to the king.

Mid-July: John writes to Pope Innocent III requesting annulment of the Magna Carta.

On August 24, the pope declares the charter null and void and excommunicates rebel barons and the citizens of London.

September: War with the barons resumes. John lays siege to Rochester Castle, held by Archbishop Langton. Barons ask Prince Louis to invade.

October: Northern barons pay homage to Alexander II, King of Scots, who is invited to invade England.

November 30: Rochester Castle falls to John.

December: The first French troops begin to arrive in England.

1216

January–March: John's determined offensive in the north and East Anglia begins successfully, but his ships fail to blockade the French invasion fleet across the Channel.

May 22: Prince Louis of France invades, landing at Sandwich in Kent.

June–August: Louis is admitted to the City of London; his forces also besiege Dover, Lincoln, and Windsor while Scottish forces re-enter England, besieging royal castles.

October 10: John falls ill with dysentery in Norfolk.

October 12: The king loses a large portion of his baggage train and treasure in the Wash.

October 18–19: John dies overnight at Newark, Nottinghamshire.

October 28: John's nine-year-old son is crowned Henry III at Gloucester, with royal government in the hands of William Marshal, Earl of Pembroke, and a council of thirteen.

November 12: The Magna Carta is reissued by papal legate Guala Bicchieri and William Marshal in the name of Henry III, but war continues.

1217

May 20: The Battle of Lincoln against the rebellious barons ends in victory for William Marshal and the royal loyalists.

August 24: At sea, the Battle of Sandwich against the French ends in victory for Hubert de Burgh and the forces of the young Henry.

September 20: By the terms of the Treaty of Lambeth, France's Prince Louis agrees to leave England.

November 6: The Magna Carta is reissued for a second time, now with the Charter of the Forest.

1225

The Magna Carta and the Charter of the Forest are reissued in definitive versions in return for the grant of a tax on "movables."

1237

The Magna Carta is reconfirmed by Henry III at a Westminster meeting described as a "parliament"; it is to be enforced by a sentence of excommunication against those who break it.

1253

The Magna Carta is reissued, again in return for taxation, and again supported by a sentence of excommunication.

1265

A parliament called by rebel baron Simon de Montfort, Earl of Leicester, reissues the Magna Carta and the Charter of the Forest, which are reconfirmed by Henry III.

1297

Edward I confirms the Magna Carta and the Charter of the Forest, along with additional articles of reform, following political dispute with leading barons.

1300

The final confirmation of the Magna Carta and the Charter of the Forest, by Edward I, takes place.

1508

The Magna Carta appears in print for the first time, issued by Richard Pynson.

1619

Barrister and parliamentarian Sir Edward Coke condemns royal abuses by the Stuart monarch James I, telling the House of Commons that they contravene the Magna Carta.

1628

Sir Edward Coke's Petition of Right seeks to emulate the Magna Carta in an attempt to bind James's successor, Charles I, to specific principles of government.

1687

The Magna Carta is published in the American colonies.

1689

The Bill of Rights is passed by Parliament, as a statement of English law and customs.

1775

Massachusetts adopts as its symbol an American patriot holding a sword in one hand and the Magna Carta in the other.

1791

An American bill of rights is ratified, designed to limit the powers of the newly independent country over its citizens.

1863

The Statute Law Revision Act strikes many clauses of the Magna Carta from the British statute book.

1948

The new United Nations Organization produces its Universal Declaration of Human Rights, described by former U.S. first lady Eleanor Roosevelt as "the international Magna Carta for all men everywhere."

1957

The American Bar Association erects a permanent monument to the Magna Carta at Runnymede.

1970

New British legislation strikes all but four clauses of the Magna Carta from the statute book.

2007

A copy of the Magna Carta 1297 is purchased at auction in New York City for $21.3 million.

2015

This year sees the 800th anniversary of the Magna Carta.

Notes

Introduction

1. Magna Carta 1215, clause 61.
2. Printed in D. C. Douglas, ed., *English Historical Documents*, vol. 3 (London/New York: 1975), 324–26.
3. Magna Carta 1215, clause 63.
4. N. Vincent, *Magna Carta: The Foundation of Freedom, 1215–2015* (London: 2014), 13.
5. J. Stevenson, ed., *Radulphi de Coggeshall Chronicon Anglicanum* (London: 1875), 170.
6. "De principis instructione liber," in *Giraldi Cambrensis Opera*, ed. G. F. Warner, vol. 8 (London: 1891), 328.

Chapter 1: The Devil's Brood

1. M. R. James, ed. and trans., *Walter Map: De Nugis Curialium: Courtiers' Trifles*, rev. C. N. L. Brooke and R. A. B. Mynors (Oxford: 1983), 477.
2. Ibid.
3. P. Walsh and M. Kennedy, eds. and trans., *William of Newburgh: The History of English Affairs*, book 2 (Warminster: 2007), 15.
4. G. M. Garmonsway, trans., *The Anglo-Saxon Chronicle* (2nd ed.) (London: 1972), 265.
5. E. Amt and S. D. Church, eds. and trans., *Dialogus de Scaccario and Constitutio Domus Regis* (new ed.) (Oxford: 2007), 3–4
6. T. K. Keefe, "King Henry II and the Earls: The Pipe Roll Evidence," *Albion: A Quarterly Journal Concerned with British Studies* 13, no. 3 (Autumn 1981): 215–17 (table 1).
7. P. Brand, "Finance and the Economy in the Reign of Henry II," in *Henry II: New Interpretations*, ed. C. Harper-Bill and N. Vincent (Woodbridge, UK: 2007), 249.
8. A. J. Duggan, ed. and trans., *The Correspondence of Thomas Becket, Archbishop of Canterbury, 1162–1170* (Oxford, 2000), 157.
9. R. A. Brown, *Allen Brown's English Castles* (new ed.) (Woodbridge, UK: 2004), 162–63.

10. R. Howlett, ed., *Chronicles of the Reigns of Stephen, Henry II and Richard I*, vol. 1 (London: 1884) 283.

11. H. M. Thomas, "Shame, Masculinity and the Death of Thomas Becket," *Speculum* 87 (2012): 1065.

12. J. S. Brewer, J. F. Dimock, and G. F. Warner, *Giraldi Cambrensis, Opera*, vol. 8 (London: 1891), 295–96. This translation is from W. L. Warren, *Henry II* (new ed.) (New Haven, CT/London: 2000), 601.

Chapter 2: Lionheart and Softsword

1. H. T. Riley, ed., *The Annals of Roger de Hoveden II* (London: 1853), 114.

2. Ibid., 120.

3. N. Barratt, "The English Revenues of Richard I," *English Historical Review* 116 (2001): 637. The 1188 pipe roll shows total income of £21,233, compared with £31,089 two years later, a rise of 47.6 percent.

4. Riley, *Annals of Roger de Hoveden II*, 290–91.

5. Ibid., 290–92.

6. William Marshal's biography is a rich source of detail for this period. See A. J. Holden, S. Gregory, and D. Crouch, eds., *History of William Marshal*, 3 vols. (London: 2002–6).

7. Barratt, "English Revenues of Richard I," 637.

8. V. Green, *An Account of the Discovery of the Body of King John in the Cathedral Church of Worcester, July 17th 1797, from Authentic Communications, with Illustrations and Remarks* (London/Worcester: 1797), 4. The average height of medieval male skeletons excavated in Britain is 5'7¼." J. Schofield, *London 1100–1600: The Archaeology of a Capital City* (Sheffield UK: 2011), 199.

9. T. D. Hardy, *A Description of the Patent Rolls in the Tower of London* (London: 1835), 60.

10. J. T. Appleby, ed. and trans., *The Chronicle of Richard of Devizes* (London: 1963), 32.

11. BL MS Cotton Claudius DII, f.116. The image dates from the fourteenth century.

12. T. D. Hardy, *Rotuli Litterarum Clausarum in Turri Londinensi asservati*, vol. 1 (London: 1837), 184.

13. See G. Gillingham, "The Anonymous of Béthune, King John and Magna Carta," in *Magna Carta and the England of King John*, ed. Loengard (Woodbridge, UK: 2010), passim.

14. T. Wright, ed., *The Political Songs of England* (London: 1839), 6.

15. R. Howlett, ed., *Chronicles of the Reigns of Stephen, Henry II and Richard I*, vol. 1 (London: 1884), 390.

16. Hardy, *Description of the Patent Rolls*, 41.

17. T. Wright, ed. and trans., *The Historical Works of Giraldi Cambrensis* (London: 1894), 315.

18. J. Holt, *King John* (London: 1963), 20.

19. W. Stubbs, ed., *The Historical Works of Gervase of Canterbury*, vol. 2, (London: 1872–73), 92–3.

20. H. R. Luard, ed., *Annales Monastici I* (London: 1864), 27.

21. J. A. Giles, *Roger of Wendover's Flowers of History*, vol. 2 (London: 1849), 206.

22. The *Rotulus de valore terrarum Normannorum* is analyzed at length in T. Moore, "The Loss of Normandy and the Invention of Terre Normannorum, 1204," *English Historical Review* 125 (2010): 1071–109.

23. When John visited York in 1200, he was the first English king to have been there for at least fourteen years. His visit to Newcastle the following year was the first since 1158. J. Holt, *King John* (London: 1963), 13.

24. J. Masschaele, "The English Economy in the Age of Magna Carta," in *Magna Carta and the England of King John*, ed. J. S. Loengard (Woodbridge, UK: 2010), 156. On prices see P. Latimer, "Early Thirteenth-Century Prices," in *King John: New Interpretations*, ed. S. D. Church (Woodbridge, UK: 1999), passim, but especially 69–73, figs. 1–9.

25. Masschaele, "English Economy in the Age of Magna Carta," 156–65.

26. E. Amt and S. D. Church, eds. and trans., *Dialogus de Scaccario: The Dialogue of the Exchequer by Richard fitzNigel* (Oxford: 2011), 86–87.

27. For John's annual revenue broken down by year, see table 1 in N. Barratt, "The Revenue of King John," *English Historical Review* 111 (1996): 839.

Chapter 3: Interdict and Intimidation

1. W. Stubbs, ed., *Memoriale fratris Walteri de Coventria*, vol. 2 (London: 1872), 203.

2. On Langton's thought see D. A. Carpenter, "Archbishop Langton and Magna Carta: His Contribution, His Doubts and His Hypocrisy," *English Historical Review* 126 (2011); J. A. Baldwin, "Master Stephen Langton, Future Archbishop of Canterbury: The Paris Schools and Magna Carta," *English Historical Review* 123 (2008); N. Fryde, "The Roots of Magna Carta: Opposition to the Plantagenets," in *Political Thought and the Realities of Power in the Middle Ages*, ed. J. Canning and O. G. Oexle (Göttingen: 1998), 3–65.

3. Baldwin, "Master Stephen Langton," 815.

4. R. Bartlett, *England Under the Norman and Angevin Kings: 1075–1225* (Oxford: 2000), 435.

5. N. Barratt, "The Revenue of King John," *English Historical Review* III (1996): 839.

6. S. D. Church, *King John* (London: 2015), 163–64.

7. See S. Ambler, "The Witness Lists to Magna Carta, 1215–1265," Magna Carta Project, July 2014, http://magnacarta.cmp.uea.ac.uk/read/feature_of_the_month/Jul_2014.

8. Bartlett, *England Under the Norman and Angevin Kings*, 213.

9. N. Fallows, trans., *The Book of the Order of Chivalry: Ramon Llull* (Woodbridge, UK, and Rochester, NY: 2013), 44–55.

10. The Lewis Chessmen are split between the National Museum of Scotland in Edinburgh and the British Museum in London (where they are assigned collection number 1831,1101.78-144).

11. King John's statement is printed and translated in D. Crouch "The Complaint of King John Against William de Briouze (c. September 1210)," in *Magna Carta and the England of King John*, ed. J. S. Loengard (Woodbridge, UK: 2010), 169–79.

12. The Treaty of Falaise, such as it is known from later transcriptions, appears in E. L. G. Stones, ed. and trans., *Anglo-Scottish Relations: 1174–1328: Some Selected Documents* (Edinburgh: 1965), 1–5. Richard's quitclaim of 1189 may be found in the same source at pages 6–8.

13. The latest discussion of the Treaty of Norham, along with a transcription of a letter from John discussing its terms, is to be found in D. A. Carpenter, *Magna Carta* (London: 2015), 237–41 and appendix I.

14. J. Holt, *The Northerners* (Oxford: 1961), 79.

Chapter 4: Crisis and Catastrophe

1. J. A. Giles, ed. and trans., *Roger of Wendover's Flowers of History*, vol. 2 (London: 1849), 274.

2. J. W. Baldwin, "Master Stephen Langton, Future Archbishop of Canterbury: The Paris Schools and Magna Carta," *English Historical Review* 123 (2008): 825.

3. J. C. Holt, *Magna Carta*, 2nd ed. (Cambridge: 1992), 190–91.

4. William the Breton's account of Bouvines may be found conveniently translated into English at http://deremilitari.org/2014/03/the-battle-of-bouvines-1214/, along with many other contemporary and near-contemporary accounts. See also J. Bradbury, *Philip Augustus: King of France 1180–1223* (London: 1998); and G. Duby, *The Legend of Bouvines: War, Religion and Culture in the Middle Ages* (Cambridge: 1990) for detailed accounts of the battle based on original sources.

5. See "The Marchiennes Account of the Battle of Bouvines," http://der emilitari.org/2014/03/the-battle-of-bouvines-1214.

6. Ibid.

7. Ibid.

8. A. J. Holden, S. Gregory, and D. Crouch, *History of William Marshal*, vol. 2 (London: 2004), 242–43. This was theoretically hearsay, as Marshal was not present at Bouvines. All the same, it is a pithy and accurate assessment.

9. Ibid.

Chapter 5: Trouble at the Temple

1. The *laudes* of Worcester is printed with musical notation in E. H. Kantorowicz, *Laudes Regiae: A Study in Liturgical Acclamations and Mediaeval Ruler Worship* (Berkeley: 1946), 217–19.

2. T. D. Hardy, ed., "Itinerary of King John," in *A Description of the Patent Rolls in the Tower of London* (London: 1835).

3. Gerald of Wales, *The Journey Through Wales* (Harmondsworth: 1976), 234–43.

4. According to Gerald of Wales, Henry II wrote this in a letter to Manuel Comnenus, Emperor of Constantinople. Ibid., 234.

5. D. A. Traill, ed. and trans., *Walter of Châtillon: The Shorter Poems: Christmas Hymns, Love Lyrics, and Moral-Satirical Verse* (Oxford: 2013), 84–85.

6. T. D. Hardy, ed., *Rotuli Litterarum Clausarum in Turri Londinensi asservati*, vol. 1 (London: 1833), 139.

7. S. Ambler, "Christmas at the Court of King John," Magna Carta Project, December 9, 2013, magnacartaresearch.blogspot.com/2013/12/christmas-at-court-of-king-john.html.

8. These recipes date from fourteenth- and fifteenth-century cooks' manuscripts. One of many useful modern editions of medieval recipes, complete with twenty-first-century adaptations for home cooking, is M. Black, *The Medieval Cookbook* (London: 1992).

9. Hardy, *Rotuli Litterarum Clausarum*, quoted in N. C. Vincent, "King John's Diary & Itinerary," Magna Carta Project, http://magnacarta.cmp.uea.ac.uk.

10. A month later Hugh de Neville claimed back from the Exchequer the money for the ninety beasts he brought to Worcester for the Christmas feasting. Hardy, *Rotuli Litterarum Clausarum*, 184.

11. See, for example, royal orders on January 29, 1215, ordering the distribution of barrels and casks of red and white wine across the realm, from Wallingford in the Thames valley to Wakefield in Yorkshire. Ibid., 185.

12. See, for example, archaeological findings in D. Keene, *Survey of Medieval Winchester*, vol. 1 (Oxford: 1985), 53.
13. "The City of Worcester: Introduction and Borough," *A History of the County of Worcester*, vol. 4 (London: 1924), 376–90 and n. 50.
14. J. A. Giles, ed. and trans., *Roger of Wendover's Flowers of History*, vol. 2 (Llanerch: 1849), 304.
15. On medieval roads see B. P. Hindle, *Medieval Roads and Tracks* (Oxford: 2008). On the legacy of Roman roads, however, see D. Harrison, *The Bridges of Medieval England* (Oxford: 2004), 48–52.
16. M. R. James, ed. and trans., *Walter Map: De Nugis Curialium, Courtiers' Trifles*, rev. C .N. L. Brooke and R. A. B. Mynors (Oxford: 1983), 370–71.
17. John's baggage train was infamously lost in the Wellstream, near the Wash in East Anglia, shortly before his death in 1216. For a convenient collation of chroniclers' accounts of the accident (and thus descriptions of John's baggage train itself) see W. L. Warren, *King John* (new ed.) (New Haven, CT: 1997): 278.
18. James, *Walter Map, De Nugis Curialium*, 477 and 103.
19. Nicholas Vincent suggests Guiting, correcting T. A. Hardy's earlier itinerary, which read "Geiting" as "Geddington," in Northamptonshire. Vincent, "King John's Diary & Itinerary."
20. Hardy, *Rotuli Litterarum Clausarum*, 182. The King of Norway at this time was Inge Bårdsson, also known as Inge II.
21. Fulk's legend may be read in modern translation in T. Ohlgren ed., *Medieval Outlaws: Ten Tales in Modern English* (Stroud, England: 1998).
22. J. Upton-Ward, *The Rule of the Templars* (Woodbridge, UK: 1992), 25, 30, 32, and 36.
23. R. Griffith-Jones and D. Park, *The Temple Church in London: History, Architecture and Art* (Woodbridge, UK: 2010), 4.
24. Ibid., 10
25. T. D. Hardy, *Rotuli Chartarum in Turri Londinensi asservati*, vol. 1 (London: 1837), 203–4.
26. J. A. Giles, ed., *Roger of Wendover's Flowers of History*, vol. 2 (Llanerch: 1849), 303–4.
27. Ibid.
28. D. C. Douglas, ed., *English Historical Documents* (2nd ed.), vol. 2 (London: 1981), 432–34.
29. On the Bury St Edmunds meeting Nicholas Vincent expresses strong doubts about "the entirely unsubstantiated account of a baronial meeting at Bury" as related by Wendover. N. C. Vincent, "King John's Diary & Itinerary," Magna Carta Project, http://magnacarta.cmp.uea.ac.uk/read/itinerary/Drama_and_jokes_at_Bury_St_Edmunds. D. A. Carpenter

makes a strong case for its happening on October 19. D. A. Carpenter, *Magna Carta* (London: 2015), 292. J. W. Baldwin argues for Langton's interest in the coronation charter and his suggestion to the English barons that it might form a basis for resistance from as early as the summer of 1213. J. W. Baldwin, "Master Stephen Langton, Future Archbishop of Canterbury: The Paris Schools and Magna Carta," *English Historical Review* 123 (2008).

30. W. Stubbs, ed., *Memoriale fratris Walteri de Coventria*, vol. 2 (London: 1872), 218.

31. T. D. Hardy, ed., *Rotuli litterarum patentium in Turri londinensi asservati* (London: 1835) 126, but note the important correction in N. C. Vincent, "The Conference at the New Temple, January 1215," Magna Carta Project, January 2015, http://magnacarta.cmp.uea.ac.uk/read/feature_of_the_month/Jan_2015.

Chapter 6: Taking the Cross

1. Matthew Paris's glorious map is in the British Library: "Historia Anglorum, Chronica majora, Part III," 1250–59, Royal MS 14 C VII, f2v–2r. It is digitized and may be viewed online at bl.uk/manuscripts/FullDisplay.aspx?ref=Royal_MS_14_c_vii. For a discussion of this and alternative routes to Rome, see D. A. Birch, *Pilgrimage to Rome in the Middle Ages* (Woodbridge, UK: 2000), 42–55.

2. P. Chaplais, *English Diplomatic Practice in the Middle Ages* (London: 2003), 28, trans. N. C. Vincent in "The Conference at the New Temple, January 1215," Magna Carta Project, http://magnacarta.cmp.uea.ac.uk/read/feature_of_the_month/Jan_2015_2.

3. C. M. Rosseau, "Neither Bewitched nor Beguiled: Philip Augustus's Alleged Impotence and Innocent III's Response," *Speculum* 89 (2014).

4. Dante Alighieri, *Paradiso*, canto XXXI:35–36.

5. Chaplais, *English Diplomatic Practice*, 28–29.

6. Ibid.

7. J. Stevenson, ed. and trans., *Gerald of Wales: On the Instruction of Princes* (London: 1858), 63.

8. According to the Arab historian Beha ed-Din and the anonymous Christian author of *De Expugatione Terrae Sanctae per Saladinium*. Both are printed and translated in A. Holt and J. Muldoon, *Competing Voices from the Crusades* (Oxford/Westport: 2008), 114–18.

9. A. J. Andrea, "Innocent III, the Fourth Crusade and the Coming Apocalypse," in S. J. Ridyard, *The Medieval Crusade* (Woodbridge, UK: 2004), 105.

10. W. Stubbs, *Memoriale fratris Walteri de Coventria*, vol. 2 (London: 1872), 219.

11. J. Bird, E. Peters, and J. M. Powell, *Crusade and Christendom: Annotated Documents in Translation from Innocent III to the Fall of Acre, 1187–1291* (Philadelphia: 2013), 114–19.

12. V. G. Berry ed. and trans., *Odo of Deuil, De profectione Ludovici VII in Orientem* (New York: 1948), 14–19.

13. R. C. Finucane, *Soldiers of the Faith: Crusaders and Moslems at War* (London: 1983), 42.

14. P. A. Throop, *Criticism of the Crusade: A Study of Public Opinion and Crusade Propaganda* (Amsterdam: 1940), 103.

15. J. Stevenson, ed. and trans. *Gerald of Wales on the Instruction of Princes* (London: 1858), 21.

16. N. Housley, *Fighting for the Cross* (New Haven, CT/London: 2008), 53.

17. Printed in K. Pennington, "The Rite for Taking the Cross in the Twelfth Century," *Traditio* 30 (1974); translated in Bird, Peters, and Powell, *Crusade and Christendom*, 42–47.

18. T. D. Hardy, *Rotuli Litterarum Clausarum in Turri Londinensi asservati*, vol. 1 (London: 1833), 188–92.

19. Ibid., 184–85, 189, 191.

20. Ibid., 191.

Chapter 7: Confrontation

1. H. J. Feasey, *Ancient English Holy Week Ceremonial* (London: 1897), passim; R. Hutton, *Stations of the Sun: A History of the Ritual Year in Britain* (Oxford: 1997), 182–97.

2. Ibid, 114–15.

3. T. D. Hardy, *Rotuli Litterarum Clausarum in Turri Londinensi asservati*, vol. 1 (London: 1833), 196.

4. Ibid., 195.

5. Ibid.

6. D. C. Carpenter, *Magna Carta* (London: 2015), 298.

7. C. R. Cheney and W. H. Semple, *Selected Letters of Pope Innocent III Concerning England (1198–1216)* (Edinburgh: 1953), 194–95.

8. Ibid, 196.

9. F. Michel, ed., *Histoire des ducs de Normandie et des rois d'Angleterre* (Paris: 1840), 115.

10. W. Stubbs, ed., *Memoriale fratris Walteri de Coventria*, vol. 2, (London: 1872), 219.

11. F. Michel, ed., *Histoire des ducs de Normandie et des rois d'Angleterre* (Paris: 1840), 145. On the naming of the Northerners more generally see J. C. Holt, *The Northerners* (Oxford: 1961), 8–16.

12. J. A. Giles, ed. and trans., *Roger of Wendover's Flowers of History*, vol. 2 (Llanerch: 1849), 305.

13. A. J. Holden, S. Gregory, and D. Crouch, eds. and trans., *History of William Marshal*, vol. 2 (London: 2004), 63, 65, 121.

14. A. J. Holden, S. Gregory, and D. Crouch, eds. and trans., *History of William Marshal*, vol. 1 (London: 2002) , 83–95.

15. Giles, *Roger of Wendover's Flowers of History*, 306.

16. The Unknown Charter is held at the Archives Nationales in Paris, where it is classified J.655. It is printed in Latin and discussed in J. C. Holt, *Magna Carta* (2nd ed.) (Cambridge: 1992), 418–28, where its provenance is dated to between January and June 1215. An English translation of John's supposed concessions is in H. Rothwell, ed., *English Historical Documents III, 1189–1327* (London/New York: 1975), 310–11. David Carpenter suggests that the Unknown Charter was written sometime between the New Temple meeting in January and the fall of London on May 17 and errs toward an earlier date within this window. Carpenter, *Magna Carta*, 314.

17. D. Starkey, *Magna Carta: The True Story Behind the Charter* (London: 2015), 40–42, suggests a date shortly after May 10 for the production of the Unknown Charter, seeing it as a response to John's suggestion of a commission of arbitration, headed by the pope, which was made on May 9.

18. Giles, *Roger of Wendover's Flowers of History*, 306.

19. John's offers of reconciliation were described in a letter to the pope the following month, printed in T. Rymer, ed., *Foedera, Conventiones, Litterae et cujuscumque generis Acta Publica*, etc., I.i (The Hague: 1745), 66–67.

20. Cheney and Semple, *Selected Letters of Pope Innocent III*, 214–15.

21. M. Tyson, "The Annals of Southwark and Merton," *Surrey Archaeological Collections* 36 (1925): 49.

22. Both are printed in Latin in Holt, *Magna Carta*, 492–93.

23. Hardy, *Rotuli Litterarum Clausarum*, 204.

Chapter 8: London

1. W. Stubbs, *Memoriale Fratris Walteri De Coventria*, vol. 2 (London: 1873), 219.

2. J. A. Giles, ed., *Roger of Wendover's Flowers of History*, vol. 2 (Llanerch: 1849), 307.

3. On Northampton Castle see H. M. Colvin, ed., *The History of the King's Works II* (London: 1963), 750–53, and W. Page, ed., "The Borough of Northampton: Description," in *A History of the County of Northampton*, vol. 3 (London: 1930), 30–40.

4. N. C. Vincent, "King John's Diary & Itinerary: 15–24 February," Magna Carta Project, http://magnacarta.cmp.uea.ac.uk, citing N. C. Vincent, "The

Seals of King Henry II and his Court," in *Seals and Their Context in the Middle Ages*, ed. P. R. Schofield (Oxford: 2015), 7–33, esp. 17, figure 2.11, and 19.

5. T. D. Hardy, *Rotuli litterarum patentium in Turri londinensi asservati* (London: 1835), 129.

6. Geoffrey de Martigny would be named in clause 50 of the Magna Carta as one of the kinsmen of Gérard d'Athée who was to be removed from England. The others included Engelard de Cigogné; Peter, Guy, and Andrew de Chanceaux; Guy de Cigogné; Martigny's brothers; and Philip Marc and his brothers and a nephew called Geoffrey.

7. Giles, *Roger of Wendover's Flowers of History*, 307. William de Beauchamp was one of the rebels who were excommunicated by Pope Innocent III for defying John.

8. Ibid.

9. A. J. Holden, S. Gregory, and D. Crouch, eds. and trans., *History of William Marshal*, vol. 2 (London: 2004), 255.

10. Wendover erroneously gives the date as Sunday, May 24.

11. Giles, *Roger of Wendover's Flowers of History*, 307.

12. Ibid. See also Stubbs, *Memoriale Fratris Walteri De Coventria*, 220.

13. C. Dyer, "The Economy and Society," in *The Oxford Illustrated History of Medieval England*, ed. N. Saul (Oxford: 1997), 155.

14. A. J. Holden, S. Gregory, and D. Crouch, eds. and trans., *History of William Marshal*, vol. 1 (London: 2002), 482–83.

15. Fitzstephen's description of London is printed in slightly truncated form in D. C. Douglas, et al., eds. *English Historical Documents*, vol. 2, 2nd ed. (London: 1981), 1024–30, and in its full Latin transcription in J. C. Robertson, *Materials for the History of Thomas Becket*, vol. 3 (London: 1877), 2–13.

16. T. Baker, *Medieval London* (London: 1970), 163–67.

17. T. H. Ohlgren, ed., *Medieval Outlaws: Twelve Tales in Modern English Translation* (Stroud, England: 1998), 144.

18. L. Thorpe, ed. and trans., *Geoffrey of Monmouth: The History of the Kings of Britain* (London: 1966), 262.

19. T. D. Hardy, *A Description of the Patent Rolls* (London: 1835), 67–68.

20. J. Schofield, *London 1100–1600: The Archaeology of a Capital City* (Sheffield, UK: 2011), 159–62.

21. Ibid., 109.

22. M. D. Lobel, *Historic Towns Atlas: The City of London From Prehistoric Times to c. 1520*, vol. 3 (Oxford: 1989), 31.

23. J. T. Appleby, *The Chronicle of Richard of Devizes of the Time of King Richard the First* (London: 1963), 64–67.

24. H. T. Riley, ed., *Chronicles of the Mayors and Sheriffs of London: 1188–1274* (London: 1863), 179–87.

25. Ibid., 1–8.

26. The assize is translated in H. Rothwell, ed., *English Historical Documents III, 1189–1327* (London/New York: 1975), 849–54.

27. R. Bartlett, *England Under the Norman and Angevin Kings: 1075–1225* (Oxford, 2000): 345.

28. H. M. Chew and M. Weinbaum, eds., *The London Eyre of 1244* (London: 1970), items 40 and 180.

29. Ibid., items 121, 48, 85, 57, and 71.

30. Douglas, et al., eds. *English Historical Documents*, 1024.

31. Stubbs, *Memoriale Fratris Walteri De Coventria*, 220.

32. For a concise survey of London's relationship with the Norman and Plantagenet kings, see Bartlett, *England Under the Norman and Angevin Kings*, 342–44.

33. Giles, *Roger of Wendover's Flowers of History*, 307–8.

34. Hardy, *Rotuli litterarum patentium*, 138, 142.

Chapter 9: Runnymede

1. A. D. Mills, *A Dictionary of British Place Names* (Oxford: 2011). Thanks to Dr. Kate Wiles for this reference and for her advice on the origins of Runnymede's name.

2. H. R. Luard, *Matthew Paris: Flores Historiarum*, vol. 2 (London: 1890), 153.

3. J. R. Maddicott, "Edward the Confessor's Return to England in 1041," *English Historical Review* 119 (2004): 661–63.

4. J. Stevenson, *Radulphi de Coggeshall Chronicon Anglicanum* (London: 1875), 172.

5. T. D. Hardy, *Rotuli Litterarum Clausarum in Turri Londinensi asservati*, vol. 1 (London: 1833), 193.

6. H. M. Colvin, *The History of the King's Works*, vol. 2 (London: 1963), 864–65.

7. H. R. Luard, *Matthaei Parisiensis, Monachi Sancti Albani: Chronica Majora* (London: 1872–73), 611.

8. Hardy, *Rotuli Litterarum Clausarum*, 213–14.

9. Ibid., 213.

10. Ibid., 214.

11. The Articles of the Barons are printed in Latin in J. C. Holt, *Magna Carta* (2nd ed.) (Cambridge: 1992), 429–40, and in English in H. Rothwell, ed., *English Historical Documents III 1189–1327* (new ed.) (London/New York: 1996), 311–16.

12. D. A. Carpenter, "The Dating and Making of Magna Carta," in *The Reign of Henry III* (London/New York: 1996), 16; D. A. Carpenter, *Magna Carta* (London: 2015), 342.

13. R. M. Thompson, ed. and trans., *The Chronicle of the Election of Hugh, Abbot of Bury St Edmunds and Later Bishop of Ely* (Oxford: 1974), 170–71. Hugh's purpose in visiting the king was to attempt to achieve royal approval for his election to the abbacy: a tortuous process that took the best part of three years to achieve.

14. Ibid.

15. Carpenter, *Magna Carta*, 361.

16. Revelations 4:1–11.

Chapter 10: The Magna Carta

1. D. A. Carpenter, *Magna Carta* (London: 2015), 366–67.

2. This secondary agreement is printed in J. C. Holt, *Magna Carta*, 2nd ed. (Cambridge: 1992), 490–91.

3. W. Stubbs, ed., *Memoriale fratris Walteri de Coventria*, vol. 2 (London: 1872), 222.

4. Ibid., 221.

5. T. D. Hardy, *Rotuli Litterarum Clausarum in Turri Londinensi asservati*, vol. 1 (London: 1833), 215.

6. T. D. Hardy, ed., *Rotuli litterarum patentium in Turri londinensi asservati* (London: 1835), 144.

7. J. A. Giles, ed., *Roger of Wendover's Flowers of History*, vol. 2 (Llanerch: 1849), 338.

8. Carpenter, *Magna Carta*, 388–89.

9. Printed in Holt, *Magna Carta*, 498.

10. F. Michel, ed., *Histoire des ducs de Normandie et des rois d'Angleterre* (Paris: 1840), 151.

11. H. R. Luard, *Matthaei Parisiensis, Monachi Sancti Albani: Chronica Majora*, vol. 2 (London: 1874), 611.

12. H. R. Luard, *Annales Monastici*, vol. 3 (London: 1866), 43.

13. C. R. Cheney and W. H. Semple, eds., *Selected Letters of Pope Innocent III Concerning England (1198–1216)* (London: 1953), 212–16.

Chapter 11: England Under Siege

1. H. R. Luard, *Annales Monastici*, vol. 3 (London: 1864), 44.
2. For this and the account that follows see J. A. Giles, *Roger of Wendover's Flowers of History*, vol. 2, (London: 1849), 336; W. Stubbs, ed., *Memoriale fratris Walteri de Coventria*, vol. 2 (London: 1873), 226.
3. Giles, *Roger of Wendover's Flowers of History*, 337.
4. L. J. Downer, ed. and trans., *Leges Henrici Primi* (Oxford: 1972), 109, 117.
5. H. M. Colvin, ed., *The History of the King's Works* (London: 1963), 59–60.
6. For an overview of castles and castle building in this age see ibid., 64–81, which follows R. A. Brown, "Royal Castle-Building in England, 1154–1216," *English Historical Review* 70 (1955): 353–98. See also R. A. Brown, *Allen Brown's English Castles* (new ed.) (Woodbridge, UK: 2004), chapter 3, 34–63.
7. R. A. Brown, "Rochester Castle," in *Castles of England and Wales* (Woodbridge, UK: 2004), supp. 1, 8–10.
8. Giles, *Roger of Wendover's Flowers of History*, 335.
9. See, for example, the great square keep at Dover Castle, ninety-five feet in height, with a splayed base and original entrances on the first and second floors. Dover was constructed in the 1180s by John's father, Henry II, and was subsequently improved by John.
10. Giles, *Roger of Wendover's Flowers of History*, 335.
11. Ibid.
12. Ibid.
13. Ibid., 336.
14. J. Bradbury, *The Medieval Siege* (Woodbridge, UK: 1992), 10–11. This seems extremely unlikely but is at least intended to be symbolic of the horrendous conditions outside the walls of the city.
15. Stubbs, *Memoriale fratris Walteri de Coventria*, 226.
16. Giles, *Roger of Wendover's Flowers of History*, 337–38.
17. T. D. Hardy, *Rotuli Litterarum Clausarum in Turri Londinensi Asservati*, vol. 1 (London: 1837), 238.
18. Giles, *Roger of Wendover's Flowers of History*, 338.
19. Ibid., 338–39.
20. Ibid., 339.
21. Ibid.

Chapter 12: Endgame

1. An English translation of the Canons of the Fourth Lateran Council may be found in H. Rothwell, ed., *English Historical Documents, 1189–1327* (London/New York: 1975), 643–76.

2. M. R. James, ed. and trans., rev. C. N. L. Brooke and R. A. B. Mynors, *Walter Map: De Nugis Curialium: Courtiers' Trifles* (Oxford: 1983), 118–21.

3. This translation from Peter of Cornwall's *Liber revelationum* may be found in R. Bartlett, *England Under the Norman and Angevin Kings, 1075–1225* (Oxford: 2000), 478.

4. M. H. Kerr, R. D. Forsyth, and M. J. Plyley, "Cold Water and Hot Iron: Trial by Ordeal in England," *Journal of Interdisciplinary History* 22 (1992): 582–83.

5. On this subject in general see M. Rubin, *Corpus Christi: The Eucharist in Late Medieval Culture* (Cambridge: 1991).

6. J. A. Giles, *Roger of Wendover's Flowers of History*, vol. 2 (London: 1849), 344.

7. C. R. Cheney and W. H. Semple, *Selected Letters of Pope Innocent III Concerning England (1198–1216)* (London: 1953), 220.

8. Giles, *Roger Wendover's Flowers of History*, 348.

9. Ibid.

10. A. J. Holden, S. Gregory, and D. Crouch, eds. and trans., *History of William Marshal*, vol. 2 (London: 2004), 255–56.

11. W. Stubbs, *Memoriale fratris Walteri de Coventria*, vol. 2 (London: 1872), 227.

12. J. D. Hosler, "Mercenaries," in *The Oxford Encyclopedia of Medieval Warfare and Military Technology*, vol. 3, ed. C. J. Rogers (Oxford: 2010), 1–3.

13. James, Brook, and Mynors, *Walter Map*, 118.

14. Holden, Gregory, and Crouch, *History of William Marshal*, vol. 2 (London: 2004), 256–57.

15. See, for example, T. D. Hardy, *Rotuli Litterarum Clausarum in Turri Londinensi asservati*, vol. 1 (London: 1833), 238.

16. Giles, *Roger Wendover's Flowers of History*, 349.

17. C. Dyer, *Everyday Life in Medieval England* (new ed.) (London/New York: 2000), 134.

18. Bartlett, *England Under the Norman and Angevin Kings*, 184.

19. C. T. Flower, *Curia Regis Rolls of the Reigns of Richard I and John*, VII (London: 1935), 467–68.

20. British Library Add MS 8167, transcribed and translated in M. Carlin and D. Crouch, eds. and trans., *Lost Letters of Medieval Life: English Society, 1200–1250* (Philadelphia: 2013), 274–77.

21. Bartlett, *England Under the Norman and Angevin Kings*, 252.

22. Translation from M. Bennett, "Wace and Warfare," in *Anglo-Norman Warfare: Studies in Late Anglo-Saxon and Anglo-Norman Military Organization and Warfare*, ed. M. Strickland (Woodbridge, UK: 1992), 233.

23. This biblical wisdom was noted by the royal treasurer Richard FitzNigel in the introduction to his *Dialogue of the Exchequer*. E. Amt and S. D.

Church, eds. and trans., *Dialogus de Scaccario and Constitutio Domus Regis* (new ed.) (Oxford: 2007), 3.

24. J. Stevenson, ed., *Radulphi de Coggeshall Chronicon Anglicanum* (London: 1875), 177.

25. Holden, Gregory, and Crouch, *History of William Marshal*, vol. 2 (London: 2004), 256–57.

26. Ibid., 256–59.

27. On John's losses in the Wash, including these translations of Coggeshall and Wendover, see W. L. Warren, *King John* (new ed.) (London/New Haven, CT: 1997), appendix C, 278–85.

28. Translation from D. A. Carpenter, *Magna Carta* (London: 2015), 405.

29. Holden, Gregory, and Crouch, *History of William Marshal*, vol. 2 (London: 2004), 260–61.

30. R. Darlington, *The Vita Wulfstani of William of Malmesbury: To Which Are Added the Extant Abridgements of This Work and the Miracles and Translation of St. Wulfstan* (London: 1928), 35–43 passim.

31. V. Green, *An Account of the Discovery of the Body of King John in the Cathedral Church of Worcester, July 17, 1797, from Authentic Communications, with Illustrations and Remarks* (London/Worcester: 1797): 4–5; Carpenter, *Magna Carta*, 406, identifies this as perhaps being the cap of unction worn by the king at his coronation.

32. H. R. Luard, ed., *Matthaei Parisiensis, Monachi Sancti Albani: Chronica Majora*, vol. 2 (London: 1873), 669.

Chapter 13: The Magna Carta Reborn

1. A. J. Holden, S. Gregory, and D. Crouch, eds. and trans., *History of William Marshal*, vol. 2 (London: 2004), 256–57.

2. J. A. Giles, *Roger of Wendover's Flowers of History*, vol. 2 (London: 1849), 205.

3. The text of the Charter of the Forest is translated and printed in D. C. Douglas, et al., eds., *English Historical Documents III 1189–1327* (London: 1975), 337–40.

4. Holden, Gregory, and Crouch, *History of William Marshal*, vol. 2 (London: 2004), 406–7.

5. The 1225 edition of the Magna Carta is translated and printed in Douglas, et al., *English Historical Documents*, 341–49.

6. F. Hill, "Magna Carta and Excommunication in 1253," Magna Carta Project, May 2014, http://magnacartaresearch.blogspot.co.uk/2014/05/magna-carta-and-excommunication-in-1253.html.

7. D. Carpenter, "The Cerne Abbey Magna Carta," Magna Carta Project, April 2014, http://magnacartaresearch.org/read/feature_of_the_month/ Apr_2014.

8. Matthew Paris's account of this episode may be found in H. Luard, *Matthaei Parisiensis, monachi Sancti Albani Chronica Majora*, vol. 4 (London: 1873), 185–87.

9. S. Ambler, "Henry III's Confirmation of Magna Carta in March 1265," Magna Carta Project, March 2014, http://magnacarta.cmp.uea.ac.uk/ read/feature_of_the_month/Mar_2014.

Chapter 14: Then and Now

1. C. Given-Wilson, et al., eds., *Parliament Rolls of Medieval England*, January 1497, item 9, http://british-history.ac.uk/no-series/parliament -rolls-medieval.

2. Pynson's book is held in the British Library under classmark BL C.112.a.2.

3. On Tudor attempts to rehabilitate John see C. Levin, "A Good Prince: King John and Early Tudor Propaganda," *Sixteenth Century Journal* 11 (1980): 24–25.

4. The manuscript is British Library Cotton Titus B I f.430r. It is printed in C. Breay and J. Harrison, eds., *Magna Carta: Law, Liberty, Legacy* (London: 2015), 116.

5. Levin, "A Good Prince," 29 –31.

6. Coke is quoted in F. Thompson, *Magna Carta: Its Role in the Making of the English Constitution 1300–1629* (Minneapolis: 1948), 302.

7. A. Cromartie, "The Constitutionalist Revolution: The Transformation of Political Culture in Early Stuart England," *Past & Present* 163 (May 1999): 101.

8. R. V. Turner, "The Meaning of Magna Carta Since 1215," *History Today* 53 (2003), http://www.historytoday.com/ralph-v-turner/meaning-magna-carta -1215.

9. The full text of Mandela's speech is to be found on the African National Congress Web site at http://www.anc.org.za/show.php?id=3430.

10. David Cameron, "British Values Aren't Optional, They're Vital. That's Why I Will Promote Them in EVERY School," *Daily Mail*, June 15, 2014, http:// www.dailymail.co.uk/debate/article-2658171/DAVID -CAMERON-British-values-arent-optional-theyre-vital-Thats-I-promote -EVERY-school-As-row-rages-Trojan-Horse-takeover-classrooms-Prime -Minister-delivers-uncompromising-pledge.html.

11. See, for example, an interview with Web pioneer Tim Berners-Lee: J. Kiss, "An Online Magna Carta: Berners-Lee Calls for Bill of Rights for Web,"

Guardian, March 12, 2014, http://www.theguardian.com/technology/2014/mar/12/online-magna-carta-berners-lee-web.

12. A. Rickell, "A New Magna Carta," disabilitynow, 2009, http://www.disabilitynow.org.uk/article/new-magna-carta; T. Kahle, "Miners for Democracy and the Planet," SocialistWorker.org, June 24, 2014, http://socialistworker.org/2014/06/24/miners-fighting-for-the-planet; J. Casillas, "Magna Carta for Medical Banking," HIMSS, no date, http://www.himss.org/files/HIMSSorg/content/files/medicalBankingProject/MBP_Magna_Carta_Aligning_Banks_Healthcare.pdf; J. Galolo, "BPOs, Workers Back Proposal to Exempt OT, Graveyard Pay from Taxes," *Sun Star Cebu*, July 7, 2014, http://www.sunstar.com.ph/cebu/business/2014/07/07/bpos-workers-back-proposal-exempt-ot-graveyard-pay-taxes-352400.

Bibliography

Primary

Amt, E., and S. D. Church, eds. and trans. *Dialogus de Scaccario and Constitutio Domus Regis*. New ed., Oxford: Oxford University Press, 2007.

Appleby, J. T. *The Chronicle of Richard of Devizes of the Time of King Richard the First*. London: Thomas Nelson and Sons, 1963.

Berry, V. G., ed. and trans. *Odo of Deuil, De profectione Ludovici VII in Orientem*. New York: W. W. Norton, 1948.

Bird, J., E. Peters, and J. M. Powell. *Crusade and Christendom: Annotated Documents in Translation from Innocent III to the Fall of Acre 1187–1291*. Philadelphia: University of Pennsylvania Press, 2013.

Brewer J, S., J. F. Dimock, and G. F. Warner. *Giraldus Cambrensis, Opera*. London: Longman, 1879–80.

Carlin, M., and D. Crouch. *Lost Letters of Medieval Life*. Philadelphia: University of Pennsylvania Press, 2013.

Chaplais, P., ed. *Diplomatic Documents Preserved in the Public Record Office*. London: H. M. Stationery Office, 1964.

Cheney, C. R., and W. H. Semple, eds. *Selected Letters of Pope Innocent III Concerning England (1198–1216)*. London: Thomas Nelson and Sons, 1953.

Chew, H. M., and M. Weinbaum, eds. *The London Eyre of 1244*. London: London Record Society, 1970.

Craw, W. "An Edition of the Histoire des ducs de Normandie et rois d'Angleterre Contained in the French MS.56 of the John Rylands Library, Manchester University." PhD thesis, University of Glasgow, 1999.

Darlington, R., ed. *The Vita Wulfstani of William of Malmesbury: To Which Are Added the Extant Abridgements of This Work and the Miracles and Translation of St. Wulfstan*. London: Offices of the Society, 1928.

Douglas, D. C., et al., eds. *English Historical Documents*. Vol. 2. 2nd ed., London: Metheun, 1981.

———. *English Historical Documents III 1189–1327*. London: Eyre & Spottiswoode, 1975.

Dubin, N. E. *The Fabliaux*. New York/London: W. W. Norton, 2013.

Fairweather, J., ed. and trans. *Liber Eliensis: A History of the Isle of Ely*. Woodbridge, UK: Boydell Press, 2005.

Fallows, N. *The Book of the Order of Chivalry by Ramon Llull*. Woodbridge, UK/Rochester, NY: Boydell Press, 2013.

Flavius Vegetius Renatus, *De Re Militari* [Concerning Military Affairs]. Driffield, UK: Leonaur Press, 2012.

Flower, C. T., et al. *Curia Regis Rolls of the Reigns of Richard I and John.* London: Stationery Office, 1922.

Garmonsway, G. M. *The Anglo-Saxon Chronicle.* 2nd ed., London: Everyman Press, 1972.

Giles, J. A., ed. and trans. *Matthew Paris's English History.* London: Henry G. Bohn, 1852–54.

———. *Roger of Wendover's Flowers of History.* London: Henry G. Bohn, 1849.

———, ed. and trans. *William of Malmesbury's Chronicle of the Kings of England.* London: Henry G. Bohn, 1847.

Hardy, T. D. *A Description of the Patent Rolls in the Tower of London.* London: Record Commission, 1835.

———. *Rotuli Chartarum in Turri Londinensi asservati I 1199–1216.* London: Record Commission, 1837.

———, ed. *Rotuli Litterarum Clausarum in Turri Londinensi asservati.* London: Record Commission, 1833–34.

———, ed. *Rotuli litterarum patentium in Turri londinensi asservati.* London: Record Commission, 1835.

Holden, A. J., S. Gregory, and D. Crouch. *History of William Marshal.* Oxford: Anglo-Norman Text Society, 2002–6.

Holt, A., and J. Muldoon, *Competing Voices from the Crusades.* Oxford/Westport, NY: Greenwood World Publishing, 2008.

James, M. R., ed. and trans. Revised by C. N. L. Brooke and R. A. B. Mynors. *Walter Map: De Nugis Curialium: Courtiers' Trifles.* Oxford: Clarendon Press, 1983.

Luard, H. R., ed. *Annales Monastici.* London: Longman, 1864–69.

———. *Flores Historiarum: Matthew Paris.* London: 1890.

———, ed. *Matthaei Parisiensis, Monachi Sancti Albani: Chronica Majora.* London: H. M. Stationery Office, 1872–73.

Michel, F., ed. *Histoire des ducs de Normandie et des Rois d'Angleterre.* Paris: Chez Jules Renovard, 1840.

Riley, H. T., ed. *The Annals of Roger de Hoveden: Comprising the History of England, and of Other Countries of Europe from AD 732 to AD 1201.* London: Henry G. Bohn, 1853.

———, ed. *Chronicles of the Mayors and Sheriffs of London: 1188–1274.* London: Trübner and Co., 1863.

Robertson, J. C., ed. *Materials for the History of Thomas Becket.* Rolls Series. London: Longman, 1875–1885.

Rymer, T., ed. *Fœdera, conventiones, literæ, et cujuscunque generis acta publica.* Vol. I.i. The Hague: Neaulme, 1745.

Stevenson, J. *Chronica de Mailros.* Edinburgh: Typis Societatis Edinburgensis, 1835.

———, ed. and trans. *The Church Historians of England.* Pre-Reformation Series. London: Seeley, 1853.

———, ed. and trans. *Gerald of Wales on the Instruction of Princes.* London: Seeley, 1858.

———. *Raduphi de Coggeshall Chronicon Anglicanum.* London: Longman, 1875.

Stubbs, W. *The Historical Works of Gervase of Canterbury.* London: Longman, 1872–73.

———. *Memoriale fratris Walteri de Coventria.* London: Longman, 1872.

Thomson, R. M. *The Chronicle of the Election of Hugh, Abbot of Bury St Edmunds and Later Bishop of Ely.* Oxford: Clarendon Press, 1974.

Thorpe, L., ed. and trans, *Geoffrey of Monmouth: The History of the Kings of Britain.* London: Penguin Books, 1966.

Traill, D. A., ed. and trans. *Walter of Châtillon: The Shorter Poems: Christmas Hymns, Love Lyrics, and Moral-Satirical Verse.* Oxford: Oxford University Press, 2013.

Tyson, M., "The Annals of Southwark and Merton," *Surrey Archaeological Collections* 36 (1925): 24–57.

Walsh, P., and M. Kennedy, eds. and trans. *William of Newburgh: The History of English Affairs.* Warminster UK: Aris & Phillips, 1998–2007.

Secondary

Baker, T. *Medieval London.* London: Littlehampton, 1970.

Barron, C. M. *London in the Later Middle Ages: Government and People, 1200–1500.* Oxford: Oxford University Press, 2004.

Bartlett, R. *England Under the Norman and Angevin Kings.* Oxford: Oxford University Press, 2000.

———. *Trial by Fire and Water.* Oxford: Clarendon Press, 1986.

Benham, W. *Old St Paul's Cathedral.* London: Seeley, 1902.

Bradbury, J. *The Medieval Siege.* Woodbridge, UK: Boydell and Brewer, 1992.

———. *Philip Augustus: King of France 1180–1223.* London: Longman, 1998.

Breay, C., and J. Harrison. *Magna Carta: Law, Liberty, Legacy.* London: British Library, 2015.

Brown, A. R. *Allen Brown's English Castles.* New ed., Woodbridge, UK: Boydell Press, 2004.

Burke, J. *Life in the Castle in Medieval England.* London: British Heritage Press, 1978.

Canning J., and O. G. Oexle, eds. *Political Thought and the Realities of Power in the Middle Ages.* Göttingen: Vandenhock & Ruprecht, 1998.

Carlin, M. *Medieval Southwark.* London: Hambledon Press, 1996.

Carpenter, D. A. *Magna Carta.* London: Penguin Books, 2015.

———. *The Reign of Henry III.* London/New York: A & C Black, 1996.

Castles of England and Wales, Supplement I.

Chaplais, P. *English Medieval Diplomatic Practice.* London: H. M. Stationery Office, 1975–82.

Church, S. D. *King John: England, Magna Carta and the Making of a Tyrant.* London: Macmillan, 2015.

———. *King John: New Interpretations.* Woodbridge, UK: Boydell Press, 1999.

Clarke, P. D. *The Interdict in the Thirteenth Century: A Question of Collective Guilt.* Oxford: Oxford University Press 2007.

Colvin, H. M., ed. *The History of the King's Works.* Vol. 1. London: H. M. Stationery Office, 1963.

Crouch, D. *The English Aristocracy 1070–1272: A Social Transformation.* New Haven, CT/London: Yale University Press, 2011.

Dodson, A. *The Royal Tombs of Great Britain: An Illustrated History.* London: Duckworth, 2004.

Duby, G. *The Legend of Bouvines: War, Religion and Culture in the Middle Ages.* Berkeley: University of California Press, 1990.

Dyer, C. *Everyday Life in Medieval England.* New ed., London/New York: A & C Black, 2000.

Feasy, H. J. *Ancient English Holy Week Ceremonial.* London: Thomas Baker, 1897.

Gravett, C. *Norman Stone Castles (2): Europe 950–1204.* Oxford: Osprey Publishing, 2004.

Green, V. *An Account of the Discovery of the Body of King John in the Cathedral Church of Worcester, July 17, 1797, from Authentic Communications, with Illustrations and Remarks.* London/Worcester: V. and R. Green, 1797.

Griffith-Jones, R., and D. Park, eds., *The Temple Church in London: History, Art and Architecture.* Woodbridge, UK: Boydell Press, 2010.

Haag, M. *The Templars: History and Myth.* London: Harper 2008.

Harper-Bill, C., and N. Vincent, eds. *Henry II: New Interpretations.* Woodbridge, UK: Profile Books, 2007.

Harrison, D. *The Bridges of Medieval England: Transport and Society, 400–1800.* Oxford: Oxford University Press, 2004.

Harvey, J. H. *The Medieval Architect.* Wayland: St. Martin's Press, 1972.

Hiley, D. *Western Plainchant: A Handbook.* Oxford: Clarendon Press, 1993.

Hindle, B. P. *Medieval Roads and Tracks.* Princes Risborough: Shire, 1998.

Holt, J. C. *Magna Carta.* Cambridge: Cambridge University Press, 1992.

———. *The Northerners: A Study in the Reign of King John.* Oxford: Oxford University Press, 1961.

Hughes, R. *Rome.* London: Vintage 2011.

Hunt R. W., and M. Gibson. *The Schools and the Cloister: The Life and Writings of Alexander Nequam (1157–1217).* Oxford: Clarendon Press, 1984.

Hutton, R. *The Stations of the Sun: A History of the Ritual Year in Britain.* Oxford: Oxford University Press, 1996.

Jobson, A., ed. *English Government in the Thirteenth Century.* Martlesham, UK: Boydell Press, 2004.

Jones, D. *Magna Carta: The Making and Legacy of the Great Charter.* London: Head of Zeus, 2014.

Jope, E. M., ed. *Studies in Building History: Essays in Recognition of the Work of B.H. St. J. O'Neil.* London: Odhams Press, 1961.

Kantorowicz, E. H. *Laudes regiae: A Study in Liturgical Acclamations and Mediaeval Ruler Worship.* Berkeley, CA: University of California Press, 1958.

Keen, M. *Medieval Warfare: A History.* Oxford: Oxford University Press, 1999.

Keene, D. *Survey of Medieval Winchester.* Oxford: Oxford University Press, 1985.

Labarge, M. W. *A Baronial Household of the Thirteenth Century.* Brighton, UK: Eyre & Spottiswoode 1965.

Lobel, M. D. *Historic Towns Atlas: The City of London From Prehistoric Times to c.1520.* Vol. 3. Oxford: Oxford University Press, 1989.

Loengard, J. S., ed. *Magna Carta and the England of King John.* Woodbridge, UK: Boydell Press, 2010.

MacCulloch, D. *A History of Christianity.* London: Viking, 2009.

McGrail, S. *Boats of the World: From the Stone Age to Medieval Times.* Oxford: Oxford University Press, 2004.

McLynn, F. *Lionheart & Lackland: King Richard, King John and the Wars of Conquest.* London: Vintage, 2007.

McSheffrey, S. *Marriage, Sex and Civic Culture in Late Medieval London.* Philadelphia: University of Pennsylvania Press, 2006.

Malden, H. E., ed. *Magna Carta Commemoration Essays.* London: Royal Historical Society, 1917.

Moore, J. C. *Pope Innocent III: To Root Up and Plant.* Leiden, The Netherlands: Brill, 2003.

Norwich, J. J. *The Popes: A History.* London: Chatto & Windus, 2011.

Piponnier, F., and P. Mane. *Dress in the Middle Ages.* Translated by C. Beamish. New Haven, CT/London: Yale University Press, 1997.

Postles, D. *Naming the People of England, c.1100–1350.* Newcastle, UK: Cambridge Scholars Press, 2006.

Purton, P. *A History of the Late Medieval Siege.* Woodbridge, UK: Boydell Press, 2010.

Robinson, J. *Masterpieces of Medieval Art.* London: British Museum Press, 2008.

Rogers, C. J. *The Oxford Encyclopedia of Medieval Warfare and Military Technology.* Oxford: Oxford University Press, 2010.

Rubin, M. *Corpus Christi: The Eucharist in Late Medieval Culture.* Cambridge: Cambridge University Press, 1991.

Sandoz, E. *The Roots of Liberty: Magna Carta, Ancient Constitution and the Anglo-American Tradition of Rule of Law.* Indianapolis, IN: Liberty Fund, 1993.

Schofield, J. *London 1100–1600.* Sheffield UK: Equinox Publishing, 2011.

Serjeantson, D., and H. Rees. *Food, Craft and Status in Medieval Winchester.* Winchester: Winchester Museums, 2009.

Starkey, D. *Magna Carta: The True Story Behind the Charter.* London: Hodder & Stoughton, 2015.

Strickland, M., ed. *Anglo-Norman Warfare: Studies in Late Anglo-Saxon and Anglo-Norman Military Organization and Warfare.* Woodbridge, UK: Boydell Press, 1992.

Vincent, N., ed. *Magna Carta: The Foundation of Freedom 1215–2015.* London: Third Millennium, 2014.

———. *Peter des Roches: An Alien in English Politics 1205–1238.* Cambridge: Cambridge University Press, 1996.

Warren, W. L. *Henry II.* New ed., New Haven, CT/London: Yale University Press, 2000.

———. *King John.* New ed., New Haven, CT/London: Yale University Press, 1997.

Weiser, F. X. *Handbook of Christian Feasts and Customs.* New York: Harcourt, 1958.

Yates, R. *History and Antiquities of the Abbey of St Edmund's Bury.* London: J. B. Nichols and Son, 1843.

Articles

Baldwin, J. W. "Master Stephen Langton, Future Archbishop of Canterbury: The Paris Schools and Magna Carta." *English Historical Review* 123 (2008).

Barratt, N. "The English Revenues of Richard I." *English Historical Review* 116 (2001).

———. "The Revenue of King John." *English Historical Review* 111 (1996).

Bradley, R. S., M. K. Hughes, and H. F. Diaz. "Climate in Medieval Time." *Science* 2003.

Broadberry, S., B. M. S. Campbell, and B. van Leeuwen. "English Medieval Population: Reconciling Time Series and Cross Sectional Evidence." qub.ac.uk. 2010.

Carpenter, D. A. "Archbishop Langton and Magna Carta: His Contribution, His Doubts and His Hypocrisy." *English Historical Review* 126 (2011).

Church, S. D. "King John's Last Testament and the Last Days of His Reign." *English Historical Review* 125 (2010).

Crockford, J. "Peripatetic and Sedentary Kingship: The Itineraries of John and Henry III." *Thirteenth Century History* 13 (2011).

Hansen, P. V. "Reconstructing a Medieval Trebuchet." *Military History Illustrated Past and Present* 27 (1990).

Keefe, T. K. "King Henry II and the Earls: The Pipe Roll Evidence." *Albion* 13 (1981).

Kerr, M. H., R. D. Forsyth, and M. J. Plyley. "Cold Water and Hot Iron: Trial by Ordeal in England." *Journal of Interdisciplinary History* 22 (1992).

Levin, C. "A Good Prince: King John and Early Tudor Propaganda." *Sixteenth Century Journal* 11 (1980).

Masschaele, J. "Transport Costs in Medieval England." *Economic History Review* 46 (1993).

Moore, T. "The Loss of Normandy and the Invention of Terre Normannorum, 1204." *English Historical Review* 125 (2010).

Pennington, K. "The Rite for Taking the Cross in the Twelfth Century." *Traditio* 30 (1974).

Rousseau, C. M. "Neither Bewitched nor Beguiled: Philip Augustus's Alleged Impotence and Innocent III's Response." *Speculum* 89 (2014).

Steiner, E. "Naming and Allegory in Late Medieval England." *Journal of English and German Philology* 106 (2007).

Thomas, H. M. "Shame, Masculinity and the Death of Thomas Becket," *Speculum* 87 (2012).

Index

Crusaders

The Epic History of the Wars for the Holy Lands

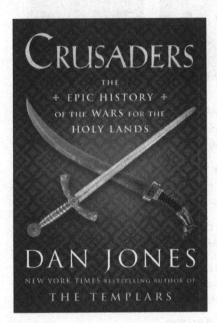

For more than one thousand years, Christians and Muslims lived side by side, sometimes at peace and sometimes at war. When Christian armies seized Jerusalem in 1099, they began the most notorious period of conflict between the two religions. Depending on who you ask, the fall of the holy city was either an inspiring legend or the greatest of horrors. In *Crusaders*, Dan Jones interrogates the many sides of the larger story, charting a deeply human and avowedly pluralist path through the crusading era.

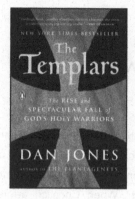 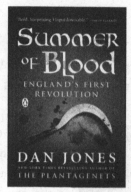